OCS EIS/EA
MMS 2008-008

Site-Specific Environmental Assessment for an FPSO Facility

Site-Specific Evaluation of Petrobras America Inc.'s Initial Development Operations Coordination Document, N-9015

**Cascade-Chinook Project
Walker Ridge Blocks 205, 206, 249, 250, 425, 426, 469, and 470**

Author

Minerals Management Service
Gulf of Mexico OCS Region

U.S. Department of the Interior
Minerals Management Service
Gulf of Mexico OCS Region

**New Orleans
March 2008**

SITE-SPECIFIC ENVIRONMENTAL ASSESSMENT DETERMINATION/ FINDING OF NO SIGNIFICANT IMPACT

Petrobras America Inc.'s Initial Development Operations Coordination Document (DOCD) and its amendments to develop the Cascade and Chinook Fields using a floating production, storage, and offloading (FPSO) facility to be located in Walker Ridge Block 249 has been reviewed. Petrobras proposes a phased development with two wells in the Cascade Field (drill centers east and west) and a single well in the Chinook Field at its respective drill center. The subsea production wells would be tied back to the FPSO using dual, piggable 9 5/8-inch (in) (24.4-centimeter (cm)) flowlines and free-standing hybrid risers (FSHR's). Production is enhanced by subsea booster pumps that are located downstream from the gathering manifolds. The FPSO will separate and treat the production and store the liquid hydrocarbon with offloading to shuttle vessels for ultimate transport to shore receiving facilities. Produced gas that is not used and fuel for the FPSO will be transported via a FSHR and export pipeline that ties into the existing pipeline infrastructure.

Our site-specific environmental assessment (SEA) on this proposed action (N-9015) is complete and results in a Finding of No Significant Impact. Based on this SEA, we have concluded that the proposed action will not significantly affect the quality of the human environment (40 CFR 1508.27). Preparation of an environmental impact statement is not required. The following mitigation is necessary to ensure environmental protection, consistent environmental policy, and safety as required by the National Environmental Policy Act, as amended, or is a recommended measure needed for compliance with 40 CFR 1500.2(f) regarding the requirement for Federal agencies to avoid or minimize any possible adverse effects of their action upon the quality of the human environment.

Mitigation

Mitigation 19.02—ROV Survey Required—DOCD

In accordance with Notice to Lessees and Operators No. 2003-G03, conduct the Remotely Operated Vehicle surveys you proposed in your plan for the facility location approved under this plan. Submit your pre- and post-installation survey reports within 60 days after the facility installation is completed.

Gary Goeke
Supervisor, NEPA/CZM Coordination Unit
Leasing and Environment, Gulf of Mexico OCS Region

3/20/08
Date

Dennis Chew
Chief, Environmental Assessment Section
Leasing and Environment, Gulf of Mexico OCS Region

3/20/08
Date

Joseph A. Christopher
Regional Supervisor
Leasing and Environment, Gulf of Mexico OCS Region

3/20/08
Date

TABLE OF CONTENTS

FIGURES

TABLES

ABBREVIATIONS AND ACRONYMS

ac	acre
API	American Petroleum Institute
ATB	articulated tug barge
bbl	barrel
BOD	biochemical oxygen demand
BOPD	barrel(s) of oil per day
BP	British Petroleum
BPD	barrels(s) per day
Btu	British thermal unit
CFR	Code of Federal Regulations
cm	centimeter
CO	carbon monoxide
CPA	Central Planning Area
CZM	Coastal Zone Management
DOCD	development operations coordination document
DOI	Department of the Interior
DP	dynamically positioned
EA	environmental assessment
EFH	Essential Fish Habitat
EIA	economic impact area
EIS	environmental impact statement
EP	exploration plan
ESA	Endangered Species Act
EWTA	Eglin Water Test Area
FEL	from the east block line
FMP	Fishery Management Plan
FNL	from the north block line
FPSO	floating production, storage, and offloading
FSHR	free-standing hybrid risers
FSL	from the south block line
ft	feet
FWL	from the west block line
FWS	Fish and Wildlife Service
GMFMC	Gulf of Mexico Fishery Management Council
ha	hectares
hp	horsepower
IBT	integrated tug barge
in	inch
km	kilometer
L	liter
LA Hwy 1	Louisiana Highway 1
m	meter
MARPOL	International Convention for the Prevention of Pollution from Ships
MEXUS	Mexican-United States
mi	mile
mm	millimeter
MMS	Minerals Management Service
MMscfd	million standard cubic feet per day
MODU	mobile offshore drilling unit
NAAQS	National Ambient Air Quality Standards
NEPA	National Environmental Policy Act
NMFS	National Marine Fisheries Service
NO_2	nitrate
NO_X	nitrogen oxides

NOAA	National Oceanic and Atmospheric Administration
NPDES	National Pollutant Discharge Elimination System
NRC	National Research Council
NTL	Notice to Lessees and Operators
NWR	National Wildlife Refuge
OCS	Outer Continental Shelf
OCSLA	Outer Continental Shelf Lands Act
OPA 90	Oil Pollution Act of 1990
Petrobras	Petrobras America Inc.
PSD	Prevention of Significant Deterioration
ROV	remotely operated vehicle
SBF	synthetic-based fluid
SEA	site-specific environment assessment
SOX	sulfur oxides
SOP	suspension of operations
SOV	spill occurrence variable
SPM	single-point mooring
TV	transport variable
U.S.	United States
U.S.C.	United States Code
USCG	U.S. Coast Guard
USDOI	U.S. Department of the Interior
USEPA	U.S. Environmental Protection Agency
VOC	volatile organic compound
WPA	Western Planning Area
WR	Walker Ridge
yr	year

INTRODUCTION

Under the Outer Continental Shelf Lands Act (OCSLA), as amended, the U.S. Department of the Interior (DOI/USDOI) is required to manage the leasing, exploration, development, and production of oil and gas resources on the Federal Outer Continental Shelf (OCS). The Secretary of the Interior oversees the OCS oil and gas program and is required to balance orderly resource development with protection of the human, marine, and coastal environments while simultaneously ensuring that the public receives an equitable return for these resources and that fair-market competition is maintained.

This site-specific environmental assessment (SEA) assesses the specific impacts associated with the proposed development of two fields with a floating production, storage, and offloading (FPSO) facility to be located in Walker Ridge Block 249 (OCS-G 16969). This SEA implements the tiering process outlined in 40 CFR 1502.20, which encourages agencies to tier environmental documents, thereby eliminating repetitive discussions of the same issue.

This SEA tiers directly from the *Proposed Use of Floating Production, Storage, and Offloading Systems on the Gulf of Mexico Outer Continental Shelf; Western and Central Planning Areas: Final Environmental Impact Statement* (FPSO EIS) (USDOI, MMS, 2001), which specifically considered areawide resources and impacts from exploration and development related to an FPSO facility. This SEA also tiers from the *Gulf of Mexico OCS Oil and Gas Lease Sales: 2007-2012; Western Planning Area Sales 204, 207, 210, 215, and 218; Central Planning Area Sales 205, 206, 208, 213, 216, and 222; Final Environmental Impact Statement; Volumes I and II* (Multisale EIS) (USDOI, MMS, 2007).

1. PROPOSED ACTION

1.1. REGULATORY FRAMEWORK

Federal laws mandate the OCS leasing program and the environmental reviews for the actions proposed by operators that seek to explore, develop, and produce hydrocarbons from Federal waters. An explanation of applicable statutes and regulations that comprise the regulatory framework for OCS activity and this proposed action is contained in Chapter 1.5 of the FPSO EIS (USDOI, MMS, 2001) and in Chapter 1.3 of the Multisale EIS (USDOI, MMS, 2007), and it is hereby incorporated by reference into this SEA and is described below.

Because of the uniqueness of the proposed action, that is, the inclusion of an FPSO, the operator will also have to comply with the U.S. Coast Guard's (USCG) regulations as well. The applicable Federal laws and policies are addressed in Chapter 1.5.1 of the FPSO EIS (USDOI, MMS, 2001) and in Chapter 1.3 of the Multisale EIS (USDOI, MMS, 2007), and they are hereby incorporated by reference into this SEA.

The applicable Federal laws addressed in the FPSO EIS and Multisale EIS include the Outer Continental Shelf Lands Act (OCSLA), the National Environmental Policy Act (NEPA) and the associated Council on Environmental Quality guidelines, the Marine Mammal Protection Act, the Magnuson-Stevens Act of 1976, the Endangered Species Act (ESA), the Marine Protection Research and Sanctuaries Act, the Oil Pollution Act of 1990 (OPA 90), the Clean Water Act, the Clean Air Act, the Resource Conservation and Recovery Act, the Marine Plastic Pollution Research and Control Act, the Coastal Zone Management Act, the Ports and Waterways Safety Act, the Jones Act, and Executive Order 12898: Environmental Justice.

1.2. PURPOSE OF THE PROPOSED ACTION

The proposed action in Petrobras America Inc.'s (Petrobras) Initial Joint Development Operations Coordination Document (DOCD) (Petrobras America Inc., 2007) and its amendments is to develop two fields using an FPSO production facility. Petrobras proposes a phased development with two wells in the Cascade Field (drill centers east and west) and a single well in the Chinook Field at its respective drill center. The subsea production wells would be tied back to the FPSO using dual, piggable 9 5/8-inch (in) (24.4-centimeter (cm)) flowlines and free-standing hybrid risers (FSHR's). Production is enhanced by subsea booster pumps that are located downstream from the gathering manifolds. The FPSO will separate and treat the production and store the liquid hydrocarbon with offloading to shuttle vessels for ultimate transport to shore receiving facilities. Produced gas that is not used and fuel for the FPSO will be transported via a FSHR and export pipeline that ties into the existing pipeline infrastructure. The recovery and production of the hydrocarbon resources is consistent with national energy policy and would help satisfy the Nation's need for energy supplies.

The Minerals Management Service's (MMS's) purpose is to ensure the balance of orderly development and production of the hydrocarbon resources with the protection of human, coastal, and marine environments. The MMS shall also ensure the public receives an equitable and fair-market return for the hydrocarbon resources.

1.3. NEED FOR THE PROPOSED ACTION

Consistent with its obligation to the Federal Government, Petrobras filed its Initial Joint DOCD with MMS. Listed below are some of the reasons for filing the plan with MMS:

- leaseholders have a legal right to pursue exploration, development, and production of hydrocarbon resources on the OCS;

- commercial quantities of hydrocarbons resources have been encountered;

- leaseholders are obligated via lease terms to diligently develop and produce the hydrocarbon resources; and

- a limited lease term and failure to develop and produce the hydrocarbon resources could lead to loss of lease(s) as well as income to the U.S.

1.4. DESCRIPTION OF THE PROPOSED ACTION

1.4.1. Project Background

1.4.1.1. Cascade and Chinook Fields

The Cascade and Chinook Fields are located in Walker Ridge in the Central Planning Area (CPA) of the Gulf of Mexico. The Cascade Field (Walker Ridge Block 206 Unit) is located approximately 250 miles (mi) (402 kilometers (km)) south of New Orleans and about 136 mi (219 km) from the Louisiana coastline in approximately 8,200 feet (ft) (2,499 meters (m)) of water. The Chinook Field (Walker Ridge Block 425 Unit) is located about 16 mi (26 km) south of the Cascade Field at a water depth of approximately 8,800 ft (2,682 m). **Figure 1** shows the approximate location of the Cascade and Chinook Fields.

Table 1 depicts the blocks contained in the Cascade and Chinook Units. The FPSO will be located in the southeast corner of Walker Ridge Block 249. All of the blocks in the units are located in Walker Ridge.

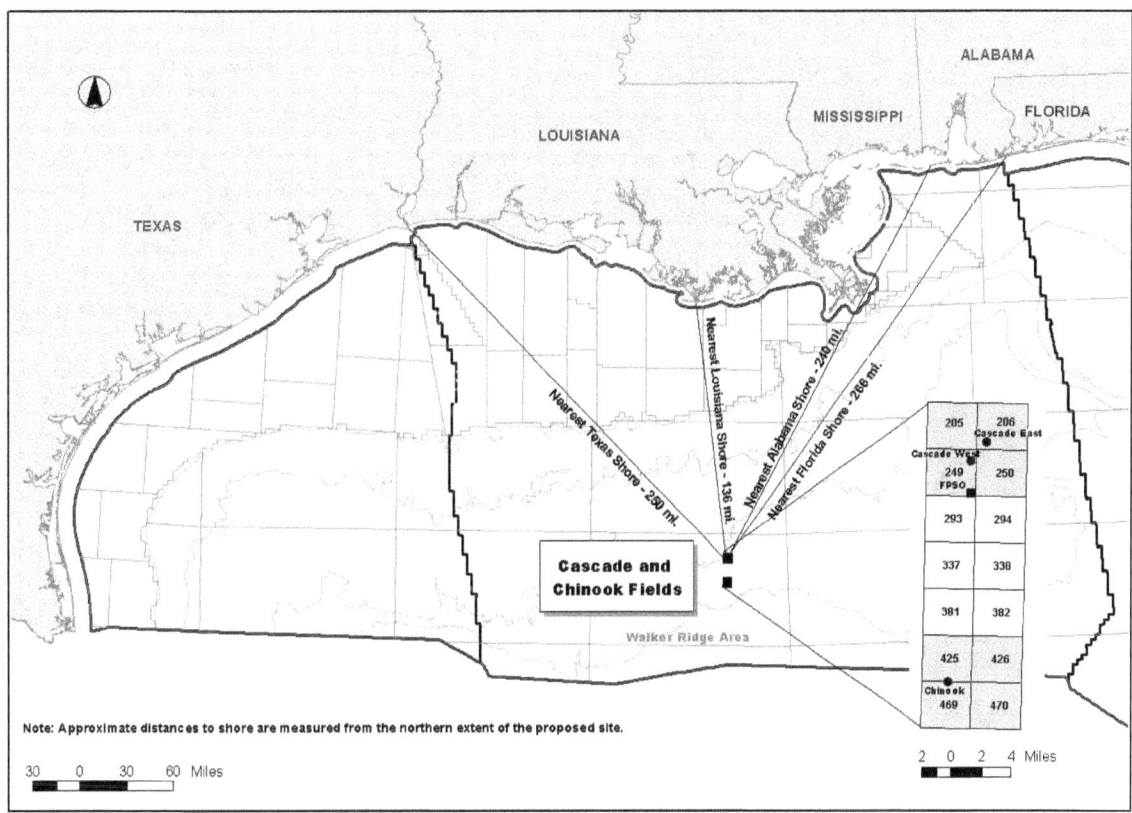

Figure 1. Location of the Cascade and Chinook Fields.

Table 1

Blocks and Lease Numbers Contained in Each Unit

Cascade – Walker Ridge Block 206 Unit		Chinook – Walker Ridge Block 425 Unit	
Block	Lease Number	Block	Lease Number
205	OCS-G 16964	425	OCS-G 16987
206	OCS-G 16965	426	OCS-G 16988
249	OCS-G 16969	469	OCS-G 16997
250	OCS-G 16970	470	OCS-G 16998

1.4.1.2. Development Operations Coordination Document

The Joint Initial DOCD addresses the first phase of the developments for both fields. The primary goal of the initial phase is to produce hydrocarbons from the fields and to gather sufficient data and information about the reservoirs and well productivity to enable the optimization of future phases of development within the fields, if they are warranted. Potentially, this will include the optimization of

- the number and type of wells required in a full field development,
- the completion design,
- the production system capacity and type,

3

- the subsea layout and boosting system, and

- the potential secondary recovery.

The fields are being developed in phases because there is very little known about the reservoir performance of Walker Ridge. There are no production analogs on similar reservoirs for Cascade or Chinook. To date, only the extended flow test for the Jack 2 well (Jack Prospect, Walker Ridge Block 758) has been conducted on an analog reservoir in Walker Ridge. Seismic surveys and well data (i.e., logs, cores, and fluid samples) provide the present support for the Cascade and Chinook reservoir interpretations.

The initial development phase of the Cascade and Chinook Fields consists of drilling and completing two new wells in the Cascade Field and one new well in the Chinook Field. The units will be developed concurrently with production to a single, FPSO facility located in Walker Ridge Block 249. The development activities' schedule in Petrobras' DOCD project simultaneous "first oil" production from the Cascade and Chinook Units in November 2009. Produced oil from the fields will be transported by shuttle vessels from the FPSO to a port of convenience along the U.S. Gulf Coast. Produced gas will be used to fuel the common process facilities on the FPSO. Excess gas will be transported from the FPSO via an export pipeline that will connect into the existing Gulf of Mexico pipeline infrastructure.

In the DOCD, Petrobras states that Phase 1 subsea and facility infrastructure can be easily expanded to accommodate additional wells and production should the reservoir and well performance justify additional investment. The subsea and facility system concepts for Phase 1 already contain many elements necessary for a full-field development. Petrobras states that they selected these elements to enhance flexibility in the systems and to minimize incremental infrastructure requirements in subsequent project phases. The flexibility is the result of using standard modular equipment concepts that can be expanded, as well as having adequate capacity in the production facility to handle the future production potential.

If needed, subsequent DOCD's will be submitted to MMS to address additional development phases as they are conceptualized. A phased development approach is part of the SOP Activity Schedule approved by MMS (letter dated July 31, 2006).

1.4.1.3. Layout

Figure 2 is an artistic rendering that depicts the proposed two-field development infrastructure and displays the FPSO and shuttle vessel in a tandem configuration. The FPSO is located in the southeast corner of Walker Ridge Block 249. There are three drill centers planned in Phase 1 of the development – two drill centers are located in the Cascade Field and one is located in Chinook Field. The Cascade East drill center is located in Walker Ridge Block 206, approximately 3.4 mi (5.5 km) from the FPSO. The Cascade West drill center is located in Walker Ridge Block 249, a little more than 2 mi (3.2 km) from the FPSO and about 1.3 mi (2.1 km) from the Cascade East drill center. The Cascade East infrastructure is connected to the Cascade West infrastructure via dual, piggable flowlines. The Cascade West drill center is connected to the FPSO via dual, piggable flowlines. The Chinook drill center is located in Walker Ridge Block 469, approximately 11.5 mi (18.5 km) from the FPSO. The Chinook drill center is also connected to the FPSO via dual, piggable flowlines. At the start of these flowlines within the Cascade West and Chinook infrastructures are 25,000 barrels of oil per day (BOPD) subsea boosting modules that are used to enhance flow rates and well production.

Both fields will be operated and controlled by an electro-hydraulic control system with both power and control umbilicals running from the FPSO to the drill centers. At the terminus of the flowlines near the FPSO are four FSHR's to transport the production from both fields from approximately an 8,200-ft (2,500-m) water depth to the FPSO at sea level.

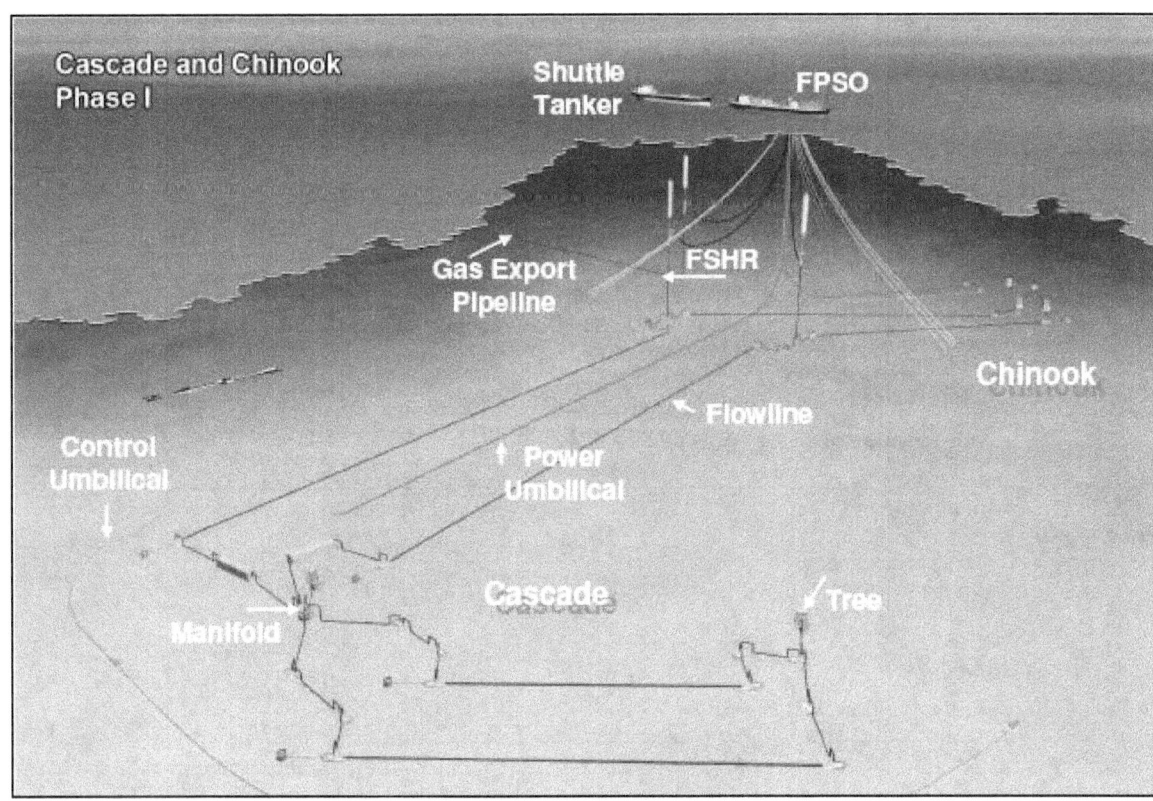

Figure 2. Artistic Rendering of the Cascade and Chinook Developments.

1.4.1.4. *Activity on the Units*

To date, three wells have been drilled on each unit. **Table 2** shows the well history for the two fields.

Table 2

Well Histories of the Cascade and Chinook Fields

Field	Area/Block/Well	Spud Date	Total Depth Date	Water Depth (ft)
Cascade	WR 206 #1[1]	01/31/2002	04/14/2002	8,143
	WR 206 #1BP1	04/23/2002	05/16/2002	8,143
	WR 206 #2	03/19/2005	05/29/2005	8,160
	WR 250 #2ST1	10/09/2005	11/24/2005	8,160
Chinook	WR 469 #1[2]	01/13/2003	06/19/2003	8,831
	WR 425 #1	10/17/2000	10/19/2000	8,845
	WR 425 #2	10/22/2000	01/01/2001	8,835

[1]   This was the Cascade discovery well.
[2]   This was the Chinook discovery well.
Note: WR is Walker Ridge.

The surface locations for the proposed new wells to be drilled under the DOCD are provided below in **Table 3**.

Table 3

Proposed New Well Locations

Development Well	Lease Number	Area/Block	Block Line Departures (ft)	Lambert Coordinates	Latitude/Longitude
Chinook	OCS-G 16997	WR 469	7,310 FEL 32 FNL	X: 2,447,890.00 Y: 9,630,688.00	Lat. 26°31'10.78" Long. 90°31'48.95"
Cascade West	OCS-G 16969	WR 249	1,623 FEL 3,984 FNL	X: 2,453,577.00 Y: 9,705,936.00	Lat. 26°43'34.53" Long. 90°30'30.24"
Cascade East	OCS-G 16965	WR 206	2,440 FSL 3,289 FWL	X: 2,458,489.00 Y: 9,712,360.00	Lat. 26°44'37.17" Long. 90°29'35.77"

Notes: FEL is from the east line.
FNL is from the north line.
FSL is from the south line.
FWL is from the west line.
WR is Walker Ridge.

Both new wells in the Cascade Field are projected to be drilled and completed by the *Ocean Endeavor*, a moored, semisubmersible mobile offshore drilling unit (MODU). The *Petrorig 1* is scheduled to drill and complete the new well on the Chinook Field. It is a dynamically positioned, semisubmersible MODU. Petrobras stated in its DOCD that wells in the Cascade and Chinook Fields will be drilled and completed applying Gulf of Mexico best practices and technologies. See **Chapter 1.4.5**, "Wells, Drilling Rigs, and Flowlines to the FPSO," for further details regarding the drilling rigs and wells.

1.4.1.5. Subsea Systems

Cascade and Chinook will be developed using clustered, subsea production wells. The production trees will be connected to 4-slot, subsea production manifolds or directly to two flowlines via pipeline end termination sleds and jumpers. The manifolds will have fixed, suction pile bases and retrievable components (e.g., control module, well and flowline jumpers, and pig loops). Production from the wells in the two fields will be commingled at the subsea manifolds and transported to the FPSO by two flowlines (7.5-in or 19-cm internal diameter nominal). The flowlines terminate at the base of the two FSHR's. The two FSHR's move the production from the seafloor upward to the disconnectable turret buoy in the FPSO. Allocation and tests will be carried out based on subsea multiphase meters installed on the wells.

The flowlines will be looped to facilitate pigging. The production FSHR's will be equipped with a pig diverter close to its base to allow pigging of both fields' pipes. Subsea boosting pumps will be installed on the flowlines downstream from each manifold to boost flow rates and production from the subsea wells.

1.4.1.6. FPSO

The production facility for the Cascade-Chinook development project will be a converted tanker FPSO. It will be modified for the expected conditions in Walker Ridge and will be configured for the production requirements of the fields' wells. The vessel will be of double-hull construction, with a double bottom and double sides, and it shall be in compliance with OPA 90. See **Chapter 1.4.2**, "FPSO Description," for a more in-depth discussion of the FPSO.

The FPSO will be located in the southeast corner of Walker Ridge Block 249 in approximately 8,200 ft (2,500 m) of water. The FPSO will be able to separate, treat, and measure fluids; store oil; process natural gas (export via a gas pipeline); and offload the stored oil to a shuttle vessel (shuttle tanker or integrated tug barge (ITB) or articulated tug barge (ATB)). The oil offloading station will be located at the FPSO's stern and will transfer crude to a tandem-moored shuttle vessel. **Figure 3** shows an actual FPSO during its tandem offloading operation.

Figure 3.   Actual FPSO during a Tandem Offloading Operation.

The FPSO's topside design capacities are 80,000 BOPD, 16,000 barrels per day (BPD) of produced water, and 16 million standard cubic feet per day (MMscfd) of gas. The storage capacity of the FPSO will be approximately 600,000 barrels (bbl) of crude oil. Two natural gas pipeline route options are being considered for export transmission.

The FPSO will be equipped with a disconnectable, single-point mooring system with a conventional passive turret that provides full weathervaning capability. The mooring system will be designed to easily disconnect from the FPSO. This feature enables the vessel to separate from the mooring system and sail away from impending severe storms and hurricanes. When disconnected, the remaining infield infrastructure will be lowered to a specific depth below sea level, thus minimizing severe surface environmental loads.

When connected to the buoy/riser system, the FPSO, including the hull, process facilities, risers, umbilicals, and subsea components, will be designed to continue operation uninterrupted during a 5-year return metocean condition and a 1-year return Loop Current. However, offloading operations are designed for a 1-year return metocean condition. The FPSO, facilities, and buoy/riser mooring system will be designed to remain intact and on-station for a 100-year return metocean condition, including eddy/Loop Current conditions.

When disconnected from the FPSO, the submerged buoy, mooring lines, anchors, and risers are designed for the 1,000-year return period hurricane condition, along with a 100-year Loop Current condition. When submerged, the buoy mooring system shall also be designed to avoid clashing between the mooring lines, risers, and umbilicals.

Figure 4 depicts the FPSO mooring system, showing the disconnectable buoy, anchor mooring lines, riser, hybrid riser, and floats.

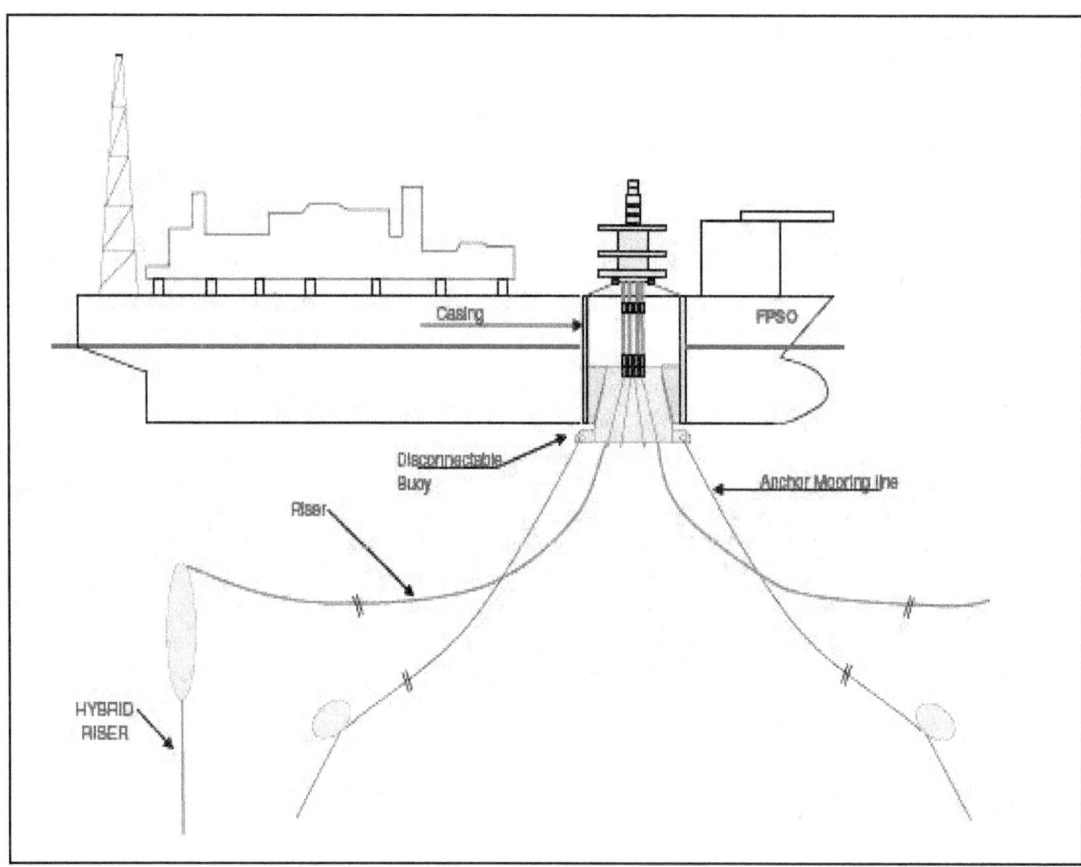

Figure 4. FPSO Mooring System Concept.

1.4.2. FPSO Description

1.4.2.1. Design

Phase 1 of the development plan proposes to use a ship-shaped FPSO with topside processing facilities as the production host for the Cascade and Chinook Fields. Produced hydrocarbons from the Cascade and Chinook Fields will be separated, treated, and measured, and the liquids will be temporarily stored on the FPSO prior to transshipment to market via shuttle vessels.

Through correspondence with MMS after the DOCD was submitted, Petrobras stated that they had signed a contract with Bergesen Worldwide for a tanker that will be converted into an FPSO for the Cascade-Chinook development project (Roland, personal communication, 2007). The vessel planned for use is the *M/T Sarasota*; however, a name change is being contemplated once the tanker is converted into an FPSO. The tanker was built in 1992 by Namura Shipbuilding Co. in Japan and it currently operates as a trading tanker in U.S. waters. Major modifications to the tanker will include fabrication and the installation of the buoy mooring system, process plant, helideck, and accommodations modules. The cargo storage capacity for the *M/T Sarasota* will be 600,000 bbl after the conversion.

Other characteristics of the FPSO include its double-hulled design with segregated cargo and ballast tanks. Stationkeeping for the FPSO will be via a disconnectable, single-point mooring (SPM) system that will allow full, passive weathervaning of the vessel. The SPM system will allow the FPSO to disconnect and motor away from named storms and hurricanes under its own power. After disconnecting from the FPSO, the buoy will be submerged to prevent damage to it from the storms. The FPSO would return to its station when operational conditions are safe to reconnect to the SPM system.

The nominal topside production design capacities for the FPSO are

- oil – 80,000 BPD,

- produced water – 16,000 BPD,

- total fluids – 80,000 BPD, and

- gas compression – 16 MMscfd.

The process facilities on the FPSO will be similar to those used in existing deepwater facilities in the Gulf of Mexico, except that

- the design will consider motion analysis because of the dynamic environment to be encountered with a ship-shaped FPSO hull and

- the process system will have special features in the turret (a swivel) to accommodate weathervaning of the FPSO.

The nature of the FPSO will require additional systems on the facilities that are not usually used on existing deepwater structures in the Gulf of Mexico. Examples of these systems include cargo monitoring, crude heating, cargo tank inerting, ballasting, and a stern discharge system for offloading to shuttle vessels. In addition, the FPSO will be designed for uninterrupted operation without the need of dry-docking during its operational life.

1.4.2.2. Overview

The FPSO receives the production from subsea wells and has production plant facilities to process crude oil, to stabilize it, and to separate the produced water and natural gas. Processed crude oil will be metered, temporarily retained in the vessel cargo storage tanks, and offloaded to shuttle vessels (tankers or special barges). Initially, the crude will be offloaded to a shuttle vessel once every 2 weeks. In subsequent years, Petrobras expects to offload to a shuttle vessel once a week. A small amount of the crude will be used as fuel. Produced water will be disposed of after appropriate treatment, and it will meet all discharge requirements. The associated gas will be compressed, dehydrated, and used for fuel gas, as required. Surplus natural gas will be exported through a gas pipeline that will be connected back to the existing pipeline infrastructure in the Gulf.

The FPSO will be equipped to transfer a minimum of approximately 500,000 bbl of oil to the shuttle vessel in no more than 24 hours. This interval does not include time for the shuttle's approach, connection, ramping up, top-off, and disconnection.

The cargo transfer system will have one standby pump to enable maintenance of the cargo pumps during offloading operations without affecting the offloading operation or the production/processing capacity of the FPSO. Individual submerged pumps (deep-well) in each tank or the conventional cargo transfer system will be used.

The design of the connection system (fluid, electrical, and optical) will allow for verification (e.g., testing or equivalent) of the connection integrity after each reconnection before exposure to operational conditions.

The design of the components and facilities allows for the offloading system to be cleaned immediately after every cargo transfer (offloading). Cleaning will be either by pumping seawater through a hose from the FPSO to the shuttle vessel or from the shuttle vessel to the FPSO.

Based on the USCG's weighing of the risk for any particular FPSO operation, the District Commander has the authority to establish a safety zone of 1,640 ft (500 m) around an FPSO operation in accordance with the regulations presented in 33 CFR 147. Petrobras states that an exclusion zone, subject to USCG approval, will be established around the FPSO marine spread to further mitigate marine traffic (Petrobras America Inc., 2007). The exclusion zone should be double the length of the FPSO, hawser, shuttle vessel, tug line, tug, and the safety buffer (including a "far condition" assuming a damaged mooring line). Petrobras will also have a dedicated field vessel that can assist in case of a possible allision.

1.4.3. Location

Figure 5 shows an overall view of the locations of the proposed Cascade-Chinook development facilities. A detailed view of the FPSO site and its nearby infrastructure are shown in **Figure 6**. **Figures 7 and 8** show the proposed anchor positions for the drilling rig at the Cascade East and West drilling centers. **Figures 5 and 6** also portray a portion of the mooring system for the FPSO. There are no anchor patterns for the Chinook well since the operator proposes to drill it with a dynamically positioned MODU.

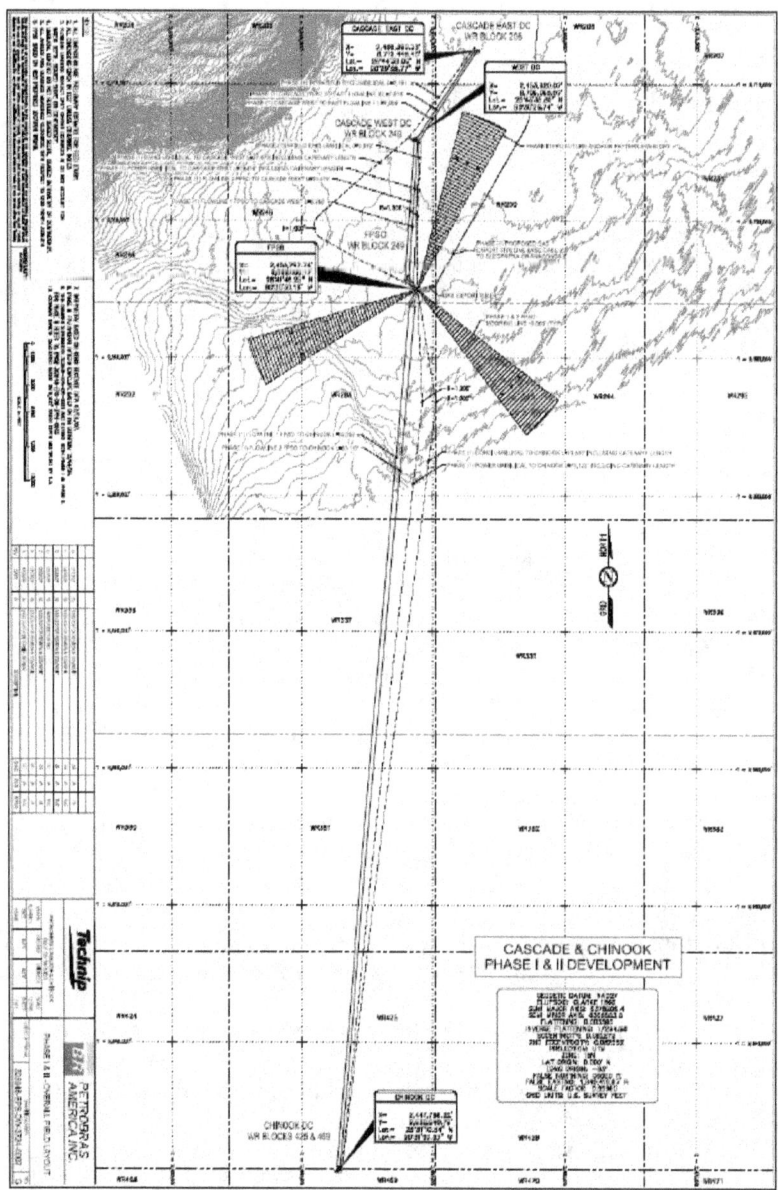

Figure 5.   Layout of the Overall Cascade-Chinook Field Development.

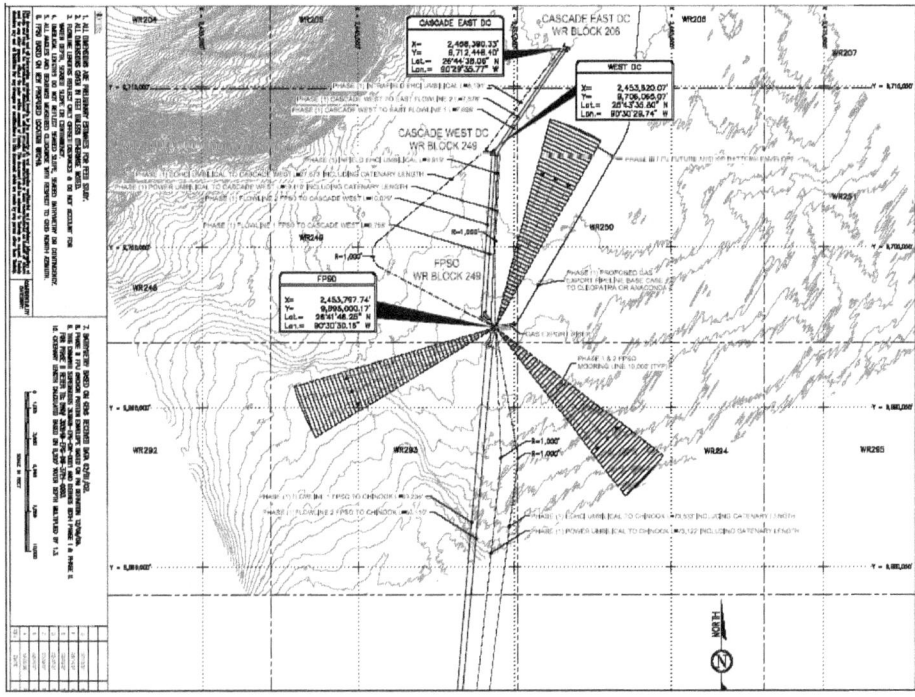

Figure 6.   Detailed View of the FPSO Site and Its Nearby Infrastructure.

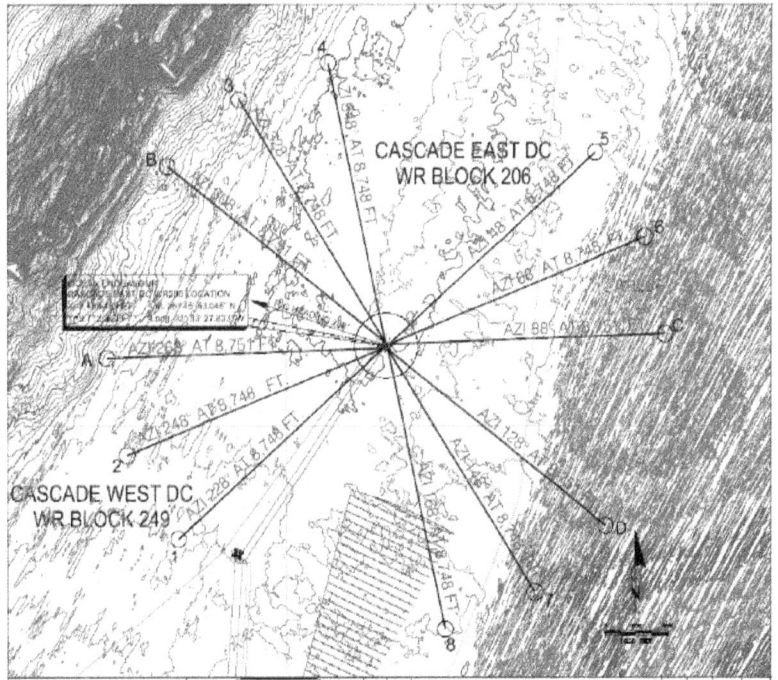

Figure 7.   Proposed Anchor Patterns for the Drilling Rig for the Cascade
East Center and a Portion of the FPSO Anchor Array Window.

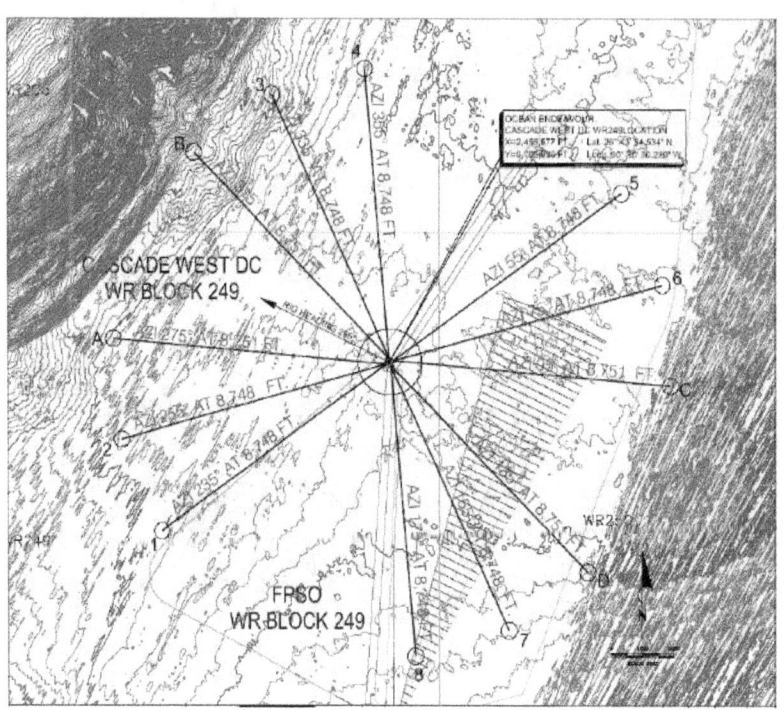

Figure 8.   Proposed Anchor Patterns for the Drilling Rig for the Cascade West Center and a Portion of the FPSO Anchor Array Window.

1.4.4.   Schedule of Activities

Table 4 portrays the schedule of activities provided by Petrobras in their DOCD for the Cascade-Chinook development project.

Table 4

Proposed Schedule of Activities

Proposed Activity	Start Date	End Date	Days
Drill and Complete 3 Wells (2 in Cascade and 1 in Chinook)	Jun 08	Dec 09	570
Install Cascade Flowlines and Gas Export Pipeline	Jun 09	Jul 09	60
Install Chinook Flowlines	Aug 09	Aug 09	30
Install Risers	Jul 09	Sep 09	75
Install Subsea Equipment (heavy lifts, umbilicals/flying leads)	Sep 09	Oct 09	60
Install FPSO (mooring system and FPSO connection)	Oct 09	Nov 09	60
First Oil from Cascade and Chinook	Nov 09	Nov 09	0

1.4.5.   Wells, Drilling Rigs, and Flowlines to the FPSO

Wells and Drilling Rigs

The three wells proposed under Phase 1 of the DOCD will be directionally drilled, cased, and perforated with multizone frac-pacs. Petrobras states in the DOCD that, although there are some well engineering challenges due to reservoir characteristics, well engineering will use proven Gulf of Mexico practices and there are no extraordinary safety or environmental considerations to be addressed. The

MMS will evaluate each proposed well when the operator submits the required application for permit to drill and the subsequent completion documentation.

Petrobras anticipates the temporary transfer of operatorship of the two proposed Cascade wells to Devon Energy Inc., its lease partner, so that they may be drilled and completed using Diamond's *Ocean Endeavor* MODU. Upon completion of the second Cascade well, Devon Energy Inc. would transfer the operatorship of the two Cascade wells back to Petrobras. Petrobras will serve as the operator for the Chinook well.

Petrobras will drill and complete the Chinook well using Seadrill's *Petrorig 1* MODU. The Seadrill's *West Sirius* (sister ship to the *Petrorig 1*) is the first alternate for Diamond's *Ocean Endeavor* while Seadrill's *Petrorig 1* will serve as the second alternative.

Flowlines to the FPSO

Phase 1 of the development plan will include drill centers at Cascade East (Walker Ridge Block 249), Cascade West (Walker Ridge Block 206), and Chinook (Walker Ridge Block 425). Cascade's drill centers are located in approximately 8,200 ft (2,500 m) of water, while Chinook's drill center is in about 8,800 ft (2,680 m) of water. Production from the well in Cascade East will be gathered and transported approximately 1.5 mi (2.4 km) to Cascade West. Production from the well in Cascade West is also gathered and is commingled with the production from Cascade East before being transported approximately 2.5 mi (4 km) to the FPSO via two 9 5/8-in (24.4-cm) flowlines and two production FSHR's. Production from the Cascade East and West drill centers is enhanced by skid-mounted booster pumps that are located immediately downstream of the Cascade West gathering manifold. The dual flowlines will allow for round-trip pigging.

Production from the Chinook well is gathered and transported approximately 12 mi (19 km) to the FPSO via two flowlines and two production FSHR's. Like the Cascade East and West development scenario, production is enhanced by a skid-mounted booster pump that is located immediately downstream of the gathering manifold. The dual flowlines facilitate round-trip pigging. The Chinook production flowline will be a pipe-in-pipe (9 5/8-in or 24.4-cm inner pipe outer diameter) configuration for flow assurance.

The gas export pipelines, along with shuttle vessels, are discussed in **Chapter 1.4.7**, "Transportation Operations."

1.4.6. Support Facilities

Petrobras proposes to use Port Fourchon, Louisiana, for its onshore support bases. Both marine and aviation support activities will be based out of this location. Petrobras believes that the existing facilities are adequate to support the operational needs of Phase 1 of the development plan and that no expansion to the onshore facilities will be required.

The marine shore base would be equipped with facilities related to warehouse, outside storage spaces, material handling equipment, marine vessel dock space, fuel storage, water storage, drilling fluid storage, communications equipment, security, offices, and vehicle parking lot.

The aviation facilities would be equipped with a helipad, office space, waiting room, and vehicle parking lot.

As a contingency, Petrobras expects to occasionally use secondary onshore support facilities located in Texas or another terminal in Louisiana when conditions warrant such actions, e.g., weather, market availability of marine vessels, helicopters, security, and/or safety.

1.4.7. Transportation Operations

1.4.7.1. Shuttle Vessels

In Phase 1 of the development plan, Petrobras proposes to charter two dedicated shuttle vessels to transport produced oil to market. Petrobras defines the term shuttle vessels in its DOCD as either shuttle tankers or ATB's. Both types of vessels will be Jones Act and OPA 90 compliant vessels. Shuttle vessels will be double hulled with segregated cargo tanks and will have a cargo capacity of between 185,000 and 500,000 bbl. Petrobras may use ATB's of 200,000- to 350,000-bbl capacity for its initial shuttling operations.

The frequency of offloading to the shuttle vessels will vary over time. During the production ramp-up interval (the first year of production operations), a single shuttle vessel will be used to perform one offload from the FPSO every 2 weeks (26 per year). In subsequent years of production, two shuttle vessels on a staggered schedule are likely to perform one offload every week (52 per year). The frequency of offloads will be determined by reservoir and topside performance. Offloads from the FPSO to the shuttle vessels are expected to take approximately 24 hours. This interval does not include the time required for the shuttle vessel to approach, moor, and disconnect.

During offloading, the FPSO and shuttle vessel will be in a tandem configuration (**Figure 3**). A shuttle vessel will maneuver to a downwind location to connect to the FPSO via a hawser system with the offloading hose connected between the shuttle vessel's bow and the FPSO's stern. This will allow the shuttle vessel to weathervane in a similar manner as the FPSO. A dedicated field support tug will be used to support offloading operations.

Shuttle vessels will transport produced oil to the terminals of choice all along the Gulf Coast. These terminals include facilities in Texas, Louisiana, Mississippi, and Alabama. Petrobras does not anticipate the need to expand or modify any of the existing terminals to receive the production from the FPSO.

Figure 9 shows the potential shuttle-vessel routes to the Gulf Coast refineries that are being considered to receive produced crude oil from the Cascade-Chinook development project.

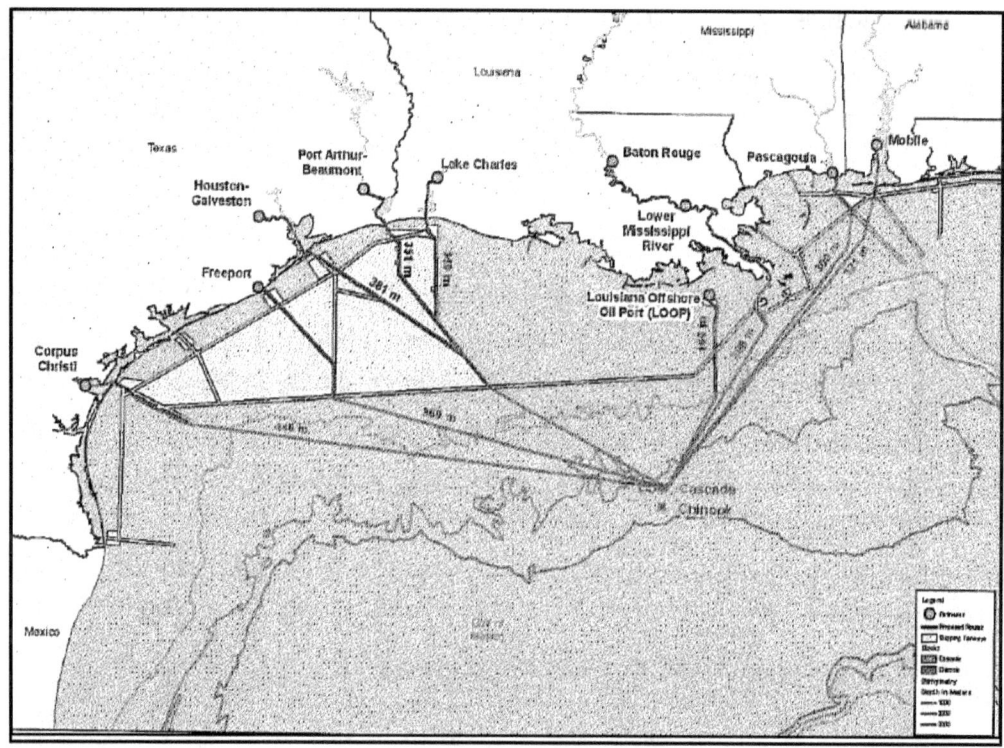

Figure 9.   Potential Shuttle-Vessel Routes to Gulf Coast Refineries.

1.4.7.2. Export Gas Pipeline

There are no existing pipelines in Walker Ridge. In Phase 1 of the development plan, Petrobras proposes to install a 6-in (25-cm) gas export pipeline that will take unused associated gas (gas that is not consumed on the FPSO) to existing pipeline infrastructure in Green Canyon. At present, Petrobras is considering two tie-in options in the DOCD: the "Cleopatra Option" (operated by BP) is located in Green Canyon Block 829 and is approximately 43 mi (69 km) from the FPSO; and the "Anaconda Option" (operated by Enterprise) is located in Green Canyon Block 606 and is approximately 66 mi (106 km) from the FPSO. A pipeline application will be submitted separately once the export pipeline route is finalized. **Figure 10** shows the two proposed export gas pipeline options contained in the DOCD.

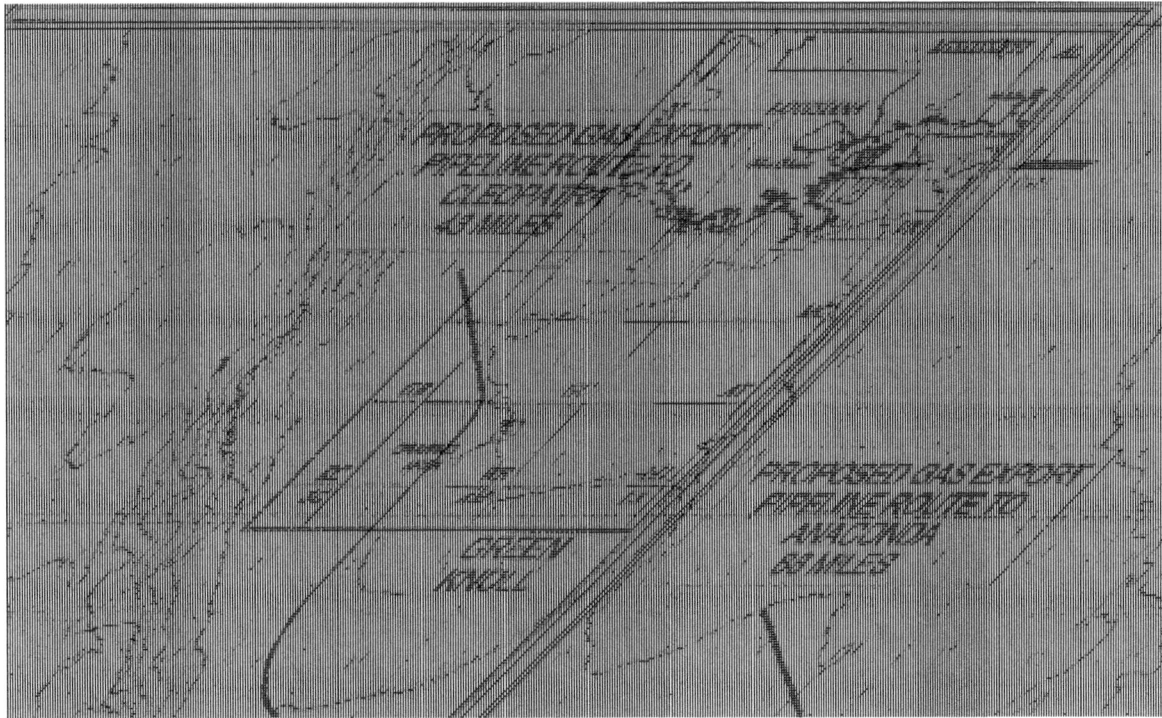

Figure 10.   Proposed Export Pipeline Route Options.

1.4.8.   New and Unusual Technology

Petrobras proposes to use five new and unusual technologies in the development of the Cascade and Chinook Fields. They may be characterized into two major areas – facilities and subsea.

Facilities

- A disconnectable, single-point, turret buoy-moored FPSO.
- Crude transportation from the FPSO to shore via a shuttle vessel.

Subsea

- The use of FSHR's to transport production fluids from the seabed to the FPSO and gas from the FPSO to the export pipeline system.
- The use of subsea, electric-driven booster pumps located on the seabed near the wells to increase production.
- The potential use of torpedo piles for attaching the vessel mooring system to the seabed.

A discussion of the potential environmental consequences of these new and unusual technologies to the Gulf of Mexico can be found below. After careful examination and evaluation, a finding is included in the discussion as to how each of the new and unusual technologies may interface with the environment.

1.4.8.1. Disconnectable, Single-Point, Turret Buoy-Moored FPSO

The FPSO EIS used a permanent, fixed mooring for the base-case FPSO scenario. The FPSO EIS noted that a ". . . few existing FPSO systems have been designed to be disconnectable under impending

15

severe weather circumstances or approaching icebergs. However, experience has shown that both the FPSO and permanent mooring systems can be designed to withstand severe weather such as hurricanes."

The FPSO EIS states that the choice of mooring systems depends on many factors needed to reduce risk and to meet design requirements (e.g., preferences in stationkeeping and mooring methods, water depth, environmental criteria, and distance from shore). Although a permanent, fixed mooring system was considered by MMS to be the most likely configuration, the FPSO EIS also recognized that some operators may propose a disconnectable, buoy mooring system.

The proposed system for the Cascade-Chinook development project is a permanently fixed, internally disconnectable, single-point, turret buoy-mooring system that allows passive weathervaning. The buoy would disconnect only during emergencies and severe weather conditions such as hurricanes. This mooring system offers significant safety advantages because it allows both personnel and liquid hydrocarbon production to be transported out of harm's way during harsh environmental conditions.

Since the time that the base-case scenario for disconnectable buoy turrets was developed, more than 7 years ago, new disconnectable turret buoy-mooring systems technology has rapidly advanced. These types of mooring systems are used all over the world, including the North Sea, where severe weather systems and icebergs can be common. The systems are also being used off the coast of Newfoundland, Canada, and China.

The FPSO EIS indicated that there is an increased risk of riser release (0.4% of potential spills by volume) during connection and disconnection operations. However, in the disconnectable turret that Petrobras plans to use, the risers and mooring system are permanently attached to the underside of the cone-shaped, disconnectable turret buoy, not to the vessel. This should minimize these risks. The risers and mooring lines remain connected to the underside of the buoy after disconnection, and the entire riser (and mooring system) is left behind, submerged under the wave action and out of danger. Therefore, the accidental disconnection of the risers, once installed, is expected to be a very low probability event.

Petrobras' use of a disconnectable buoy turret with the riser and mooring lines attached to the detachable buoy makes the riser system similar to other deepwater production systems.

Riser failure can be more likely attributed to corrosion, fatigue, or impact, but this is not FPSO specific. These issues will be dealt with in the design and operation of the import and export risers. The MMS's Notice to Lessees and Operators (NTL) 2007-G14 requires that risers connected to floating platforms be subject to the platform verification program as associated structures. The separate verification process necessitates the use of an independent Certified Verification Agent specifically for the pipeline risers. Guidelines are set forth in this NTL. In addition, MMS's inspection program will examine and evaluate the wells, subsea systems, pipelines and risers, and production systems.

Significant damages to offshore facilities from hurricanes occurred after the FPSO EIS was published. Hurricanes Katrina and Rita (in 2005) were 1,000-year return period storms with estimated 83-ft (25 m) waves, and Hurricane Ivan (in 2004) was a 2,000-year return period storm with estimated 95-ft (29 m) waves. The effects from the hurricanes included 123 fixed platforms and 1 floating platform destroyed, and dozens more suffered significant damage. Both semisubmersible and jackup drilling rigs suffered significant damage as well.

The FPSO EIS noted that the primary benefit of abandoning a facility during a hurricane is the reduced potential for loss of life in the event of a failure rather than any reduction in oil-spill risk. However, evacuating personnel by helicopter is not a risk-free operation and helicopter accidents are one of the major fatality risks of offshore operations.

The FPSO will operate in conditions up to a 100-year hurricane storm, when it will disconnect from the turret buoy and motor out of the way. After disconnection, the mooring system (which is permanently attached to the turret buoy) and the turret buoy submerge to a predetermined depth (between 80 and 150 ft [24 and 30 m] below sea level). The submerged buoy and riser systems are designed to handle any submerged sea state during storm conditions. **Figures 11 and 12** show a typical FPSO connected to and then disconnected from a disconnectable, single-point mooring buoy.

In a planned shutdown, the crude product in the flowlines will be partially displaced prior to disconnecting with an inert fluid (such as dead oil), which will not present flow assurance issues on restarting the facility.

In summary, MMS believes that the disconnectable, single-point mooring system adds no more risks to the environment than those systems currently employed in the Gulf of Mexico for other deepwater operations. This assumes the operator properly inspects and maintains the mooring system.

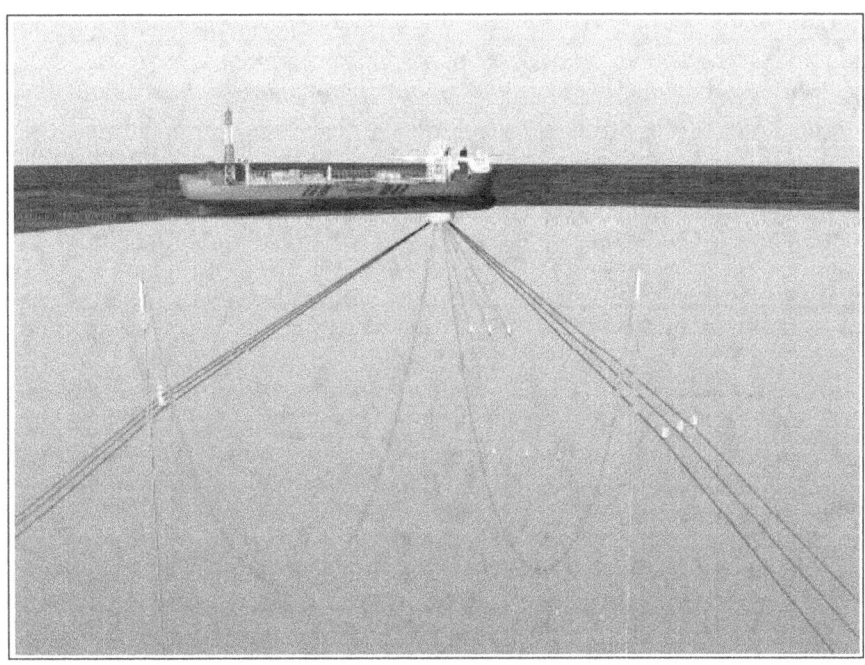

Figure 11.   Typical FPSO Connected to a Disconnectable, Single-Point Mooring Buoy.

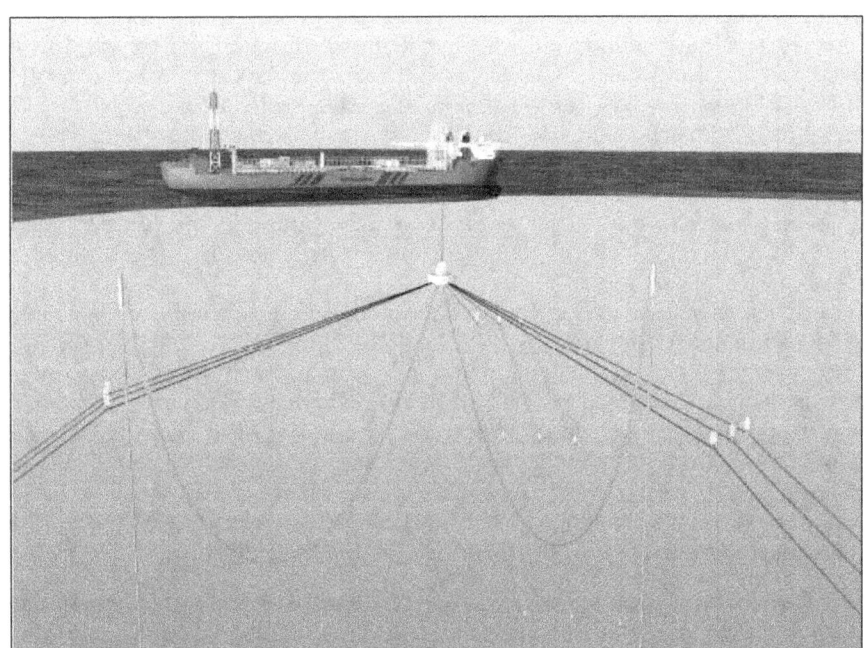

Figure 12.   Typical FPSO Disconnected from a Disconnectable, Single-Point Mooring Buoy.

1.4.8.2. *Shuttle Vessels*

The FPSO EIS outlined several advantages of using FPSO's at offshore, deepwater Gulf of Mexico oil-production sites. One of the biggest advantages was using marine vessels to transport product to shore in lieu of pipelines. While shuttle vessels (i.e., shuttle tankers, ITB's, and ATB's) can vary in size, the base-case scenario for the FPSO EIS considered a 500,000-bbl capacity shuttle tanker as the likely means of transporting oil cargo in Gulf of Mexico FPSO operations. Petrobras states in its DOCD that there are no Jones Act compliant shuttle tankers of the 500,000-bbl size or greater.

In its plan, Petrobras is proposing to use an internal, propulsion-system shuttle tanker, ITB, or ATB. The likely size is around the 300,000- to 425,000-bbl capacity. Petrobras has a study underway to determine which type of offloading vessel will be used, the capacity, and the locations of the offloading ports. The vessels chosen for the Cascade-Chinook project would be designed per USCG requirements and compliant with the Jones Act and OPA 90. The shuttle tanker or ITB/ATB that would be used for the Cascade-Chinook project would connect to the FPSO via a hawser mooring system between the bow of the shuttle vessel and the stern of the FPSO in a tandem offloading configuration, with the shuttle vessel lying downwind. Both the FPSO and shuttle vessel would weathervane around the turret. This is similar to the conditions analyzed in the FPSO EIS. A tug would be available for support during offloading operations.

Since 2001, considerable advances in offloading vessel design and capabilities have been made. The ITB design, in which the tug fits into a notch in the stern of the barge and pushes it, was a significant advancement in tug and barge technology. The ITB's offer features or specially designed connection systems that increase sea-keeping capabilities and increase speed and cargo capacity over the older tug and barge system.

The ATB's are the next generation of ITB's, and the USCG considers the ATB to be a specialized ITB. Crowley Maritime Corporation, Maritrans, Inc., and other companies are building and using ATB's that consist of a tank vessel (barge) and a large, powerful tug positioned in a notch in the stern of the barge in the Gulf of Mexico. The tug propels and maneuvers the barge. Unlike an ITB, where the tug and barge are locked together in a rigid connection and, for practical purposes, become one unit, the ATB has an articulated or "hinged" connection system between the tug and barge that allows movement in one axis, or plane, in the critical area of fore and aft pitch. This type of movement is not possible with an ITB unit.

Recent events in the Gulf of Mexico have proven the safety and reliability of ATB's. When hurricanes damaged pipelines in 2005, at least four companies with offshore production facilities asked for and received waivers from the USCG to use ATB's to transport product from their platforms and bring it to shore. This method of transporting oil has been satisfactory to the USCG and has so far resulted in no spills. Informal feedback from USCG has indicated they found no problems with the maneuverability of ATB's, and the transfer and transportation operations have gone very smoothly, with no spills recorded. For FPSO operations, USCG has recommended that the tug and barge not separate at any time during the transfer or movement of product, except during critical emergencies needed to save lives or prevent greater damage. Overall, there are few obstructions and little additional risk with the use of ATB's or ITB's instead of shuttle tankers.

Offloading operations will be under the jurisdiction of USCG. The FPSO is required to have a Port Operations Manual (manual) approved by USCG before any offloading operations may occur. The manual includes criteria for connecting, conducting offloading operations, and disconnecting. One of the largest concerns is the risk associated with oil spills from shuttle operations. These risks were compared and evaluated with other deepwater development systems in the FPSO EIS and in the comparative risk assessment. Conclusions from the comparative risk assessment regarding oil spills include the following:

- The average total volume of oil spilled during a deepwater facility's lifetime will be dominated by rare, large spills rather than frequent, small spills.

- The major contribution to the oil-spill risks for all systems is the transportation of oil from the production facility to the shore terminal by either pipelines or shuttle tankers. Spill risks for pipelines and shuttle tankers are comparable, although the frequencies and sizes of possible spills are different for pipelines versus shuttle tankers. The spill risks for pipelines are dominated by the possibility of spills between 10,000 and 100,000 bbl in size that are expected to occur once every 600 years on average. The spill risks for shuttle tankers are dominated by the possibility of spills between 100,000 and 500,000 bbl in size that are expected to occur on average once every 4,500 years.

- The confidence intervals in predicted oil-spill volumes range over about an order of magnitude, reflecting the limited quantity and quality of historical data available to estimate frequencies for rare events.

1.4.8.3. Free-Standing Hybrid Risers

The Cascade Field is located in approximately 8,200 ft (2,500 m) of water. The development is at the base of the Sigsbee Escarpment. The development plan proposes to produce a number of wells (3 initially) to a turret-moored FPSO vessel. The wells will be tied back to the FPSO via two production flowlines and FSHR's. Export oil will be offloaded to shuttle vessels, and unconsumed produced natural gas will be exported from the field via an FSHR and a gas export pipeline.

The FSHR concept proposed for the Cascade-Chinook development project is a proven solution for deepwater, floating production systems and has been used in West Africa in several projects (i.e., Girassol and Kizomba A & B). It also has been applied in the Gulf of Mexico in the past, in a hybrid concept with tensioners, in Placid's Green Canyon development and later in Ensearch's Garden Banks development.

The FSHR's do not appear to interact with the environment any differently than other risers currently in use with existing deepwater development projects. Although new to the Gulf of Mexico, the technology has been successfully used in other countries.

1.4.8.4. Subsea Boosting

Petrobras states in their DOCD that their experience with subsea boosting systems began with the installation of the first electric submersible pump on a subsea well in 1994. Petrobras is currently developing its Jubarte and Golfinho Fields using subsea boosting technology similar to the technology proposed for Cascade-Chinook development project. These two developments and the use of electric submersible pumps are described more extensively in the Offshore Technology Conference (OTC) Papers OTC 18198 and OTC 17398 (Figueiredo et al., 2006; Rodrigues et al., 2005, respectively).

In concept, the pumps boost the operating system pressure, lowering flowing tubing pressures at each well, thereby increasing flow rates. This production increase will likely extend the field's life and increase ultimate recovery.

The MMS has approved the use of other booster pump systems to enhance production. The adaptation proposed in this installation locates the boosting pumps at the seafloor instead of "downhole" in the well. The MMS believes that the booster pump systems will interact with the environment in a similar manner to those that are already in use.

1.4.8.5. Torpedo Piles

In the DOCD, Petrobras states that the mooring system for the FPSO is still under design development. It may involve synthetic mooring lines. The base-case design scenario for the anchor point is presently a suction pile, but torpedo piles are also under consideration. Torpedo piles are a relatively recent development that was first used in Brazil because of the lack of cost-effective installation infrastructure. Patented by Petrobras, torpedo piles are relatively easy to install and enable a much greater number of installation vessels.

Torpedo piles are a type of vertically loaded anchors that provide mooring points on the sea bottom with high horizontal and vertical resistance capability, thus eliminating the long, dead-chain section usually found in conventional catenary anchor leg systems. The dead-chain section is a necessary feature of conventional anchors systems in order to prevent anchor lift. This is also a distinct advantage of vertically loaded anchors in that the environmental impact on the seafloor is considerably less with these anchors.

Vertically loaded anchoring devices have been used offshore for a long time, but they were all pile-type anchors, being either drilled and grouted piles ("grouted piles") or suction embedded piles ("suction piles"). Petrobras, together with the manufacturers and based on its operational experience, has developed the torpedo pile, a patented technology. This new kind of pile, which has withstood tests for loads up to 1,300 tons, is positioned at a certain predetermined height over the seabed and dropped. The momentum generated by the free-fall movement of the pile is sufficient to embed it in the soil down to a depth where soil friction is enough to counteract the designed pullout load. These devices are extremely simple to fabricate and require only one standard anchor-handling vessel to install with good accuracy at the desired location. As a consequence, there is a significant drop on the total installed cost of the anchoring system using this new concept. Petrobras now has one FPSO moored with torpedo piles.

1.4.9. Lightering Zone and Operations

The area around the Cascade-Chinook development project is within the boundaries of the Gulfmex No. 2 lightering zone. The proposed development facilities are located in the southern portion of the lightering area.

Lightering zones within the Gulf of Mexico were designated by USCG (33 CFR 156.300, Subpart B) for safety reasons. The zones are located more than 60 mi (97 km) from the baseline of the territorial sea. Until 2015, single-hulled tankers may conduct lightering operations with in the Gulfmex zone.

Lightering operations involve the offloading of crude oil from very large crude carriers or ultra-large crude carriers to smaller shuttle tankers at sea. The smaller tankers then transport the crude to onshore terminals for offloading. Lightering operations are necessary because the draft of the very large crude carriers or ultra-large crude carriers exceed the water depth of channels to the Gulf ports.

Three companies currently conduct lightering activities in the Gulfmex No. 2 area (Clark, 2006). The companies and their approximate percentage of lightering operations within the zone are shown in **Table 5**.

Table 5

Companies Using the Gulfmex No. 2 Lightering Zone
and Their Percentage of Use

Company	Approximate Percentage of Use
Skaugen Petrotrans	40 to 45
American Eagle Tankers	40 to 45
Heinrich Lightering Service	15 to 20

Most of the lightering vessels that call on the zone are now double hulled and can conduct lightering operations outside of the designated area. Therefore, the lightering zone is not highly used by the industry and is only required for nondouble-hulled tankers (scheduled to be phased out of service in 2015) (Clark, 2006). Generally, the area that is used within the Gulfmex No.2 lightering zone is located closer to shore in the very northeastern corner of the designated area. Based on these current use facts, it is unlikely that the proposed Cascade-Chinook development project would affect or be affected by activities in the Gulfmex No.2 lightering zone.

1.5. MAJOR ISSUES

The major issues of concern considered and/or analyzed in this SEA include many of the same issues identified during scoping for previous MMS NEPA documents covering OCS oil and gas development, as well as issues identified specifically for FPSO's in the EIS scoping process.

Only issues unique to FPSO-based production systems were selected for detailed analysis in this SEA. Most of these issues are associated with the following unique aspects of FPSO operations: offshore storage of large volumes of OCS-produced crude oil; offloading of OCS-produced crude oil offshore; and transportation of OCS-produced crude oil via surface vessel (versus transport via marine pipeline).

Issues of concern include potential impact-producing factors associated with FPSO operations and support activities; sensitive environmental resources that could be impacted by FPSO installation, operation, decommissioning, and associated transportation and support activities; and socioeconomic activities that could be affected by FPSO-related activities. Examples of impact-producing factors include air emissions, seafloor disturbance from mooring, anchoring, and structure/pipeline emplacement, ocean discharges, onshore waste disposal, and accidental events such as oil spills and blowouts.

The environmental resources that are potentially vulnerable to impacts from construction, installation, operation, and decommissioning of an FPSO in the Gulf of Mexico are air quality, water and sediment quality, coastal habitats, benthic communities, marine mammals, sea turtles, coastal and marine birds, fish, commercial and recreational fisheries, social and economic conditions, recreational resources and beach use, cultural resources, and other uses.

2. ALTERNATIVES CONSIDERED

2.1. NONAPPROVAL OF THE PROPOSAL

The "nonapproval" alternative refers to the continuation of the existing conditions of the affected environment, i.e., without implementation of the proposed Cascade-Chinook development project. Inclusion of the "nonapproval" alternative is prescribed by the Council on Environmental Quality's implementing NEPA regulations. It serves as the benchmark against which the proposed action can be evaluated. Under the "nonapproval" alternative, Petrobras would not be allowed to drill, complete, and produce the proposed wells as specified in its Cascade-Chinook DOCD (Phase 1). Selection of this alternative would result in no impacts to the environment from the proposed action because no action would take place, but it could preclude the development of much-needed hydrocarbon resources from known discoveries, thereby, resulting in a loss of energy for American citizens and royalty income for the U.S. In addition, it is entirely likely that, if these fields are not produced as part of the joint development plan, they may individually be abandoned because the cost of producing any single discovery might be uneconomic for the operator to undertake. This may be especially true for the Chinook Field since only one well is envisioned in Phase 1 of the development. Considering these aspects and the fact that MMS anticipates minor environmental and human impacts resulting from the proposed action, this alternative was not selected for further analysis.

2.2. APPROVAL WITH EXISTING MITIGATION

The MMS's lease stipulations, OCS Operating Regulations, NTL's, as well as other regulations and laws were identified throughout this environmental assessment as existing mitigation to minimize potential environmental effects associated with the proposed action. Additional mitigation measures are described below. This alternative was selected for evaluation in this SEA.

2.3. APPROVAL WITH EXISTING AND/OR ADDITIONAL MITIGATION

The MMS believes an additional mitigation measure is warranted for the proposed action. The mitigation below is required to be implemented by the operator for the proposed developmental activities.

Mitigation

Mitigation 19.02—ROV Survey Required—DOCD

In accordance with Notice to Lessees and Operators No. 2003-G03, conduct the Remotely Operated Vehicle surveys you proposed in your plan for the facility location approved under this plan. Submit your pre- and post-installation survey reports within 60 days after the facility installation is completed.

3. DESCRIPTIONS AND IMPACT ANALYSES OF THE AFFECTED RESOURCES

This chapter describes the physical and biological resources, as well as providing impact and cumulative analyses of these resources, in and adjacent to Walker Ridge Blocks 205, 206, 249, 250, 425, 426, 469, and 470. These resources could be potentially affected by exploration and production activities for the proposed Cascade-Chinook project. The descriptions of the environmental resources provide baseline information for further analyses of potential impacts from the Cascade-Chinook project in Walker Ridge. Discussions in the Multisale EIS (USDOI, MMS, 2007), the FPSO EIS (USDOI, MMS, 2001), and the *Gulf of Mexico Deepwater Operations and Activities: Environmental Assessment*

(Deepwater EA) (USDOI, MMS, 2000a) are summarized and are hereby incorporated by reference into this SEA, where appropriate.

Impact-Producing Factors

Impact-producing factors from the Cascade-Chinook project in Walker Ridge Blocks 205, 206, 249, 250, 425, 426, 469, and 470 include (1) waste and discharges from vessel operations and drilling activities (**Appendix A**), (2) air emissions, (3) bottom disturbances, and (4) noise from vessel and helicopter transportation and drilling activities. Potential impacts from accidents include (1) vessel collisions with marine mammals and sea turtles, (2) oil spills and blowouts (**Appendix B**), (3) vessel and helicopter collisions with coastal and marine birds, and (5) bottom impacts to benthic communities. The impact-producing factors described above were considered in the Multisale EIS (USDOI, MMS, 2007), FPSO EIS (USDOI, MMS, 2001), and Deepwater EA (USDOI, MMS, 2000a) and are hereby incorporated by reference into this SEA where appropriate. Site-specific analyses of potential impacts to resources are described below. The subregional oil-spill-response plan is also discussed in **Appendix B**.

3.1. PHYSICAL RESOURCES

The descriptions of the physical environment located in Appendix A of the Multisale EIS (USDOI, MMS, 2007) and are hereby incorporated by reference into this SEA, where appropriate. Appendix A of the Multisale EIS discusses the following components of the physical environment: (1) geologic and geographic setting; (2) physical oceanography; (3) meteorological conditions; and (4) existing OCS-related infrastructure.

Physical environments in the CPA and Western Planning Area (WPA) are characterized in the Deepwater EA (USDOI, MMS, 2000a), FPSO EIS (USDOI, MMS, 2001), and Multisale EIS (USDOI, MMS, 2007) and are hereby incorporated by reference into this SEA. Summaries of these resources follow and include water quality and air quality.

3.1.1. Water Quality

3.1.1.1. Coastal Waters

3.1.1.1.1. Description

The coastal water quality of Texas, Louisiana, Mississippi, and Alabama could be affected by the proposed development and production activities in the eight blocks of Walker Ridge that comprise the Cascade-Chinook project. The most likely service bases for this project are located on the coast at Port Fourchon, Louisiana, and Galveston, Texas. Marine transportation to and from Walker Ridge would traverse coastal waters to reach these bases, and accidental spills could make landfall along the coastline. The shuttle tankers or articulated barges that will transport liquid hydrocarbon production to the Gulf Coast for refining could use any of the existing receiving terminals from Texas to Alabama. Discharges to coastal waters would be similar to those from existing tanker and other vessel traffic, but spills that would affect coastal water quality could occur.

A detailed description of offshore and nearshore water quality can be found in Chapter 3.1.2 of the Multisale EIS (USDOI, MMS, 2007). The description incorporates information on the general water quality along the Gulf Coast and a broad description of the estuarine water quality, as well as sediment and population growth effects.

The bays, estuaries, and nearshore coastal waters of the north-central Gulf are important in that they provide important feeding, breeding, and/or nursery habitat for many commercially important invertebrates and fishes, as well as for sea turtles, birds, and marine mammals. Water quality governs the suitability of these waters for animal as well as human use. Furthermore, the egg, larval, and juvenile stages of marine biota dependent upon these coastal areas are typically more sensitive to water quality degradation than their adult stages.

In June 2007, the U.S. Environmental Protection Agency (USEPA) issued the National Estuary Program Coastal Condition Report (USEPA, 2007). The report described conditions at four Gulf Coast estuaries near the MMS CPA and WPA—Mobile Bay, the Barataria-Terrebonne Estuary, Galveston Bay, and Coastal Bend Bays and Estuaries (Corpus Christi Bay Estuary). A water quality rating was determined, and the Barataria-Terrebonne Estuary and Mobile Bay were ranked fair.

The priority water quality issues identified by the Gulf of Mexico Alliance are bacterial-related beach and shellfish bed closures, estuarine hypoxia, harmful algal blooms, and seafood, particularly mercury, contamination. Several of these issues are linked to economic consequences for the Gulf Coast States as well. Nutrient loading was also identified as a regional action item (Gulf of Mexico Alliance, 2005). The hypoxic zone is discussed in Chapter 3.1.1.2.1 of the Multisale EIS (USDOI, MMS, 2007).

Harmful algal blooms form intermittently in some areas of Gulf waters. Red tide occurs naturally and has reached bloom concentrations in Gulf Coast waters. The red tide organism produces a toxin that, at sufficient concentrations, can cause fish kills and marine mammal deaths. When the bloom is transported towards the coast, beach and oyster bed closures may occur.

Other pollutant source categories include (1) agricultural runoff, (2) municipal point sources, (3) landfill leachate, (4) hydromodification, (5) petrochemical plants and refineries, (6) power plants, (7) pulp and paper mills, (8) fish or livestock processors, (9) nonrefinery industrial discharge, and (10) shipping activities. Hydromodification includes dredging and spoil disposal; channelization (channel straightening); dam, levee, or floodgate construction; and river bank and shoreline modifications that change river flow patterns or sediment load.

The National Research Council (NRC, 2003; Table I-4) estimated that approximately 942 metric tons of oil/year (yr) (about 6,600 bbl/yr) entered Gulf waters from petrochemical and oil refinery industries in Louisiana and Texas. Further, NRC (2003) calculated an estimate for oil and grease loads from all land-based sources per unit of urban land area for rivers entering the sea. The Mississippi River introduced approximately 525,600 metric tons of oil/yr (about 3.7 million bbl/yr) (NRC, 2003; Table I-9) into the waters of the Gulf.

Vessels from the shipping and fishing industries, as well as recreational boaters, add contaminants to coastal water in the form of bilge water, liquid and solid waste, spills, and chemicals leached from antifouling paints.

Many millions of cubic feet of sediments are moved each year in coastal areas as a result of channelization, dredging, spoil disposal, and other hydromodifications. Water quality may be affected by these activities because they can lead to saltwater intrusion, increased turbidity, and the release of contaminants.

Water quality in coastal waters of the northern Gulf of Mexico is highly influenced by season. For example, salinity in open water near the coast may vary between 29 and 32 parts per thousand during fall and winter but decline to 20 parts per thousand during spring and summer due to increased runoff (USDOI, MMS, 2000a). Oxygen and nutrient concentrations also vary seasonally.

3.1.1.1.2. Impact Analysis

Sources that originate upriver from the Mississippi River Delta, as well as coastal sources, contribute to water quality degradation in nearshore and offshore environments of the Gulf of Mexico. These sources can be broadly characterized as industrial, agricultural, municipal, and point or nonpoint sources.

A discussion of impacts to coastal and offshore water quality from OCS activity is provided in Chapters 4.1.3.4, 4.2.1.1.2, and 4.2.2.1.2 of the Multisale EIS (USDOI, MMS, 2007). The impact analysis in the Multisale EIS examined the effects of domestic and sanitary wastes, service vessels, river borne hydrocarbons, and coastal spills.

The impact-producing factors associated with the development and production of hydrocarbons at the Cascade-Chinook project in Walker Ridge that could affect coastal water quality include (1) effluents from onshore support bases and discharges from the shuttle tanker/ATB and OCS service vessels, such as sanitary and domestic wastes; (2) turbidity increases from vessel traffic; and (3) accidental spills of crude oil, diesel fuel, or chemicals associated with development or production, or other materials from service vessels or the shuttle tankers/ATB's in coastal waters. Water-based drilling mud discharges, water-based and synthetic-based cuttings discharges, treated completion fluids, and produced-water discharges are impact-producing factors that originate and are discharged at the Cascade-Chinook development sites over 100 mi (160 km) from the coast. These discharges are regulated by USEPA and will not impact coastal waters.

The Cascade-Chinook project is located approximately 136 mi (219 km) from the nearest Louisiana coastline and greater distances from the other coastal states. The distance of this project from coastal waters introduces lengthy spill travel times and tremendous dilution factors for any accidental spills of crude oil, diesel fuel, or other materials. Any spill from a shuttle tanker/ATB in the area around the selected receiving terminal in Texas, Louisiana, Mississippi, or Alabama could have an effect on the local environment.

Spills that may occur in the associated blocks of Walker Ridge present an extremely small likelihood of affecting coastal water resources. Spills of crude oil and diesel fuel can occur in offshore waters from vessel and transfer accidents, and well blowouts. Although a large spill ($\geq$1,000 bbl) is highly unlikely, if a large spill were to occur at the surface or originate from a well blowout (a <0.5% chance), the oil would form a surface slick. Response efforts can recover or disperse some of the slick, and wave action could contribute to its break up while at sea. Weathering and evaporation of volatile organics can degrade a slick while at sea. Slicks existing for 10 days or more have a small chance to wash ashore. Spills associated with the Cascade-Chinook project are expected to be few (if any), volumetrically small, and take place near or in Walker Ridge.

Some wastes not permitted for offshore disposal are brought ashore for disposal or recycling and can present spill hazards if not handled properly. The disposal of synthetic-based fluids (SBF) from development drilling in Walker Ridge are governed by the USEPA Region 6 General National Pollutant Discharge Elimination System (NPDES) permit, which does not allow the fluid fraction to be discharged overboard on the OCS. Development and production waste include oil-based drilling fluids and cuttings, liquid wastes ("fracing" fluids, i.e., fluids forced into formations to fracture, dissolve cement, or prop open pore throats, emulsifiers, workover fluids, mud additives, etc.), and possibly well test solids and produced sand are also transported across coastal waters to shore for disposal. These wastes are taken to transfer stations and on to State-regulated disposal locations in Texas and Louisiana. The recycling or disposal facilities for these waste products generally lie inland rather than directly on the coasts. Spillage or improper storage of these wastes at dockside facilities can adversely impact surrounding coastal waters and wetland areas.

Conclusion

No significant long-term impacts on coastal water quality would be expected from the proposed Cascade-Chinook project. The proposed action would use existing onshore support bases and one or more existing oil receiving terminals. Discharges from the support bases, service vessels, and shuttle tanker/ATB could impact coastal waters. The contribution by the proposed action to the level of these impacts is expected to be very minor, transient, and not contribute significantly to the decline in coastal water quality.

3.1.1.1.3. Cumulative Analysis

Cumulative impacts on water quality include sources of pollutants that affect both coastal and offshore settings. Human sources in coastal waters include effluents, wastes, or surface runoff from varied urban, rural, and industrial sources. These sources may include (1) the petrochemical industry (inclusive of OCS development and processing); (2) agriculture and animal processing; (3) agricultural and urban runoff; (4) municipal and recreational sewerage treatment; (5) marinas; (6) commercial fishing; (7) maritime shipping and cruise ships; (8) hydromodification activities; (9) wood processing, pulp, and paper mills; (10) recreational boating and fishing; (11) manufacturing activities; (12) accidental spills of oil, diesel fuel, or other material; and (13) atmospheric deposition of airborne contaminants onto the sea. Contaminants entering coastal waters can also be transported to offshore marine waters.

Human sources in offshore waters include effluents and discharges from fixed (MODU's and production platforms) and mobile sources (vessels of all types). Anchored MODU's and fixed platforms are stationary but temporary in nature. They operate for periods ranging from months to decades. Each fixed or mobile source has routine and permitted effluents and discharges. Fixed platforms and MODU's discharge (1) water-based mud and cuttings; (2) cuttings wetted with synthetic-based mud; (3) small quantities of wellbore cement and treatment, completion, and workover chemicals; (4) domestic and sanitary discharges; (5) produced water; (6) bilge, ballast, cooling, and desalinization unit water; and (7) deck wash.

Vessels such as OCS service boats and crewboats, freighters, tankers, barges, fishing boats, and cruise ships discharge (1) bilge, ballast, and cooling water; (2) domestic and sanitary discharges; and (3) deck wash. Both fixed and mobile sources can accidentally spill oil, diesel fuel, or other material, and trash and debris can be lost inadvertently overboard despite handling precautions.

Worldwide, natural seeps from geologic formations release 4,200,000 bbl (1.8×10^8 gal) of oil into the oceans each year (NRC, 2003; page 2). Natural hydrocarbon seeps are the most significant source of oil entering Gulf waters. Recent studies have suggested that seepage rates in the Gulf of Mexico are much higher than earlier estimates (NRC, 2003; page 191). Mitchell (2000) estimated that 500,000 bbl/yr of oil seeped into northern Gulf of Mexico waters (U.S. territorial waters); a figure NRC doubled to estimate seepage rates for the entire Gulf of Mexico. In the same range, if apportioned to the Gulf of Mexico, would be a recent estimate by MMS (USDOI, MMS, 2003a), which concluded that 1,700 bbl/ day are released into all U.S. territorial waters by natural seeps (620,000 bbl/yr). The NRC (2003; page 191) estimated that an average of 980,000 bbl of oil enters the entire Gulf of Mexico each year from natural seeps (with a range of 560,000-1,400,000 bbl). This average amount is four times the volume of the 1989 *Exxon Valdez* spill (USDOC, NOAA, 1992) every year.

Table 6 reports the annual contribution of oil in marine waters of North America (U.S. and Canada) from various human activities and natural sources. The NRC (2003) provided a best estimate that 1,820,000 bbl of petroleum enters North American marine waters (U.S. and Canada) each year. The majority of this amount is from natural seeps; approximately 1,120,000 bbl or 62 percent. The NRC (2003) shows that the largest fraction of oil entering the water from all sources relates to the consumption of petroleum (33%) and that only 5 percent is related to the production or transportation of oil (including refining). Subtracting the amount contributed by natural seeps, nearly 85 percent of the 627,700 bbl of oil entering North American marine waters each year from human activities comes from the following sources, in relative order: (1) land-based runoff and polluted rivers; (2) recreational boats and jet skis, particularly those with 2-cycle engines; (3) atmospheric deposition; and (4) jettisoned aircraft fuel (NRC, 2003). Approximately 9 percent of the total attributable to human activity comes from transportation, pipeline, or refining activity (NRC, 2003), and 3 percent comes from oil and gas exploration and production (NRC, 2003).

No irreversible or irretrievable impacts to the marine environment on a broad oceanic scale are caused by either natural seeps or accidental spills (NRC, 2003). Natural seeps have released oil into the Gulf of Mexico and the oceans of the world in all types of coastal and marine environments for millennia. Natural marine systems can accommodate rather substantial quantities of oil in the sea, apparently without much noticeable impact.

The Gulf Coast has been, and will continue to be, heavily used for industrial, commercial, and recreational enterprises. The Mississippi River will continue to be the major source of contamination of the Gulf. Over time, continuing coastal water quality contamination will degrade offshore water quality. If the capacity of coastal waters to assimilate contaminants is exceeded, there will be a subsequent, gradual movement of the area of degraded waters farther offshore over time. This degradation could cause short-term loss of the designated uses of large areas of shallow offshore waters due to the contamination itself or the effects of contamination such as lingering hypoxia or episodes of harmful algal blooms. The signs of environmental stress are already evident, among them high nutrient loads, low-dissolved oxygen, toxic contamination, high bacteria counts that close shellfish grounds, and wetland loss. Degradation of coastal water quality is expected to continue because no cessation or reduction in any of the sources that contribute to degradation is likely to occur in the near future. Efforts to improve water quality progress slowly because of a complex regional regulatory structure with State and Federal responsibilities, land-use issues, and the costs associated with implementing additional controls.

Cumulative impacts on the water quality of the coastal waters result from the addition of discharges from supply-vessel and infrastructure discharges. The incremental contribution of the proposed action to the cumulative impacts to coastal water quality is not expected to be significant as long as all regulations are followed.

Table 6

Average Annual Releases of Oil in North American Marine Waters (1990-1999) in Barrels

Source	Best Estimate (bbl)	Minimum (bbl)	Maximum (bbl)	Percent of Best Estimate
Natural Seeps	**1,120,000**	**560,000**	**1,680,000**	**62.0**
Platforms	1,120	1,050	1,260	0.06
Atmospheric Deposition	840	490	3,150	+
Produced Water	18,900	1,470	2,590	1.0
Total Extraction Activity	**21,000**	**16,100**	**30,100**	**1.5**
Pipeline Spills	13,300	11,900	14,700	0.7
Tank Vessel Spills	37,100	28,000	44,800	2.0
Coastal Facility Spills	13,300	11,900	15,400	0.7
Atmospheric Deposition	70	†	140	+
Total Transportation Activity	**63,700**	**51,800**	**77,000**	**3.5**
Land-Based (river, runoff)	378,000	18,200	13,300,000	20.7
Recreational Vessels	39,200	15,400	63,000	2.1
Commercial Vessel Spills	8,400	7,700	9,800	0.4
Operational Discharges	154	420	4,200	+
Atmospheric Deposition	147,000	63,700	567,000	8.0
Aircraft Dumping	10,500	7,000	30,800	0.5
Total Consumption Activity	**588,000**	**133,000**	**14,000,000**	**33.0**

Notes: *denotes <0.001%.
　　　　**denotes <70 bbl.
　　　***does not add to 100 due to independent rounding.

Source: Modified from Table 3-2 of NRC, 2003. (Table 3-2 was converted from metric tons to barrels (1 metric ton = 7 bbl)).

3.1.1.2. Offshore Waters

3.1.1.2.1. Description

The water offshore of the Texas and Louisiana coasts can be divided into two regions: the continental shelf and the slope west of the Mississippi River (<1,000 ft or 305 m) and deep water (>1,000 ft or 305 m). The continental shelf off the modern Mississippi River Delta is narrow because of the outbuilding of sediment from the river onto the shelf. To the west, the shelf broadens and is about 100 mi (161 km) wide in western Louisiana. Waters on the continental shelf and slope are heavily influenced by the Mississippi and Atchafalaya Rivers, the primary sources of freshwater, sediment, and pollutants from a huge drainage basin encompassing 55 percent of the continental U.S. (Murray, 1998). Lower salinities are characteristic nearshore where freshwater from the rivers mix with Gulf waters. While the average discharge from the Mississippi River exceeds the input of all other rivers along the Texas-Louisiana coast by a factor of 10, during low-flow periods the Mississippi River can have a flow less than all these rivers combined (Nowlin et al., 1998).

A zone of hypoxia on the Louisiana-Texas shelf is one of the largest areas of low oxygen in the world's coastal waters (Murray, 1998). Increased nutrient loading in the Mississippi and Atchafalaya River systems since the turn of the 19th century correlates with the increased magnitude and frequency of hypoxic events (Eadie et al., 1992) and supports the interpretation that hypoxia zones are related to nutrient input into the Gulf of Mexico. Phosphorus is believed to play a larger role than originally suspected and, in the 2005 reassessment, the Hypoxia Task Force suggested the occurrence of

26

phosphorous may contribute to the hypoxic conditions in the Gulf of Mexico (USEPA, 2005). Hypoxic zones are discussed in detail in Chapter 3.1.2.2 of the Multisale EIS (USDOI, MMS, 2007).

The presence or extent of a nepheloid layer at the sea bottom affects water quality on the shelf and slope. A nepheloid layer is a zone of suspended clay-sized particles that may play a role in transporting fine-grained sediment and contaminants from nearshore to offshore waters. The nepheloid layer can be thin and near-bottom or very thick, depending on factors such as water depth, depth of water-column mixing, season, and sediment input. Freshwater from the Mississippi/Atchafalaya River systems may carry trace amounts of organic pollutants including polynuclear aromatic hydrocarbons; herbicides such as atrazine, chlorinated pesticides, and polychlorinated biphenyls; and trace inorganic (metals) pollutants.

The concentration of hydrocarbons in slope sediments (except in seep areas) is lower than concentrations reported for shelf and coastal sediments (Gallaway et al., 2003). No consistent decrease with increasing water depth is apparent below 300 m (984 ft). In general, the Central Gulf has higher levels of hydrocarbons in sediment, particularly those from terrestrial sources, than the Western and Eastern Gulf (Gallaway and Kennicutt, 1988). Total organic carbon is also highest in the Central Gulf. Hydrocarbons in sediments have been determined to influence biological communities of the Gulf slope, even when present in trace amounts (Gallaway and Kennicutt, 1988).

Hydrocarbon seeps are extensive throughout the continental slope and contribute hydrocarbons to the surface sediments and water column, especially in the Central Gulf (Sassen et al., 1993a and b). Natural hydrocarbon seepage is considered to be a major source of petroleum into Gulf slope waters (Kennicutt et al., 1987; Gallaway et al., 2003), and the NRC (2003) considers seeps to be the predominant source. Hydrocarbon seeps are discussed in detail in Chapter 3.1.2.2 of the Multisale EIS (USDOI, MMS, 2007).

In addition to hydrocarbon seeps, other fluids leak from the underlying sediments into the bottom water along the slope. These fluids have been identified to have three origins: (1) seawater trapped during the settling of sediments; (2) brine from dissolution of underlying salt diapirs; and (3) deep-seated formation waters (Fu and Aharon, 1998; Aharon et al., 2001). The first two fluids are the source of carbonate for hardground deposits, while the third is rich in barium and is the source of barite deposits in chimneys.

Produced water (formation water) is the volumetrically largest waste stream from the oil and gas industry that enters Gulf waters. Produced water is commonly treated to separate free oil and is either injected back into the reservoir or discharged overboard according to NPDES permit limits. The NRC has estimated the quantity of oil in produced water entering the Gulf per year to be 473,000 bbl (NRC, 2003; Table D-8).

The Walker Ridge blocks that comprise the Cascade-Chinook project are entirely in deep water, for which limited information is available on water quality. Generally, the water quality in deep water could be considered significantly better than that of the coastal waters (USDOI, MMS, 2002a). Water at depths >1,400 m (4,593 ft) is relatively homogeneous with respect to temperature, salinity, and oxygen (Nowlin, 1972; Pequegnat, 1983; Gallaway and Kennicutt, 1988). Offshore Texas, Louisiana, and Alabama show detectable levels of petroleum hydrocarbons, likely from natural seeps (Regg, 1998; USDOI, MMS, 2000b). Pequegnat (1983) pointed out the importance of water-column mixing and flush time for the Gulf of Mexico. Oxygen in deep water must originate from the surface and be mixed into deep water by some mechanism, but the time for turnover or the mechanism by which oxygen replenishment takes place in the deep Gulf of Mexico is essentially unknown.

Deepwater sediments, with the exception of barium concentrations in the vicinity of previous drilling, do not appear to contain elevated levels of metal contaminants (Regg, 1998; USDOI, MMS, 2000b). Reported total hydrocarbons, including biogenic hydrocarbons (e.g., from plankton and other biological sources), in sediments collected from the Gulf slope range from 5 to 86 nanogram/gram (Kennicutt et al., 1987). Petroleum hydrocarbons including aromatic hydrocarbons (<5 parts per billion) were present at all sites sampled.

The MMS studied the effect of exploration and development at four drilling sites located in water depths >1,000 m (3,280 ft) (CSA, 2006). The sampling design called for before and after exploratory or development drilling and captured the drilling-related changes that occur in sediments and sediment pore water. Cuttings wetted with SBF were discharged and the effects were detected in the decrease in sediment dissolved oxygen after development drilling and the visible microbial mat growth on these cuttings.

3.1.1.2.2. Impact Analysis

The impact-producing factors associated with proposed development and production of the Cascade-Chinook project that could affect offshore water quality include (1) degradation of Gulf of Mexico offshore waters from coastal activity, runoff, and riverine inputs; (2) activities that contact or disturb the sea bottom and increase turbidity; (3) discharges during the drilling and completion of wells; (4) discharges during production, such as produced water, from offshore OCS oil and gas production; (5) disturbances during decommissions; and (6) accidental spills of crude oil, diesel fuel, chemicals or other materials from vessels in offshore waters. Impacts are discussed in greater detail in Chapter 4.3.3.1 of the FPSO EIS (USDOI, MMS, 2001).

Operations

The Walker Ridge blocks that comprise the Cascade-Chinook project are in water depths of approximately 8,200 ft (2,500 m). These deep marine waters and environments would be most directly affected by the Cascade-Chinook project's Phase 1 installation activities. Drilling will be conducted by a combination of dynamically positioned (DP) and non-DP rigs. Seafloor disturbances would occur from the anchoring of the non-DP drill rig and mooring of the FPSO. Additional seafloor disturbances would result from the installation of the subsea production equipment, including subsea booster pumps mounted on skids, manifolds, well tree, flowline sleds, and umbilical termination assemblies, and the gas export pipelines installation. These disturbances would not adversely affect offshore water quality because the area of potential disturbance is small and the effects would be most intense during the first year of the project. Elevated turbidity would be a short-term, localized, and reversible condition once the disturbance ceases.

A range of effluents and wastes would be discharged overboard from the Cascade-Chinook project. Overboard discharges and wastes intended from the project are shown in the wastes and discharge tables in **Appendix A**. The types and discharge rates will be in accordance with USEPA NPDES General Permit GMG 290000 for USEPA Region 6, or an individual NPDES permit if one is secured by Petrobras and its partners. The USEPA permit GMG 290000 was recently reissued and will expire on September 30, 2012. The 316(b) cooling water intake structure regulations recently incorporated into the USEPA Region 6 general NPDES permit do not apply to the FPSO. Wastes destined for onshore disposal or recycling pose no potential impacts to affected resources unless spilled.

Decommissioning effects would be similar in scope and magnitude with offshore construction and installation operations unless the subsea production infrastructure is left in place, in which case the impacts on the sea bottom would be reduced or eliminated. All discharges would be expected to adhere to NPDES discharge criteria designed to mitigate adverse environmental effects.

Accidental Events

Failure or disconnects of a riser system could result in the release of some or all of the fluid in the annuli. Riser system failures and disconnects, though not common, have occurred in the past (USDOI, MMS, 2000b and 2003b). A spill of SBF could accumulate on the seafloor and result in the smothering of benthic organisms directly beneath the spill and anoxic surface sediments as microbial degradation occurs.

A spill from the FSPO vessel could occur at the production site. A spill from the shuttle tanker or ATB could occur at any point from where the FPSO offloads to the oil transportation vessel to the point where the vessel offloads at the terminal. A risk assessment for the FPSO is presented in Chapter 4.4.1 of the FPSO EIS (USDOI, MMS, 2001). The risk of spills unique to FPSO operations in the Gulf of Mexico is low (0.37%). The risk of spills during offloading from the FPSO to the shuttle tanker is similar to that for lightering operations in the Gulf of Mexico, where there is a history of low spill frequency and small spill volumes. The risk of shuttle-tanker transport spills was derived from a database of all tanker spills in U.S. waters. The rate of spills for tankers in port is greater than at sea (Anderson and LaBelle, 2000). The spill rate for barges is greater than the spill rate for tankers. The risk of a spill from the shuttle tanker or barge carrying oil from Cascade-Chinook would be similar to that for other vessels importing oil. The impact of a spill would depend upon many factors including the volume of the spill, the location, meteorological conditions at the time of the spill, and the subsequent response activities.

The oil has an American Petroleum Institute (API) gravity of 17°-29°. Based on this preliminary data, the oil at Cascade-Chinook appears heavier than typical Gulf of Mexico oils. It could weather differently from typical Gulf of Mexico oils and have a shorter "window of opportunity" for effective use of dispersants.

A surface slick from an oil spill begins to weather as soon as it forms, depending on a number of factors, particularly the characteristics of the released oil and oceanographic conditions. Some of the subsurface oil may disperse within the water column. Evidence from a recent experiment in the North Sea indicated that oil released during a deepwater blowout (844-m or 2,769-ft water depth) would quickly rise to the surface and form a slick (Johansen et al., 2001). A variety of physical, chemical, and biological processes act to disperse and degrade the slick once oil enters the ocean. These include spreading, evaporation of the more volatile constituents, dissolution into the water column, emulsification of small droplets, agglomeration sinking, microbial modification, photochemical modification, and biological ingestion and excretion. Some oil from the slick would be mixed into the water and dispersed by wind and waves. The quality of marine waters on the surface or in a rising subsurface plume from a blowout would be temporarily affected by the solubility of hydrocarbon components and by small, dispersed oil droplets that do not rise to the surface due to current activity or that are mixed downward by surface turbulence. Dispersion by currents and microbial degradation remove the oil from the water column and eventually dilute the constituents to background levels.

No blowouts are projected as a result of drilling, well completions, or hydrocarbon production associated with the Cascade-Chinook project based on historical trends in the Gulf of Mexico (**Appendix B**).

Conclusion

No significant long-term impacts on offshore water quality would be expected from the proposed Cascade-Chinook project. Near-bottom water quality would be affected by increased turbidity and disturbed substrates during the period of installation of subsea infrastructure, FPSO mooring, and gas pipeline installation. Any effects from the elevated turbidity would be short term, localized, and reversible. Small numbers of bottom-dwelling invertebrates may be killed or adversely impacted.

Impacts on offshore water quality from the drilling and production discharges that would be expected to result from the Cascade-Chinook project are insignificant because of (1) existing environmental regulations, (2) great water depth, (3) distance of the project and grid from the coast, (4) spill transit times, and (5) dilution factors. An accidental oil spill would affect water quality at the surface (top few feet or meters of the water column). Spilled oil originating from the project would not be ≥1,000 bbl and is expected to be substantially recovered while still at sea. Operator-initiated activities to contain and clean up an oil spill would begin as soon as possible after an event. Small quantities of unrecovered oil would weather and largely biodegrade within 2 weeks.

Impacts on offshore water quality from the shuttle tanker or ATB would be similar to discharges from vessels in the maritime industry and would present no new type or increased volume of waste than is presently discharged. Spilled oil from the shuttle tanker or ATB increases the risk of a surface spill as opposed to a subsurface spill that could occur from pipeline rupture.

3.1.1.2.3. Cumulative Analysis

The sources identified in **Chapter 3.1.1** ("Water Quality") above contribute to cumulative water quality degradation in offshore waters. Spills of oil, diesel fuel, and other materials may occur from vessels transporting crude oil and petroleum products; from vessels involved in commercial fishing, freight, or passenger transport; and from OCS operations. Well blowouts can disturb the bottom, increase turbidity, and put oil into the sea. Should one of these blowouts occur, localized, short-term changes in water quality would be expected. Cumulative impacts would be negligible.

Bottom area disturbances resulting from non-OCS sources are not expected in Walker Ridge water depths. Bottom disturbances from anchoring the MODU and the FPSO would produce short-lived effects on water quality on small footprints of about 5 ac (2 ha) per anchor. Cumulative impacts are negligible.

Daily operational discharges to offshore waters occur from vessels moving through Gulf waters and from MODU's and production facilities (**Chapters 3.1.1.1.2 and 3.1.1.2.2**). The discharge of drilling fluid, cuttings, and produced water are the main effluents from oil and gas exploration, development, and production operations. Although not an issue for the Cascade-Chinook project, other production projects in the vicinity that follow may include the drilling of development wells. The discharges from OCS production facilities have been examined in several studies (Avanti Corporation, 1993; CSA, 1997; Kennicutt, 1995; Neff, 1997). These studies concluded that contaminants in produced water, drilling fluid, and cutting discharges should be undetectable in the water column beyond 1,000 m (3,281 ft) from the discharge point. The contaminant deposition and accumulation rate on the sea bottom from discharges is primarily dependent on the water depth and current strength. Sediment contaminants from OCS discharges may occur from several hundred to several thousand meters from the discharge point depending on volumes discharged. Biological responses to contaminant levels retained in bottom sediments are not expected to be detectable beyond a couple hundred meters, and toxic effects to the benthos would be localized, limited to within a hundred meters of the discharge, and of a relatively small magnitude. Toxic effects beyond 100 m (328 ft) should be controlled through the USEPA's NPDES permit requirements.

Well blowouts can resuspend fine-grained sediment in the water to increase turbidity. The rapid accumulation of sediment (or cuttings if well drilling is part of the development project) on the sea bottom that are thicker than 30 cm (1 ft) would be lethal for all sessile and most motile invertebrates (Frey, 1975; Basan et al., 1978; Ekdale et al., 1984). An accumulation rate of this type would not be expected in most deepwater development projects, and most soft-bottom, motile invertebrates would have a chance to react and move. Diluted and discharged slowly over large areas, these wastes contribute in a very small way to the degradation of offshore water quality.

Impacts on the water quality of the marine environment may result from the addition of discharges from supply-vessel and from the exploration, production, and removal activities of the project. However, the incremental contribution of the proposed action to the cumulative impacts to marine water quality is not expected to be significant as long as all regulations are followed.

3.1.2. Air Quality

3.1.2.1. Description

Walker Ridge Blocks 249 and 469 are located west of 87.5° W. longitude and hence falls under MMS's jurisdiction for enforcement of the Clean Air Act. The air over the OCS water is not classified, but it is presumed to be better than the National Ambient Air Quality Standards (NAAQS) for all criteria pollutants. The Cascade/Chinook project in Walker Ridge Blocks 249 and 469 is located approximately 250 mi (402 km) south of Orleans Parish, Louisiana, an area that is in attainment of the NAAQS for CO, NO_x, SO_x, and particulate matter and that, for prevention of significant deterioration (PSD) purposes, is classified as a Class II area.

The influence to onshore air quality is dependent upon meteorological conditions and air pollution emitted from operational activities. The pertinent meteorological conditions regarding air quality are the wind speed and direction, the atmospheric stability, and the mixing height (which govern the dispersion and transport of emissions). The typical synoptic wind flow for the Walker Ridge Blocks 249/469 area is driven by the clockwise circulation around the Bermuda High, resulting in a prevailing southeasterly to southerly flow, which is conducive to transporting emissions toward shore. However, superimposed upon this synoptic circulation are smaller meso-scale wind flow patterns, such as the land/sea breeze phenomenon. In addition, there are other synoptic scale patterns that occur periodically, namely tropical cyclones and mid-latitude frontal systems. Because of the routine occurrence of these various conditions, the winds blow from all directions in the area of concern (Florida A&M University, 1988).

3.1.2.2. Impact Analysis

Air quality would be affected in the immediate vicinity of the development operations, production, service vessels, and aircraft. The drilling, facility installation, and production activities are not expected to significantly affect onshore air quality. The distance from Walker Ridge Blocks 249 and 469 to any PSD Class I air quality area such as the Breton National Wildlife Refuge is >200 km (124 mi). Lafourche Parish, Louisiana, the location of the primary service, is in attainment for ozone (USEPA Greenbook, 2007; USDOI, MMS, 2007).

Air quality could be affected in the event of spilled oil. The volatile organic compounds (VOC's), which would escape to the atmosphere from a surface slick, are precursors to photochemically produced ozone. A spike in VOC's could contribute to a corresponding spike in ozone, especially if the release were to occur on a hot sunny day in a NO_2-rich environment. The corresponding onshore area is in attainment for ozone. However, due to the distance from shore, the project is not expected to have any impacts on onshore air quality. If a fire occurs, particulate and combustible emissions will be released in addition to the VOC's.

Conclusion

No significant long-term impacts on air quality would be expected from the proposed Cascade/Chinook project. The air quality in the immediate vicinity of the proposed activities would be affected by the projected emissions. The distance between Walker Ridge Blocks 249 and 469 and the shoreline introduces tremendous dilution factors for point-source emissions in Walker Ridge. No special mitigation, monitoring, or reporting requirements apply to this project.

3.1.2.3. Cumulative Analysis

Cumulative impacts on air quality within the offshore area would come primarily from sources generated outside the Walker Ridge Blocks 249/469 area and include emissions from industrial plants, power generation, and urban transportation. The location of Walker Ridge Blocks 249 and 469 is far removed from coastal populations or industrial activity. The OCS activity that takes place in the vicinity of Walker Ridge Blocks 249 and 469 would be widely spaced production platforms, all >100 mi (160 km) from shore, and would not affect the overall quality of air over the Gulf Coast. Localized air quality may be temporarily impacted by activities immediate to the Cascade-Chinook development; however, other local anthropogenic sources that impact air quality are limited this far from shore. Most of the Gulf's coastal areas are currently designated as "attainment" for all the NAAQS-regulated pollutants (USEPA, 2007). The cumulative impact from emissions for this DOCD will not exceed MMS's exemption levels. As a result, cumulative impacts as a result of the proposed action are negligible.

3.2. BIOLOGICAL RESOURCES

Descriptions of and impacts to the biology, life history, and distribution of biological resources in the CPA and WPA, including the deepwater benthic communities, are characterized in the Deepwater EA (USDOI, MMS, 2000a), the FPSO EIS (USDOI, MMS, 2001), and the Multisale EIS (USDOI, MMS, 2007) and are hereby incorporated by reference into this SEA. Summaries of these resources follow.

3.2.1. Sensitive Coastal Resources

3.2.1.1. Coastal Barrier Beaches and Associated Dunes

3.2.1.1.1. Description

The description, physical location, and formative processes that create the various coastal beaches and barrier island complexes are described in Chapter 3.2.1.1 of the Multisale EIS (USDOI, MMS, 2007). A description of integrated shoreline environments, the barrier islands, and the dune zones that comprise and delineate the various vegetated habitats along these mainland and barrier beaches can also be found in this chapter of the Multisale EIS. Therefore, the discussions that follow will only summarize the pertinent features of these resources in relation to their ability to allow, minimize, or neutralize the impact-producing factors associated with the proposed action. In addition, the post-hurricane condition of these island and beach resources, along with their integral protective features, will be described.

The Louisiana coastal barrier beaches and associated dunes form narrow, elongated landforms comprised of unconsolidated, predominantly coarse sediment that results in sandy beaches with several interrelated environments (i.e., shore face, foreshore, and backshore) that are lower in profile and therefore more susceptible to wave washover and channeling. Louisiana has both trangressive barriers (landward migration) to the east and regressive (seaward migration) barrier islands in the western waters. In coastal Louisiana, the heights of dune lines range from 1.6 to 4.3 ft (0.5 to 1.3 m) above mean high tide levels. For more detail on morphology and vegetative characteristics of these landforms, see Chapter 3.2.1.1 of the Multisale EIS (USDOI, MMS, 2007) and Chapter 3.2.1.1 of the FPSO EIS (USDOI, MMS, 2001).

The Dog Keys define the Mississippi Sound of Mississippi and Alabama. These islands, with the exception of the low-profile, transgressive Dauphin Island (Alabama), are generally regressive islands that are stable, showing some westward migration, and they are characterized by high beach ridges and prominent sand dunes. These islands may be overwashed during strong storms as was seen after Hurricanes Ivan (2004), Dennis (2005), and Katrina (2005). The Gulf coastline of Texas is about 367 mi (590 km) long and is afforded protection by a combination of low–profile, transgressive barriers to the west (i.e., Follets Island, Matagorda Peninsula, and South Padre Island) and higher profile, regressive islands flanking the eastern shoreline(Galveston Island, Bolivar Peninsula, and North Padre Island). The elevations of Galveston Island and Bolivar Peninsula's beach ridges generally range from 5 to 10 ft (1.5 to 3 m) above sea level (Fisher et al., 1972). Padre Island is moderately regressive; the shoreline is retreating and more land is being exposed. It is typically 5-10 ft (1.5-3 m) above sea level and occasionally overwashed by hurricane surges. On the northern portion, some dunes may rise 20-30 ft (6-9 m), and the dune ridge is generally continuous. On the southern portion, the dune ridge is a series of short discontinuous segments.

Hurricane Katrina in August 2005 caused severe erosion and landloss for the coastal barrier islands of the deltaic plain. The pre-storm land area of the Chandeleur Islands was reduced to half its size by Hurricane Katrina, based on aerial post-storm surveys by U.S. Geological Survey (USDOI, GS, 2005). Grand Isle was also heavily damaged by Hurricane Katrina. Although Hurricane Katrina made landfall more than 50 mi (80 km) to its east, Grand Isle received extremely high winds and a 12- to 20-ft (4- to 6-m) storm surge that caused tremendous structural damage to most of the island's camps, homes, and businesses (Louisiana Sea Grant, 2005). Boyd and Penland (1988) estimated that storms raise mean water levels 5.68-6.66 ft (1.73-2.03 m) above mean sea level 10-30 times per year. Under those conditions, the following would be overwashed: 67 percent of Timbalier Island; 100 percent of Isles Dernieres and the Barataria Bay Barriers (excluding Grand Isle); and 100, 89, and 64 percent of the southern, central, and northern portions of the Chandeleur Islands, respectively (USDOI, MMS, 2007). Hurricane Rita in September 2005 severely impacted the shoreface and beach communities of Cameron Parish in southwest Louisiana. Some small towns in this area have no standing structures remaining. A storm surge approaching 20 ft (6 m) caused beach erosion and overwash that flattened coastal dunes, depositing sand and debris well into the backing marshes. Barrier beaches and dune environments are further characterized in Chapter 3.2.1.1 of the Multisale EIS (USDOI, MMS, 2007).

Along the Mississippi Gulf Coast, the barrier islands were also severely eroded. The overall size, elevation, and vegetative cover were significantly reduced by about 15 percent (USDOC, NMFS, 2007a). Mississippi's offshore barrier islands include Petit Bois, Horn, Ship, and Cat Islands. This island chain, located 12 mi (19.3 km) south of coastal Mississippi, provides a natural first line of defense against hurricanes and other tropical storm systems. Unfortunately, these natural barriers have suffered a series of onslaughts, first by Hurricane Camille in 1969, which created a major cut through Ship Island; then by Hurricane Georges in 1998, which breached Horn Island; and then several years later by Hurricane Ivan in 2004 and Hurricane Katrina in 2005, which caused further damage. Hurricane Katrina alone destroyed more than 2,000 ac (809 ha) on these four islands and drastically reduced the functionality of the remaining acres (Barbour, 2006). Importantly, their elevations have, in many instances, been reduced to near sea level and the vegetative cover has been greatly reduced. The majority of permanent landloss (conversion to open water) occurred from what appears to be bare to slightly vegetated soil, with the exception of Petit Bois Island, which lost mostly denser vegetation (USDOC, NMFS, 2007a).

Portions of the barrier islands along the Alabama coast suffered from wind and water-induced erosion as a result of the storm surge. The majority of the damage was on Isle Aux Herbes, a barrier island in Mississippi Sound on the southwest coast of Alabama. A biological survey report prepared for the Mobile Bay Estuary Program indicated that landloss had occurred on the island as a result of shoreline erosion and that vegetative debris from the storm event was piled on some areas of the island (Barry A. Vittor & Associates, 2006). The barrier island beaches were important as sea turtle nesting sites. The U.S. Fish and Wildlife Service (USDOI, FWS, 2005) reported that about 50 sea turtle nests were lost along the Alabama coast. All 10 nests at the Bon Secour National Wildlife refuge were destroyed.

Barrier islands from Texas to Alabama incurred some type of damage from the combination of Hurricanes Katrina and Rita and, in some cases, in combination with Hurricanes Wilma, George, and Ivan as well. While Louisiana barrier islands incurred most of the damage, all of the areas experienced varying degrees of erosion, land and vegetation loss, loss in elevation or beach profile and, in some cases, movement toward shore as a result of the previous, highly active hurricane season. The resulting change in elevation and island profiles reduces the ability of these features to provide the pre-storm coastal protection to the mainland beaches and wetlands. While these barriers can rebuild to some extent naturally over time, it is the intent of both Federal and State coastal restoration projects like the Coastal Wetlands Protection, Planning & Restoration Act, Louisiana Coastal Resources Program, and Coastal Impact Assistance Program to assist in these barrier island restorations.

3.2.1.1.2. Impact Analysis

The impact-producing factors associated with FPSO exploration and development in the CPA and WPA that could affect barrier beaches and dunes include installation of the FPSO, support for construction of onshore facilities, vessel traffic, maintenance dredging, oil spills from blowouts or vessel collisions, spill response, and cleanup. The impact-producing factors described above have been considered in the FPSO EIS (USDOI, MMS, 2001), Deepwater EA (USDOI, MMS, 2000a), and the Multisale EIS (USDOI, MMS, 2007) and are hereby incorporated by reference into this SEA. A summary of the incorporated materials and site-specific analyses of potential impacts to resources are described below. The subregional oil-spill-response plan is discussed in **Appendix B**.

During installation, there are expected to be slight increases in the number of vessel transits to and from support bases and fabrication yards, resulting in minor incremental impacts to channels and coastal erosion rates. Given the limited number of vessels required and the relatively short timeframe for each phase of installation activity, such impacts are short term and extremely localized. During routine operations, the only impacts FPSO's will produce on sensitive coastal environments will be those associated with the incremental increase in vessel traffic due to the shuttle tankers. The significance of these incremental increases in impacts varies depending upon the location of the shuttle tanker destinations. For further detail, see Chapter 4.3.4.1 of the FPSO EIS (USDOI, MMS, 2001).

Vessel traffic in close proximity to barrier islands has been shown to move considerably more bottom sediment than tidal currents, thus increasing coastal and barrier island erosion rates. The magnitude of these erosion effects is dependent primarily upon ship speed and channel cross section (Renger and Bednarczyk, 1986; Kwik, 1992). The incremental increases in channel and coastal erosion associated with increased vessel traffic can be expected to be more significant in those barrier island or beach locations that are currently undergoing transgression. The erodability of some of the barrier islands off Louisiana and Mississippi has increased because of the hurricane-induced erosion and the removal or die off of the wetland vegetation. However, given the level of other tanker and vessel traffic using Gulf ports, impacts on coastal environments from FPSO-related tankering operations is considered to range from low to minor but not significant, depending upon the nature of adjacent coastal environments. At this point in time, most of the proposed tanker ports are located either offshore or are near armored or partially armored channels and flood control features (i.e., levees, etc.); therefore, erosion along the barrier islands and beaches should be minimal. Some islands (i.e., Chandeleur Islands) along the Louisiana coast that were heavily damaged by Hurricane Katrina may be evolving into a minimal island or shoal. If future tanker routes are in close proximity to these islands, recovery time could be greatly extended. However, these islands may be targeted as a State or Federal restoration project. The need for a second attending vessel to accompany tankers during lightering operations or offloading in some ports may temporarily increase the number of harbor transits. The extent of impacts caused by a few additional harbor transits would depend upon harbor characteristics, vessel hull design, transit speed, and the susceptibility of a particular channel to erosion.

No new navigation channels are planned; however, there is the potential for maintenance dredging of existing channels to assure appropriate depths for the shuttle tankers. This dredged material will be used beneficially either for wetland creation or beach restoration.

While offshore oil spills could pose problems for beaches and nearshore barrier islands, these coastal features would be the most susceptible to inshore spills associated with vessel collisions or offloading. Inshore oil spills pose a more severe threat to beaches and nearshore barrier islands than the offshore spills. As noted in the FPSO EIS (USDOI, MMS, 2001), the Oil Spill Risk Analysis models from the FPSO launch points indicate that the conditional probabilities of oil coming ashore on these barrier beaches within 30 days of release are predominantly <0.5 percent. Most oil spills from FPSO's are expected to be small, ranging from <10 to 1,000 bbl. The frequency of larger spills from FPSO's is very low. Based on the analysis in **Appendix B**, there were actually zero spills ≥1,000 bbl during the historical period of record (1985-1999). Spills of <1,000 bbl are expected to dissipate rapidly and would not reach shore unless they did so within the first several days after a spill. Given the distance of the

FPSO launch points and the proposed action from shore (136 mi or 219 km), there is <0.5 percent probability of any spill reaching shore or barrier islands along the parishes and counties of coastal Louisiana or Texas within 3, 10, or 30 days. The percent chance of a spill occurring is based on processing 80,000 bbl per day on the FPSO and the FPSO being in use for 8 years. The spill rates for FPSO's and shuttle tankers were calculated in the FPSO EIS (USDOI, MMS, 2001). The oil-spill risk for shuttle-tanker transport is comparable with and slightly less than pipeline transport. The calculated risk of spills from shuttle tankers and the FPSO is 1.2 and 0.37 percent, respectively (USDOI, MMS, 2001). These low probabilities, combined with the review of the historical data, indicate that the risk to barrier beaches from oil spills from shuttle tankers is low.

The likelihood of contact of spilled materials with the barrier beaches and dunes is dependent on the meteorological and current conditions at the time of the spill and on the quantity and location of the spill (USDOI, MMS, 2001). In coastal Louisiana, the heights of dune lines range from 1.6 to 4 ft (0.5 to 1.3 m) above mean high tide levels. For spilled oil to move onto beaches or across dunes, strong southerly winds must persist for an extended time prior to or immediately after the spill to elevate water levels. Strong winds would accelerate oil-slick dispersal, spreading, and weathering, thereby reducing impact severity at a landfall site. Any barrier beach or dune contacted by a spill associated with the proposed activity is very unlikely except during abnormally high water levels, such as might occur during a hurricane. A study in Texas showed that oil disposal on sand and vegetated sand dunes had little deleterious effects on the existing vegetation or on the recolonization of the oiled sands by plants (Webb, 1988). Oil or its components that remain in the sand after cleanup may be (1) released periodically when storms and high tides resuspend or flush beach sediments, (2) decomposed by biological activity, or (3) volatilized and dispersed during hot or sunny days.

The cleanup impacts of these spills could result in short-term (up to 2 years) adjustments in beach profiles and configurations as a result of sand removal and disturbance during cleanup operations. Some contact to lower areas of sand dunes is expected. These contacts would not result in significant destabilization of the dunes. The long-term stressors to barrier beach communities caused by the physical effects and chemical toxicity of an oil spill may lead to decreased primary production, plant dieback, and hence further erosion.

Conclusion

In summary on a local basis, oil spills from the Cascade-Chinook operations could produce either adverse (but not significant) or extended (but not irreversible) impacts on coastal barrier beaches, depending upon spill size, the nature of the oil coming ashore (e.g., highly vs. lightly weathered), and the location and characteristics of the coastal barrier beach. Impacts may be long term, depending upon spill location and the relative position of sensitive resources. However, the combined probability of a spill ≥1,000 bbl contacting coastal barrier beaches and associated dunes in any county or parish within 30 days is extremely low (<0.5%). At all offshore locations modeled, smaller spills are not predicted to reach shore.

3.2.1.1.3. Cumulative Analysis

Barrier beaches along coastal Louisiana and Texas have experienced severe erosion and landward retreat (marine transgression) because of natural processes enhanced by human activities. Louisiana, Mississippi, Alabama, and to a lesser extent Texas have experienced beach erosion and shoreline depletion in varying degrees as a result of Hurricanes Katrina, Rita, Ivan, and Wilma (USDOC, NMFS, 2007a). The cumulative effect of these barrier island losses will continue as future tropical storms and hurricanes approach these coasts and further degrade these barriers. Various beach nourishment projects in Mississippi and Louisiana will have the effect of slowing the loss or conversion of barrier beaches and dunes, but they will not arrest the natural subsidence of the deltaic plain.

Impact-producing factors from non-OCS activity that contribute to barrier beach and dune erosion, or conversion to another environment, include (1) levee construction and stabilization structures for channels and beaches; (2) natural processes such as hurricanes, erosion, and subsidence; (3) recreational vehicle use on dunes and beaches; (4) recreational and commercial development; and (5) removal of coastal vegetation. Deterioration of the Gulf's barrier beaches is expected to continue in the future.

Impact-producing factors related to OCS activity may include oil spills, beach cleanup, and vessel-induced erosion. However, because of the distance of the proposed OCS activity from shore, the absence of pipeline landfalls, and minimal shuttle tanker trips, only the following impact-producing factors could potentially affect barrier beaches and shorelines. These impact-producing factors would include the minimal (<0.5% chance) potential of beach oiling from oil spills and the minimal potential for vessel-related erosion due to the proximity of the navigation channels to the barrier islands. The incremental contribution of the proposed action's impacts to the cumulative impact on coastal barrier beaches and associated dunes is negligible and likely undetectable.

3.2.1.2. Wetlands

3.2.1.2.1. Description

Detailed descriptions of various wetland types, processes, functions, and importance can be found in Chapter 3.1.2.1 of the Multisale EIS (USDOI, MMS, 2007) and in Chapter 3.2.1.2 of the FPSO EIS (USDOI, MMS, 2001), and they are hereby incorporated by reference into this SEA.

The following is a summary of the information presented in the Multisale EIS, including any new pertinent information discovered since the publication of the Multisale EIS. Wetland habitats found specifically along the Gulf Coast of the CPA and WPA include fresh, intermediate, brackish, and saline marshes; mud and sand flats; and forested wetlands of mangrove swamps, cypress-tupelo swamps, and bottomland hardwoods. These coastal wetland habitats occur as bands around waterways and as broad expanses along the coastal bays, beaches, and barrier islands. The importance of coastal wetlands to the coastal environment can be characterized by their high organic productivity; their ability to recycle nutrients; and by the providing of diverse habitat for a wide variety of commercial and recreational aquatic, terrestrial, and avian species.

Louisiana's coastal wetlands support more than two-thirds of the wintering waterfowl population of the Mississippi Flyway, including 20-25 percent of North America's puddle duck population. Louisiana's coastal region also supports the largest fur harvest in North America (Olds, 1984). During 1997, the area of interest in Louisiana contained about 2,736 mi^2 (708,570 ha) of coastal wetlands. About 32,570 ha (126 mi^2) of this were freshwater marsh and forests; 678 mi^2 (175,560 ha) were intermediate salinity marsh; and 207,440 ha (801 mi^2) were brackish marsh (Louisiana Dept. of Wildlife and Fisheries, Fur and Refuge Division and USDOI, GS, Biological Resources Division, 1997). Presumably, the remaining 293,000 ha (1,131 mi^2) were saline marsh. These wetlands largely occur as broad expanses. More recent information is provided below by geographic area, including recent land change as a result of Hurricanes Katrina and Rita. The most notable was the 217 mi^2 (562 km^2) of Louisiana's coastal lands that were transformed to water after Hurricanes Katrina and Rita (Barras, 2006). The change to density and concentration of the previously described coastal wetland types resulting from these two hurricanes will be determined after several growing seasons.

Wetland loss rates in coastal Louisiana are well documented to have been as high as 10,878 ha/yr (42 mi^2/yr) during the late 1960's. Studies have shown that the landloss rate in coastal Louisiana for the period 1972-1990 had slowed (USDOI, GS, 1988). It was estimated in 2000 that coastal Louisiana would continue to lose land at a rate of approximately 2,672 ha/yr (10 mi^2/yr) over the next 50 years. Further, it was estimated that an additional net loss of 132,794 ha (512 mi^2) may occur by 2050, which is almost 10 percent of Louisiana's remaining coastal wetlands (Barras et al., 2003). However, Hurricanes Katrina and Rita in 2005 caused 217 mi^2 (562 km^2) of land change, primarily wetlands to open water (Barras, 2006). Based on the analysis of the latest satellite imagery (Barras, 2007), approximately 82 mi^2 (212 km^2) of new water areas were in areas primarily impacted by Hurricane Katrina (Mississippi River Delta Basin, Breton Sound Basin, Pontchartrain Basin, and Pearl River Basin), whereas 117 mi^2 (256 km^2) were in areas primarily impacted by Hurricane Rita (Calcasieu/Sabine Basin, Mermentau Basin, Teche/Vermillion Basin, Atchafalaya Basin, and Terrebonne Basin). Barataria Basin contained new water areas caused by both hurricanes, resulting in some 18 mi^2 (46.6 km^2) of new water areas.

This would be a 3 percent loss of the remaining wetland acreage when compared with the 2,077,947 ha (8,023 mi^2) of Louisiana wetlands estimated by Tiner (1984) in 1983. Using Barras' estimates (Barras et al., 2003) of wetland loss, an additional 600 mi^2 (155,399 ha) might have been lost between 1983 and 2007 (a loss rate of 6,475 ha (25 mi^2) per year for 24 years), bringing the wetland acreage down to 1,922,548 ha (7,423 mi^2) for 2007. In this case, the percent loss due to Hurricanes Katrina and Rita is still 3 percent. The most notable of these changes are the dramatic loss of emergent wetlands and areas of unconsolidated shore, and the subsequent increase of over 51,800 ha (200 mi^2) of open water. The most prominent of these changes was the loss of over 38,850 ha (150 mi^2) of estuarine emergent marsh. These changes were seen in the areas surrounding Plaquemines and St. Bernard Parishes in Louisiana. Bottomland hardwood forests were lost in the coastal areas and are now replaced by palustrine emergent species and/or their scrub/shrub understories. These coastal forests suffered uprooting and blowdown or complete defoliation (Smith, 2005).

According to Dahl (1990) and Henfer et al. (1994), during the mid-1980's, 4.4 percent of Texas (3,083,860 ha or 7,620,218 ac) (Henfer et al., 1994), 28 percent of Louisiana (3,557,520 ha or 8,790,632 ac), 14 percent of Mississippi (17,678,730 ha or 43,684,142 ac), and 8 percent of Alabama (1,073,655 ha or 2,653,002 ac) were considered wetlands. The wetland areas in these states have decreased by 1.6-5.6 percent since the mid-1970's. Along the Texas coast in the vicinity of southern Padre Island, marshes are minimal and unstable, compared with the more northern Gulf. Brackish marshes occur in less saline, inland areas and are divided into frequently and infrequently flooded marshes. Infrequently flooded marshes contain an assemblage of plants that are much more tolerant of dry conditions. Frequently flooded flats usually remain moist and may have mats of blue-green algae and an area-specific assemblage of invertebrates. Infrequently flooded flats are at higher elevations where only tides that are driven by strong wind can flood them. These are better drained and much dryer. Higher tidal flats remain barren because of the occasional saltwater flooding and subsequent evaporation that raises salt concentrations in the soil. This inhibits most plant growth; some salt-marsh plants that are tolerant of dry conditions may be found there. Some higher flats are non-tidal, barren fan deltas and barren channel margins along streams.

Freshwater marshes in Texas occur inland above tidally delivered saline waters, in association with streams, lakes, and catchments. Broken bands of black mangroves (*Avicennia germinans*) also occur in this area (Brown et al., 1977; White et al., 1986). Wind-tidal flats of mud and sand are mostly found around shallow bay margins and in association with shoals. South of Corpus Christi and into Tamaulipas, flats increasingly replace lagoonal and bay marshes. Laguna Madre of Texas is divided into northern and southern parts by the wind-tidal flats of the Land-Cut Area, just south of Baffin Bay. The Intracoastal Waterway is dredged through this area, as are a series of well access channels. Dredging has caused topographic and vegetative changes among the flats of Laguna Madre. Inland beaches of sand and shells are found along the shores of bays, lagoons, and tidal streams. The structure of these beaches is similar to, but much narrower and smaller in scale than, barrier beaches. Compared with sand beaches, shell features are typically stacked to higher elevations by storm waves and are generally more stable. Few freshwater swamps and bottomland hardwoods occur in the general vicinity of OCS-related service bases and navigation channels of the Texas barrier island area. In the southern third of this area, they are nonexistent (Brown et al., 1977; White et al., 1986).

The devastating 2005 hurricane season heavily impacted the Gulf Coast wetlands, changing both the face and hydrology of these coastal resources. Aside from physically removing some of the wetland vegetation through scour, these hurricanes changed the topography and hydrology of these wetlands, which, in turn, provided more avenues for increased erosion and landloss. The post-Katrina view of these coastal wetlands is described below.

In Louisiana, Hurricanes Katrina and Rita greatly impacted the remaining wetlands and may have caused the loss of 217 mi^2 (562 km^2) (Barras, 2006). In this one hurricane season, as much landloss took place as was predicted to occur over more than 21 years (Barras et al., 2003) and as much as 8 to 11 times the annual rate of loss between 1990 and 2000. The degree of impact incurred varied by marsh community type. Fresh and intermediate marsh types located near to or east of the hurricanes' landfalls appeared to experience extensive shearing, and estimates of the decrease in marsh area in these communities (fresh=122 mi^2 (316 km^2), intermediate=90 mi^2 (233 km^2) accounted for 71 percent of the coastwide water area increase. Intermediate and fresh marshes received most of the hurricane damage because their highly organic soils were ripped apart by the storm surge and waves (Boesch et al., 2006). Most (72% of the total) water area increase occurred on the Chenier Plain in the interior marshes located between Freshwater Bayou and Calcasieu Lake (Barras, 2006). The decrease in intermediate marsh was greater on the Deltaic Plain, primarily in the upper Breton Sound Basin (Barras, 2006). Most saline marshes appeared physically intact after the hurricanes, although some shorelines along open bays were eroded by storm-generated waves (Boesch et al., 2006). The brackish marsh turned brown from exposure to saline waters but appeared physically intact (Boesch et al., 2006). Estimates for the decreases in brackish and saline marshes by Barras (2006) were 33 mi^2 (85 km^2) and 28 mi^2 (73 km^2), respectively.

Mississippi had an estimated 1,890 ac (765 ha) of coastal marshes and forest severely damaged or destroyed by Hurricane Katrina (USDOC, NMFS, 2007a). However, in Mississippi the overall land cover change noted by the National Oceanic and Atmospheric Administration's (NOAA's) Coastal Change Analysis Program (C-CAP) was much less severe than encountered in Louisiana. The total area that changed from wetlands to water is less than 5 mi^2 (13 km^2). Compared with Louisiana, the loss of emergent marsh and unconsolidated shoreline was minimal. The greatest change was in coastal forests, especially bottomland hardwoods. While over 70 mi^2 (181 km^2) of forest (mostly evergreen) was lost or converted to grasses, an estimated 10 mi^2 (26 km^2) of bottomland hardwood forests were seen changing to palustrine scrub or emergent categories. There was also a conversion of 40 mi^2 (104 km^2) of evergreen forest to scrub/shrub cover. Estuarine marsh and wetlands suffered extensive damage from Hurricane Katrina (Mississippi Dept. of Marine Resources, 2005; Barbour, 2006).

Along the Alabama coast there was some damage to wetlands due to erosion along the shores of some of the barrier islands. There was also some damage, although not quantified, from crushed, debris-scraped, gouged, or covered wetland habitats. The land cover changes in Alabama observed by NOAA's C-CAP highlight the loss of forested land and the related increase to grassland area, which was likely caused by the 2005 hurricanes (Herold and McCombs, personal communication, 2007). There was a loss of approximately 50 mi^2 (129 km^2) of hardwood forests. The areas that were primarily evergreen stands were either damaged by Hurricane Katrina or intentionally harvested, and the areas are now dominated by scrub/shrub (approximately 15 mi^2 or 39 km^2) or grassland (approximately 17 mi^2 or 44 km^2).

Most of the wetlands and, therefore, wetland loss along the Texas coast is associated with National Wildlife Refuges (NWR) and State wildlife management areas such as Texas Point NWR, McFaddin NWR, Sea Rim State Park, and J.D. Murphree State Wildlife Management Area. These areas comprise over 60,000 ac (24,281 ha) of coastal marsh (fresh, intermediate, brackish), coastal prairie (non-saline and saline), coastal woodlands, and beach/ridge habitat in Jefferson and Chambers Counties in southeast Texas (USDOC, NMFS, 2007a). The ridge/dune system that was the main buffer between the Gulf and the wetlands has been significantly lowered by the overwash of the past hurricanes. While a remnant dune/beach system still exists post-Rita, much has been lost through erosion and shoreline retreat, leaving only a low-lying, washover terrace. The loss of the existing beach dunes and the lowering of beach ridge elevations along the Gulf shoreline of the McFaddin Complex from Hurricane Rita imperils approximately 30,000 ac (12,140 ha) of nationally significant wetlands due to the increasing frequency of saltwater inundation from the Gulf of Mexico. Ongoing shoreline retreat along the Gulf of Mexico, which was exacerbated by Hurricane Rita, is resulting in a rapid loss of valuable coastal habitats, including emergent estuarine marshes and coastal prairies. In summary, the NWR's in southeast Texas suffered wetland habitat loss, primarily as a result of wave erosion, during Hurricane Rita. Impacts to three Federal refuges were estimated to include marsh loss of more than 75 ac (30 ha), approximately 15,000 ac (6,070 ha) of marsh under increased threat by future storms, and erosion losses along 20 mi (32 km) of shoreline.

In summary, the wetlands along the Gulf Coast were severely damaged by the Hurricanes Katrina and Rita, leaving the mainland less protected. The Louisiana coast had significant changes of land to water. These new water areas represent landlosses caused by the direct removal of wetlands. They also indicate transitory changes in water area caused by remnant flooding, removal of aquatic vegetation, scouring of marsh vegetation, and water-level variation attributed to normal tidal and meteorological variation between satellite images. It was noted (Barras, 2006) that permanent losses cannot be estimated until several growing seasons have passed and the transitory impacts of the hurricanes are minimized. It is too early to estimate the actual overall marsh loss. Along the Texas coast, once viable wetlands within the NWR's that both protected the mainland and portions of coastal Texas, as well as wetlands along barrier islands, were either heavily damaged or in some cases lost.

The deterioration of coastal wetlands is an issue of Federal, State, and local concern. Federal legislation that reflects this concern includes the Clean Water Act, the Coastal Zone Management Act, and the Coastal Wetlands Planning, Protection and Restoration Act. The National Environmental Policy Act is designed to identify and, where appropriate, analyze such issues of concern. The States of Louisiana, Mississippi, Alabama, and Texas have adopted Coastal Zone Management (CZM) programs and a variety of other laws that discourage wetland destruction. Many of the coastal parishes of Louisiana have also adopted coastal management programs and other permitting procedures to discourage wetland destruction.

3.2.1.2.2. Impact Analysis

The impact-producing factors associated with the proposed exploration and development activities that could affect wetlands includes oil spills from blowouts or vessel collisions, maintenance dredging, and vessel traffic. Detailed discussions of the potential affects of OCS activities on wetland resources can be found in Chapters 4.2.2.2.3.1 and 4.2.2.3.2 of the Multisale EIS (USDOI, MMS, 2007) and in Chapter 4.3.4.2 of the FPSO EIS (USDOI, MMS, 2001), and they are hereby incorporated reference. The incorporated material is summarized below.

The addition of the proposed routine activities associated with the proposed FPSO action would have minimal to no direct effect on the coastal wetlands since the proposed action is located 136 mi (219 km) from the nearest shore. The potential for indirect impacts may exist due to the initial needs for shore-based, supply vessel support. Only a slight increase in vessel traffic is expected to occur, but vessel size may increase due to supply needs, open-sea conditions, and shuttle tankers. At present, existing ports, production facilities, and navigation channels would be used, eliminating the need for the expansion or construction of any facilities into wetland areas. While various ports may be used, some of the proposed port usage would have minimal impact because of its offshore location (Louisiana Offshore Oil Port) or because the port has an armored access channel such as Port Fourchon. Since the vessel support will be using primarily armored coastal channels, as well as existing offshore channels and sea lanes, vessel-related erosion should be minimal, and the need for channel maintenance should not significantly increase as a result of the proposed activity. If channel maintenance is required, the material can be placed in an already established disposal area or used beneficially to create or restore wetlands.

The primary accidental impact-producing factor with the potential to impact coastal wetlands is oil spills, specifically coastal and inland spills adjacent to the coastal wetlands. Barrier islands can provide protection or reduce the severity of an oil spill by intercepting the spill before it reaches the wetlands located either behind (on mainland shore) or within the interior of the islands. Due to the lower post-hurricane (Katrina and Rita) elevations of the barrier islands along the Louisiana coast, and to some extent the Texas coast, there is now a greater chance of spilled oil reaching mainland shores. Should a spill occur inshore or in nearshore waters, it presents a much greater potential for adversely impacting wetlands than an offshore deepwater spill simply due to proximity. The works of several investigators (Webb et al., 1981 and 1985; Alexander and Webb, 1983 and 1987; Lytle, 1975; Delaune et al., 1979; Fischel et al., 1989) evaluated the effects of potential spills to area wetlands. For wetlands along the central Louisiana coast, the critical oil concentration is assumed to be 0.025 gal/ft^2 (1.0 L/m^2) of marsh. Concentrations above this would result in longer-term effects to wetland vegetation, including some plant mortality and loss of land. Concentrations less than this may cause diebacks for one growing season or less, depending upon the concentration and the season during which contact occurs. Chapter 4.3 of the Multisale EIS has a complete discussion of oil spills, the various impacting factors, and risk analysis; Chapter 4.4.3.2 of the Multisale EIS specifically addresses the types and severity of wetland impacts. There are concerns that offshore spills may contribute to wetland damage; however, due to the distance offshore of the FPSO (136 mi or 219 km), the possibility of spills reaching coastal wetlands with the toxicity to significantly impact the coastal wetlands is low.

A current review of the potential for an accidental spill and impacts from the proposed Chinook-Cascade FPSO has been completed and is included as **Appendix B**. Based on this review, the probability of a large spill ($\geq$1,000 bbl) occurring and contacting identified wetland resources after 3, 10, or 30 days is less than 0.5 percent. Although a spill is unlikely, if a spill were to occur, the toxicity of the spilled oil would be greatly reduced or eliminated by weathering, wave action, and the use of dispersants if used to contain the spill in the offshore environment.

Conclusion

There is a very low probability of a spill from the proposed FPSO contacting wetland environments due to the distance to shore and the absence of pipeline emplacement. Based on the low frequency of port visits and the historically low probability of spills from shuttle tankers, the probability of impacts to coastal wetlands would be small. Should a spill make landfall and a cleanup proceed with approved procedures, impacts to wetlands would be minimal due to the weathered condition of the oil and the containment and cleanup techniques. Recovery periods longer than 2 years would be very unlikely. Therefore, no significant, long-term impacts to the structure or vitality of wetlands would be expected to occur from accidental spills of oil, diesel fuel, drilling fluids, or chemicals.

Installation activities associated with FPSO commissioning would produce slight increases in the number of vessel transits, resulting in minor incremental impacts to channels and coastal erosion rates, i.e., a negligible impact. During routine operations, ship traffic would produce an incremental increase in erosion rates, sediment resuspension, and turbidity, i.e., an adverse but not significant impact to coastal wetland and seagrass habitats. Under the range of options, increases in shuttle tanker trips into Gulf ports would produce a negligible impact to coastal wetlands. During decommissioning, slight increases in the number of vessel transits would result in minor impacts to channels and coastal erosion rates, i.e., a negligible impact.

3.2.1.2.3. Cumulative Analysis

The conversion of wetlands to agricultural, residential, recreational, and commercial uses has generally been the major cause of wetland loss. Loss of wetlands is projected to continue in the Gulf Coast States. Deltaic Louisiana will continue to experience the greatest losses; wetland loss is also expected to continue in coastal Texas, Mississippi, and Alabama, but at slower rates. Approximately 2.1 to 2.4 percent of coastal wetland losses can be attributed to OCS oil and gas activities (USDOI, MMS, 2001). The proposed action would represent a fraction of a percent contribution to these impacts.

Insignificant adverse impacts upon wetlands from maintenance dredging are expected because the large majority of the material would be disposed upon existing disposal areas. Alternative dredged material disposal methods can be used to enhance and create coastal wetlands. Depending upon the regions and soils through which they were dredged, secondary adverse impacts of canals may be more locally significant than direct impacts. Additional wetland losses generated by the secondary impacts of saltwater intrusion, flank subsidence, freshwater-reservoir reduction, and deeper tidal penetration have not been calculated due to a lack of quantitative documentation; MMS has initiated a project to document and develop data concerning such losses. A variety of mitigation efforts are initiated to protect against direct and indirect wetland loss. The nonmaintenance of mitigation structures that reduce canal construction impacts can have substantial impacts upon wetlands. These localized impacts are expected to continue.

Wetlands will continue to be impacted by natural events such as hurricanes, subsidence, saltwater intrusion, and sea-level rise. There is increasing new evidence of the importance of the effect of sea-level rise (or marsh subsidence) as it relates to the loss of marsh or changes in marsh types and plant diversity (Spalding and Hester, 2007). This study shows that the very structure of coastal wetlands will likely be altered by sea-level rise, as community shifts will be governed by the responses of individual species to new environmental conditions. In addition, the State of Louisiana has made provision for wetlands protection and restoration part of the States' plan for hurricane protection. As climatic patterns vary, drought conditions may induce a need for additional reservoir storage and, as a result, ,alter the freshwater input into the coastal wetlands. The reduction in freshwater input and salinity modifications may alter wetland types and, in some cases, allow for increased saltwater intrusion into fresh marshes. The Louisiana State legislature established the Coastal Protection and Restoration Authority and charged it with coordinating the efforts of local, State, and Federal agencies to achieve long-term and comprehensive coastal protection and restoration that integrates flood control and wetland restoration.

In summary, the effects to coastal wetlands from the primary impact-producing activities associated with the proposed action are expected to be low. Maintenance dredging of navigation channels and canals is expected to occur with minimal impacts; the proposed action is expected to contribute minimally to the need for this dredging. Alternative, dredged-material disposal methods can be used to enhance and create coastal wetlands. Vessel traffic associated with the proposed action is expected to contribute minimally to the erosion and widening of navigation channels and canals. The FPSO and shuttle tanker risks are comparable with the risks associated with existing deepwater production platforms and oil pipelines; therefore, the net increase in risk would be negligible. Therefore, the incremental contribution of the proposed action's impacts to the cumulative impact on coastal wetlands is negligible and likely undetectable among the other cumulative impacts.

3.2.1.3. Seagrass Communities

3.2.1.3.1. Description

Seagrass beds grow in shallow, relatively clear, protected waters with predominantly sand bottoms. Their distribution depends on an interrelationship among a number of environmental factors that include temperature, water depth, turbidity, salinity, turbulence, and substrate suitability. Seagrasses provide important habitat for immature shrimp, black drum, spotted sea trout, juvenile southern flounder, and several other fish species, and they provide a food source for species of wintering waterfowl. Beds of lower salinity vegetation provide important habitats for commercially important, although less diverse, communities of fish and shellfish.

Approximately 1.02 million ha (2.52 million ac) of submerged seagrass beds are estimated to exist in exposed, shallow coastal waters and embayments of the northern Gulf of Mexico. Over 80 percent of this is in Florida Bay and Florida coastal waters (Duke and Kruszynski, 1992; Zieman and Zieman, 1989). In the area from Mobile Bay to south Texas, seagrass occurs only in relatively small beds behind barrier islands.

Mississippi: In coastal Mississippi, about 20,016 ac (8,100 ha) of seagrass beds were reported in 1973. Currently, about 2,000 ac (800 ha) are found in the state. Seagrass beds primarily occur in Mississippi Sound and associated bays to the north and along the islands to the south. May (2007) discussed the distribution of seagrass in southeastern Mississippi waters, finding some burial of seagrass after Hurricane Katrina, seasonal fluctuation of *Ruppia maritima*, and persistent *Halodule wrightii*. In Biloxi Marsh, Mississippi, fish communities at sites denuded of seagrass by Hurricane Katrina resembled those of sites with no seagrass before the hurricane (Maiaro, 2007).

Alabama: Barry A. Vittor & Associates, Inc. (2004) reported approximately 6,714 ac (2,717 ha) of submerged aquatic vegetation in Alabama coastal waters. A few beds are found along the shores of Mobile Bay and in the rivers and wetlands that feed into the bay. A survey of 44 stations in Alabama seagrass beds showed seagrasses still present in 86 percent of the study sites after Hurricane Ivan's landfall at Mobile in September 2004. Seagrasses in Bayou la Batre, Alabama, exhibited reduced benthic and water-column production after Hurricane Katrina made landfall at the eastern border of Louisiana in August 2005 (Anton et al., 2006). Byron and Heck (2006) found 82 percent of Alabama seagrasses present in 2002 still present in November 2004. They also noted increases in *Ruppia maritima* and no loss of seagrasses resulting from Hurricane Katrina.

Louisiana: In Louisiana, submerged vegetation primarily consists of freshwater and low salinity vegetation. Largely due to the turbid water conditions that are caused by the Mississippi and Atchafalaya Rivers, seagrass beds in Louisiana have very low densities and are rare, with the exception of beds in the vicinity of the Chandeleur Islands. About 100,442 ha (248192 ac) of seagrass beds were found in the vicinity of these islands in 1998 (USDOI, GS, 1998). Since 1998, the Chandeleur Island chain has been hit by five major hurricanes (Michot and Wells, 2005). The land area of the Chandeleur Islands was reduced by Hurricane Katrina from 3,600 ac to 1,600 ac (1,460 ha to 648 ha) and then to 1,280 ac (518 ha) by Hurricane Rita (Silvestro, 2006). The influx of saltwater in low salinity estuaries caused by Hurricanes Katrina and Rita may lead to an increase in colonization by *Ruppia maritima* and a decrease in the abundance of freshwater species such as *Vallisineria americana* in upper bay areas. Such a fluctuation in community composition was documented for Lake Pontchartrain in Louisiana by Poirrier and Cho (2002) after the landfall of Hurricane Georges in September 1998.

Texas: Seagrasses in Texas are widely scattered beds in shallow, high-salinity coastal lagoons and bays. Although permanent meadows of perennial species occur in nearly all bay systems along the Texas Gulf Coast, most of the State's seagrass cover (79%) is found in the Laguna Madre (Pulich, 1998), with seagrasses covering about 60,047 ac (24,300 ha; 94 mi^2 or 243 km^2) in the upper portion of the Laguna Madre (Quammen and Onuf, 1993). Lower-salinity, submerged beds of aquatic vegetation are found inland and discontinuously in coastal lakes, rivers, and the most inland portions of some coastal bays. Hardegree (2007) highlighted declines in seagrass in Christmas Bay, Texas and the Lower Luguna Madre, Texas. He also analyzed propeller scarring, recovery, and regulation.

3.2.1.3.2. Impact Analysis

The activities associated with the proposed action that could adversely affect seagrass communities are vessel traffic, oil spills, spill-response, and cleanup activities. Impacts from activities resulting from the proposed action are expected to have negligible effects on seagrass communities.

Vessel traffic will generally only pose a risk to seagrass when nearshore. Beds of submerged vegetation within a navigation channel's area of influence will have already adjusted their bed configurations in response to turbidity generated there. Very little, if any, damage would then occur as a result of typical channel traffic. Propwashing of shallow navigation channels by vessel traffic resuspends sediments, increasing the turbidity of nearby coastal waters. Generally, propwash will not resuspend sediments in navigation channels beyond pre-project conditions.

Inshore oil spills pose a more severe threat to seagrass communities than offshore spills. Most seagrass communities are located behind barrier islands and are protected from the direct impact of offshore spills. Inshore spills may result from either vessel collisions that release fuel and lubricants or from pipelines that rupture. If an oil slick settles into a protective embayment where seagrass beds are found, shading may cause reduced chlorophyll production and thinning of leaf density. Increased water turbulence due to storms or vessel traffic can break apart the surface sheen and disperse some oil into the water column, potentially causing some dieback of leaves for one growing season. It may take as much as 5-10 years of community succession before faunal composition resembles pre-impact conditions.

Conclusion

Seagrass distributions inshore of the CPA and WPA have declined over the last several decades due to a number of natural and manmade factors, including recent hurricanes, flooding, dredging, trawling, dredge material disposal, water quality degradation, and levee construction, which has diverted freshwater away from wetlands (USDOI, MMS, 2001).

The activities associated with the proposed action that could adversely affect seagrass communities are vessel traffic, oil spills, spill response, and cleanup activities. Impacts from activities resulting from the proposed action are expected to have negligible effects on seagrass communities.

Oil spills from FPSO operations are not expected to produce either adverse or significant impacts on seagrass beds. The probabilities for spilled oil reaching Florida seagrass beds are very low. Smaller spills from FPSO locations offshore are not predicted to reach shore.

3.2.1.3.3. Cumulative Analysis

Pipelines, canal dredging, channelization and other water-control structures, scarring from vessel traffic, oil spills, and hurricanes can impact seagrass communities. Pipeline construction creates turbidity that reduces light availability and can cause sedimentation and direct burial of seagrass communities. Dredging generates the greatest overall risk to seagrass communities. Channel dredging to create and maintain waterfront real estate, marinas, and waterways will continue to cause the greatest impacts to higher salinity submerged vegetation. Mitigation, such as the use of turbidity curtains, may be required to reduce undesirable impacts of dredging. Large, water-control structures influence salinities in coastal areas, which can influence the location of seagrass communities and associated epifauna. Seagrass beds can be scarred by anchor drags, trampling, trawling, loggerhead turtles, occasional seismic activity, and boats operating in water that is too shallow for their keels or propellers. The greatest scarring results from small boats operating in the vicinities of large populations of humans and registered boats. Inshore oil spills present greater risks of adversely impacting submerged vegetation than do offshore spills. Wave action and extreme, low-tide events during a spill can cause direct contact of oil on seagrass. This will result in dieback of the seagrass vegetation and supported epifauna, which will be replaced, for the most part, within 1-2 growing seasons. The cleanup of slicks can cause significant scarring and trampling of submerged vegetation and seagrass beds. Hurricanes generate substantial overall risk to submerged vegetation by burial and eroding channels through seagrass beds. When combined with other stresses, impacted seagrass beds may fail to recover. The most effective mitigation for direct impacts to submerged vegetation beds is avoidance.

Seagrass beds have been repeatedly damaged by the natural processes of transgression from hurricane overwash of barrier islands. Recent hurricane impacts have produced changes in seagrass community quality and composition (Heck and Byron, 2006; Poirrier and Cho, 2002; Anton et al, 2006; May, 2007; Maiaro, 2007). Human efforts to stabilize shorelines interfere with the natural process of the shoreward transgression of associated seagrass habitats.

In general, the proposed action could potentially cause a minor incremental contribution to impacts on submerged vegetation from possible oil spills if a project-related spill reaches the isolated seagrass beds. Dredging generates the greatest overall risk to submerged vegetation, and hurricanes cause direct damage to seagrass beds, which may fail to recover in the presence of cumulative stresses. There is no dredging proposed or expected related to the Cascade-Chinook development. The proposed action would have a negligible incremental contribution to impacts on seagrass communities.

3.2.1.4. Alabama, Choctawhatchee, St. Andrew, and Perdido Key Beach Mice

3.2.1.4.1. Description

Sixteen subspecies of field mouse (*Peromyscus polionotus*) are recognized along the Gulf Coast, eight of which are collectively known as beach mice. The Alabama, Choctawhatchee, St. Andrew, and Perdido Key beach mice are designated as protected species under the Endangered Species Act (ESA) because of the loss of coastal habitat (USDOI, MMS, 2007).

Beach mice are characterized in Chapter 3.2.5 of the Multisale EIS (USDOI, MMS, 2007) and are hereby incorporated by reference into this SEA. A summary of the incorporated material follows.

Beach mice are restricted to the coastal barrier sand dunes along the Gulf Coast. Optimal overall beach mouse habitat is currently thought to be comprised of a heterogeneous mix of interconnected habitats including primary dunes, secondary dunes, scrub dunes, and interdunal areas. Beach mice dig burrows mainly in the primary, secondary, and interior scrub dunes where the vegetation provides suitable cover. Most beach mouse surveys conducted prior to the mid-1990's were in primary and secondary dunes because the investigators assumed that these habitats are the preferred habitat of beach mice.

Beach mice feed nocturnally in the dunes and remain in burrows during the day. Their diets vary seasonally but consist mainly of seeds, fruits, and insects (Ehrhart, 1978; Moyers, 1996). Changes in the availability of foods result in changes in diets between seasons and account for variability of seasonal diets between years.

Hurricanes are a natural environmental phenomenon affecting the Gulf Coast, and beach mice have evolved and persisted in coastal dune habitats since the Pleistocene. Hurricanes are part of a repeated cycle of destruction, alteration, and recovery of dune habitat. The extensive coastal dune habitat that existed along the Gulf Coast before the fairly recent commercial and residential development allowed beach mice to survive even the most severe hurricane events to repopulate dune habitat as it recovered. Beach mice are affected by the passage of hurricanes along the northwest Florida and Alabama Gulf Coast. Since records on hurricane intensity began in 1885, a total of 32 hurricanes have struck northwest Florida within the historic ranges of the four Gulf Coast beach mouse subspecies (Williams and Duedall, 1997; Doering et al., 1994; Neumann et al., 1993). In addition, 22 hurricanes have made landfall along the coast of Alabama from 1851 to 2004 (USDOC, NOAA, National Hurricane Center, 2006).

Beach mice have existed in an environment subject to recurring hurricanes, but tropical storms and hurricanes are now considered to be a primary factor in the beach mouse's decline. It is only within the last 20-30 years that the combination of habitat loss due to beachfront development, isolation of remaining beach mouse habitat blocks and populations, and destruction of remaining habitat by hurricanes have increased the threat of extinction of several subspecies of beach mice.

3.2.1.4.2. Impact Analysis

The major impact-producing factors associated with the proposed action that may affect beach mice include (1) oil spills, (2) spill-response activities, and (3) beach trash and debris from OCS activity. Chapters 4.2.2.1.7 and 4.4.7 of the Multisale EIS (USDOI, MMS, 2007) contain a discussion of impacts from OCS activity and are hereby incorporated by reference into this SEA. The incorporated materials are summarized below.

Direct contact with spilled oil that has washed ashore can cause skin and eye irritation, asphyxiation from the inhalation of fumes, oil ingestion, and reduction or contamination of food sources. Regardless of the potential for persistence of oil in beach mouse habitat, a slick cannot wash over the fore dunes unless carried by a heavy storm swell. High seas would be necessary to cause a spill slick to landfall and affect mice or their habitat. The erosion associated with high seas during storms is likely to do more damage to beach mouse habitat than oiling.

Vehicular traffic and activity associated with oil-spill cleanup can trample or bury nests and burrows or cause displacement from preferred habitat. Trash and debris may be mistakenly consumed by beach mice or it may ensnare them; however, contact between mice and trash originating from the proposed development activities in Walker Ridge is very unlikely. The impacts on beach mice from oil spills and cleanup activities are discussed in Chapter 4.4.7 of the Multisale EIS (USDOI, MMS, 2007) and are hereby incorporated by reference into this SEA. Oil spills or cleanup activity and incidental trash related to the proposed activity are not expected to significantly impact beach mice.

Conclusion

Impacts from the proposed development activities in the Walker Ridge area on the Alabama, Choctawhatchee, St. Andrew, and Perdido Key beach mice are unlikely. Impact may result from consumption of beach trash and debris. The proposed activities would deposit only a small portion of the total debris that would reach the habitat. Efforts undertaken for the removal of marine debris may temporarily scare away beach mice, destroy their food resources, or collapse the tops of their burrows.

Oil-spill response and cleanup activities could impact beach mice and their habitat if not properly regulated. However, given the low probability of a large (≥1,000 bbl) oil spill occurring, direct impacts of spills on beach mice from the proposed action are highly unlikely.

3.2.1.4.3. Cumulative Analysis

Cumulative activities have a potential to harm or reduce the numbers of Alabama, Choctawhatchee, St. Andrew, and Perdido Key beach mice. Those activities include oil spills, alteration and reduction of habitat, predation and competition, and consumption of beach trash and debris. Spills from the Petrobras Cascade_Chinook development activities, as well as oil spills stemming from service vessels, are not expected to contact beach mice or their habitats. Cumulative activities posing the greatest potential harm to beach mice are non-OCS activities (beach development and coastal spills) and natural catastrophes (hurricanes), which, in combination, could potentially deplete some beach mice populations to unsustainable levels. The expected incremental contribution of the proposed development activities to the cumulative impacts is negligible.

3.2.2. Sensitive Offshore Resources

3.2.2.1. Deepwater Benthic Communities

3.2.2.1.1. Nonchemosynthetic Communities

3.2.2.1.1.1. Description

The description of the biology, life history and distribution of nonchemosynthetic deepwater benthic communities can be found in Chapter 3.2.2.2.2 of the Multisale EIS. The vast majority of the Gulf of Mexico has a soft, muddy bottom in which burrowing infauna are the most abundant invertebrates. The Walker Ridge complex analyzed here, including Walker Ridge Blocks 205, 206, 249, 250 and 425, falls into this category and the proposed wells are at water depths between approximately 8,200 and 8,800 ft (2,500 and 2,683 m). Using complete 3D seismic seabed amplitude anomaly coverage of the area, there are no known hard-bottom areas in these blocks; however, there are some potentially exposed features on slopes of the nearby Sigsbee Escarpment.

As in all areas of the Gulf, a wide variety of organisms ranging from single-celled bacteria to invertebrates and fish inhabit soft-bottom habitat at almost every depth range in the Gulf of Mexico. These organisms can also include chemosynthetic animals, a remarkable assemblage of invertebrates found in association with hydrocarbon seeps that use a carbon source independent of photosynthesis and the sun-dependent photosynthetic food chain that supports most all other life on earth. This unique group is discussed in **Chapter 3.2.2.1.2**. Also, study results from Rowe and Kennicutt (2002) have indicated some unique areas of soft-bottom communities near the Mississippi River Delta with substantially higher community biomass and carbon flux.

The continental slope in the Gulf of Mexico extends from the edge of the continental shelf at about 200 m (656 ft) to a water depth of approximately 3,000 m (9,840 ft) (USDOI, MMS, 2007; pages A-3 through A-8). The Walker Ridge complex lies in the lower part of the continental slope, which corresponds to the upper part of the abyssal depth zone as characterized by Pequegnat (1983) and Gallaway and Kennicutt (1988). Major groups of animals that live in this habitat include (1) bacteria and other microbenthos, (2) meiofauna (0.063-0.3 millimeter (mm)), (3) macrofauna (>0.3 mm), and (4) megafauna (larger organisms such as crabs, sea pens, sea cucumbers, crinoids, and bottom-dwelling (demersal) fish). All of these groups are represented throughout the entire Gulf—from the continental shelf to the deepest abyssal depths (about 3,850 m (12,630 ft)).

Basic descriptions of typical, soft-bottom fauna (i.e., bacteria, meiofauna, macrofauna, and megafauna) are addressed in Chapter 3.2.2.2.2 of the Multisale EIS. Representatives from all of these groups would be expected in the Cascade-Chinook Walker Ridge block complex. Several publications have derived from two major, MMS-funded, deep Gulf studies (Rowe and Kennicutt, 2002; Gallaway and Kennicutt, 1998; Gallaway et al., 1988a,b), from which the majority of this summary information is derived. These two studies contain extensive background information on deepwater Gulf of Mexico habitat and biological communities.

There are some potential hard-bottom outcrops (and potential associated chemosynthetic communities) located on the Sigsbee Escarpment in Walker Ridge Blocks 205 and 249. These areas are well removed from the drill sites (>1.5 mi or 2.4 km).

3.2.2.1.1.2. Impact Analysis

The potential impacts to nonchemosynthetic, deepwater benthic communities expected to inhabit the Walker Ridge complex, excluding chemosynthetic communities (discussed in **Chapter 3.2.2.1.2**), are discussed below.

The impact-producing factors associated with the development and production of the Cascade-Chinook project that could affect deepwater benthic communities include (1) drilling discharges, including primarily cuttings with adhering drilling muds; (2) seafloor disturbance from anchoring and emplacement of facilities; and (3) blowouts during well drilling or production. The deepwater ecosystem in the Walker Ridge complex area can be characterized as vast expanses of soft-bottom faunas. The topography is gently sloping, lying just beyond the edge of the steep gradient of the Sigsbee Escarpment. Each of the blocks in the complex only slopes about 150 m or so (492 ft) from the northwest corners to the deeper, southeast corners of each block.

The most important impact-producing factors on deepwater benthic communities are physical disturbances of the seafloor caused by (1) the deposition of drilling cuttings and associated drilling fluids; (2) anchoring of the drilling rigs or FPSO; (3) installation or maintenance of subsea infrastructure such as booster pumps, flowlines, and umbilicals on the sea bottom; and (4) resuspension of sediment during a blowout from drilling or workovers of production wells. The maximum bottom area disturbed in any way is estimated to be no larger than 315 ha (778 ac), assuming the worst case of muds and cuttings discharges reaching distances of 1,000 m (3,281 ft) from the well site in every direction (CSA, 2006) (highly unlikely). Realistically, splays of discharges only move to limited directions depending on prevailing currents; a good estimate would be 1/3 of the radius of a circle or 105 ha (259 ac) out to 1,000 m (3,281 ft). Impacts will also be limited by the drilling of just single wells at each location. This would not result in a significant impact on the benthic communities because the duration and areal extent of the proposed activities would be limited and recolonization of benthic communities is facilitated from nearby surrounding areas.

Anchors and mooring lines can cause disturbances with lethal effects in small footprints on the seafloor of a few acres. Among these disturbances would be (1) crushing of benthic faunas by anchors or mooring lines; (2) burial or disruption of fauna from scraping, plowing, or redistribution of bottom sediment by mooring lines that pivot on their anchors; and (3) increased turbidity from sediment that is resuspended as a result of anchor emplacement or mooring line motion that fouls or interferes with filter-feeding organs.

The drilling MODU at the two Cascade locations will have a total of 12 anchors each, and the FPSO mooring will use a total of 9 anchors. The Chinook well will be drilled using a DP drillship. The areal extent and severity of the impact caused by anchors and anchoring are related to the size and configuration of the anchor and mooring system, the length of chain resting on the bottom, and the swing arc that a chain could have as a result of currents or winds. An estimated sea-bottom disturbance footprint for each anchor and the swing arc of its mooring line is approximately 5 ac (2 ha) for a total of 165 ac (66 ha) for 33 anchors. An additional area of sea bottom will be disturbed by the installation of subsea production facilities, such as manifolds, blowout preventers, umbilicals, and flowlines. In total, the potential sea-bottom area that can be disturbed as a result of the Cascade-Chinook project is a very small portion of this vast deepwater environment, and all impacts will occur on soft-bottom habitat only.

A blowout at the seafloor could create a crater on the sea bottom and resuspend and disperse large quantities of bottom sediments within a 300-m (984-ft) radius of the blowout site, burying both infaunal (live in the sediment) and epifaunal (live on the sediment) organisms and interfering with sessile invertebrates that rely on filter-feeding organs. Anchoring and other bottom-disturbing activities can resuspend bottom sediments but not to the degree achieved by a blowout event. Rapid burial by accumulations of sediment >1 ft (30 cm) in thickness is likely to be lethal for all benthic organisms based on analysis of escape trace fossils from the geologic record (Frey, 1975, page 135; Basan et al., 1978, page 20; Ekdale et al., 1984, page 92). Burial by thinner accumulations of sediment (or cuttings) may be lethal to some sessile (attached or immotile) invertebrates and survivable by motile organisms. Similar to impacts from drill cuttings, impacts from a blowout would be limited because the duration and areal extent would be limited and recolonization of communities is facilitated from nearby surrounding areas.

Routine surface discharges of drilling cuttings have been documented to reach the seafloor in water depths >400 m (1,310 ft); however, significant accumulation thickness will be limited to a relatively close distance from the surface discharge point. A recent study looked at both exploratory and production facility drilling discharges in water depths of 1,000 m (3,280 ft) and reported detectable accumulations at distances as far as 1 km (0.6 mi) (CSA, 2006). Geophysically mapped thicknesses of cuttings accumulations at one site showed a rapid decrease of thickness with increasing distance from the well site (CSA, 2006). Accumulation thickness was <7.6 cm (3 in) within 240 m (787 ft). The total amount of area significantly impacted by discharge accumulation could be expected to be somewhat larger at the Walker Ridge complex due to the longer descent time of muds and cuttings; however, the increased dispersion distance will also result in thinner accumulations.

Conclusion

The proposed Cascade-Chinook project is expected to have negligible impacts on the ecological function, biological productivity, or distribution of soft-bottom nonchemosynthetic communities. Bottom disturbances from discharge of drilling cuttings and associated drilling muds, (2) anchoring of the drilling MODU at two sites and the FPSO, and (3) installation or maintenance of subsea infrastructure such as flowlines, separator and boosting systems, and umbilicals on the sea bottom will not be of a sufficient size or duration to adversely affect these benthic community types to any significant or permanent degree. The crushing or burial of individual organisms could take place within small areas of a few acres. Minor and temporary impacts, such as interference with filter-feeding structures, could occur over areas inside an envelope estimated to be no more than about 165 ac (66 ha) based on the installation of the total number of anchors for the proposed project. Routine discharges are not expected to adversely impact these community types because of the water depths in the Walker Ridge complex. Bottom disturbance from a blowout during completion or workover of the production wells is not likely based on the historical record of blowout events in the Gulf. Recruitment of new organisms would take place from nearby areas, and organisms from undisturbed areas are free to migrate into disrupted areas after the disturbance ceases. or structures are removed.

3.2.2.1.1.3. Cumulative Analysis

Cumulative impacts on nonchemosynthetic, deepwater benthic communities include crushing and physical disturbance of the sea bottom from drilling discharges and the emplacement of other drilling rigs, production platforms, and subsea production infrastructure. The water depth in the Walker Ridge complex area ranges from 8,200 to 8,800 ft (2,500 to 2,683 m). These depths are too deep for anchoring by service vessels. There are no non-OCS activities (e.g., commercial bottom trawling) that could cause sea-bottom disturbances. The cumulative impacts on nonchemosynthetic benthic communities are expected to cause little damage to the ecological function or biological productivity of the expected typical communities existing on sand/silt/clay bottoms of the deep Walker Ridge complex area of the Gulf of Mexico. Large motile animals would tend to move from disturbed areas, and recolonization by populations from neighboring substrates would be expected in any areas impacted by any form of burial.

The incremental contribution of the proposed action's impacts to the cumulative impact on nonchemosynthetic, deepwater benthic communities are negligible and likely undetectable among the other cumulative impacts.

3.2.2.1.2. Chemosynthetic Communities

3.2.2.1.2.1. Description

Chemosynthetic communities are defined as persistent, largely sessile assemblages of marine organisms dependent upon symbiotic chemosynthetic bacteria as their primary food source (MacDonald, 1992). Chemosynthetic clams, mussels, and tube worms are similar to (but not identical with) the hydrothermal vent communities of the eastern Pacific (Corliss et al., 1979). Bacteria live within specialized cells in these invertebrate organisms and are supplied with oxygen and chemosynthetic compounds by the host via specialized blood chemistry (Fisher, 1990). The host, in turn, lives off the organic products subsequently released by the chemosynthetic bacteria and may even feed on the bacteria themselves. Additional information on the biology, life history and distribution of chemosynthetic deepwater benthic communities can be found in Chapter 3.2.2.2.1 of the Multisale EIS.

Hydrocarbon seep communities in the Central Gulf have been reported to occur at water depths between 951 and 8,999 ft (290 and 2,743 m). The total number of chemosynthetic communities in the Gulf is now known to exceed 60. A recent MMS-funded study, *Investigations of Chemosynthetic Communities on the Lower Continental Slope of the Gulf of Mexico* (Brooks et al., in press), has performed exploration surveys specifically targeting water depths below 1,000 m (3,280 ft). This project confirmed the presence of 12 additional chemosynthetic communities not previously known in these water depths. What was initially thought to be relatively rare occurrences of chemosynthetic communities is now known to be far more common and regularly associated with primary geophysical signatures of the seabed, including faulting with conduits for hydrocarbons to the surface from deeper depths and precipitation of carbonate deposits on the seafloor. Anomalies of seismic survey acoustic amplitudes on the seabed is one major feature related to almost all known chemosynthetic communities, and these kinds of features are now relatively well mapped throughout the entire northern Gulf of Mexico. The total number of features on the northern Gulf slope that have probable associated communities now number in the thousands.

A review for the potential occurrence of chemosynthetic communities associated with the Cascade-Chinook project was performed for this SEA. These blocks generally lie in an area generally devoid of any surface features related to underlying faulting or hydrocarbon seepage necessary for the potential presence of chemosynthetic communities, except on the steep slopes of the Sigsbee Escarpment.

3.2.2.1.2.2. Impact Analysis

Chapters 4.2.1.1.4.2.1 and 4.2.2.1.4.2.1 of the Multisale EIS contain a general discussion of impacts from OCS activity. The NTL 2000-G20, "Deepwater Chemosynthetic Communities," makes mandatory the search for and avoidance of dense chemosynthetic communities (such as Bush Hill-type communities) or areas that have a high potential for supporting these community types, as interpreted from geophysical records. The NTL is exercised on all applicable leases and is not an optional protective measure. Under the provisions of this NTL, lessees intending to explore or develop in water depths >400 m (1,310 ft) are required to conduct geophysical surveys of the area of proposed activities and to evaluate the data for indications of conditions that may support chemosynthetic communities. The drill sites for one well in each of Walker Ridge Blocks 206, 249, and 469 are all located over 1.5 mi (2 km) from any potential chemosynthetic communities sites. There are some signatures for chemosynthetic communities in areas of Walker Ridge Blocks 249 and 205 on the shallower portions of the Sigsbee Escarpment where anchor deployment was initially planned; however, the placement of anchors has been modified to locate all anchors and associated impacts away from these features. The use of an FPSO is not expected to have any possible impact on chemosynthetic communities in a region of soft mud bottom only. The mooring anchors for the FPSO in Walker Ridge Blocks 249, 250, 293, and 294 are located well away from any areas with the potential to have chemosynthetic communities. There will be no anticipated impacts to any chemosynthetic communities as a result of this project.

Conclusion

The proposed Cascade/Chinook project is not expected to impact either known or probable areas of high-density chemosynthetic communities. The nearest potential for any chemosynthetic community in proximity to the Walker Ridge impacting activities will be more than 1,000 ft (305 m) away from the anchor locations. No high-density, chemosynthetic community signatures occur in the vicinity of the proposed drilling in Walker Ridge Blocks 206, 249, or 469. Use of an FPSO will not increase the risk of impact to distant chemosynthetic communities.

3.2.2.1.2.3. Cumulative Analysis

Cumulative impacts on chemosynthetic communities include crushing and physical disturbance of the sea bottom from drilling discharges and the emplacement of other drilling rigs, production platforms, and subsea production infrastructure. No additional impacts to chemosynthetic communities from either OCS or non-OCS-related activities would be expected. Normal fishing practices should not disturb the bottom in these areas. Bottom-disturbing activities such as trawling and boat anchoring are virtually nonexistent at water depths >400 m (1,312 ft). The MMS reviews plans for exploration and development operations and pipeline applications that include geophysical evaluations of bottom characteristics or direct observations in areas planned for OCS activity. Sea-bottom areas likely to be disturbed by these projects are examined to determine if conditions exist that have the potential to host chemosynthetic communities. If these conditions exist, mitigations designed to avoid sea-bottom disturbances to chemosynthetic communities are applied. These reviews and mitigations are designed to protect these unique communities. Cumulative impacts as a result of the proposed activity in the Walker Ridge complex are expected to be negligible. No impacts from non-OCS-related activities would be expected in this deepwater area.

The incremental contribution of the proposed action's impacts to the cumulative impact on chemosynthetic deepwater benthic communities are negligible and likely undetectable among the other cumulative impacts.

3.2.2.2. Marine Mammals

3.2.2.2.1. Description

Twenty-eight cetaceans (whales and dolphins) and one sirenian (manatee) species have confirmed occurrences in the northern Gulf of Mexico (Davis and Fargion, 1996). Cetaceans are divided into two major suborders: Mysticeti (baleen whales) and Odontoceti (toothed whales and dolphins). Of the six baleen whale species occurring in the Gulf, four are listed as endangered or threatened. Of the 21 toothed whale species occurring in the Gulf, only the sperm whale is listed as endangered. The only member of the Order Sirenia found in the Gulf is the endangered West Indian manatee. The manatee has been reported in Louisiana coastal waters, but the coastal waters of Peninsular Florida and the Florida Panhandle are the manatee's normal habitat.

Information on each marine mammal species listed can be found in Chapter 3.2.3 of the Multisale EIS (USDOI, MMS, 2007) and is hereby incorporated by reference into this SEA. A summary of the incorporated material follows. The MMS has been conducting scientific research of marine mammals in the Gulf of Mexico since 1991, including GulfCet I and II and the Sperm Whale Acoustic Monitoring Program. The most recent study, Sperm Whale Seismic Study, completed four years of field work in 2005. This multifaceted program involved numerous partners and researchers. Yearly reports have been published and a synthesis report of the Sperm Whale Seismic Study will be published in 2008 (Jochens et al., in press). These studies have shown that the Gulf of Mexico has a diverse and abundant marine mammal community including a genetically-distinct resident population of the endangered sperm whale.

The distribution and abundance of cetaceans within the northern Gulf of Mexico is strongly influenced by various mesoscale oceanographic circulation patterns. These patterns are primarily driven by river discharge (primarily the Mississippi and Atchafalaya Rivers), wind stress, and the Loop Current and its derived circulation phenomena. In the north-central Gulf of Mexico, the relatively narrow continental shelf south of the Mississippi River Delta may be an additional factor affecting cetacean distribution (Davis et al., 2000). Outflow from the mouth of the Mississippi River transports large volumes of low salinity, nutrient-rich water southward across the continental shelf and over the slope. River outflow also may be entrained within the confluence of a cyclone-anticyclone eddy pair and transported beyond the continental slope. In either case, this input of nutrient-rich water leads to a localized deepwater environment with enhanced productivity and may explain the persistent presence of aggregations of sperm whales within 50 km (31 mi) of the Mississippi River Delta in the vicinity of Mississippi Canyon.

3.2.2.2.2. Impact Analysis

The impact-producing factors associated with the proposed Cascade-Chinook project that could affect marine mammals include (1) noise from vessel traffic, air traffic, and exploration and development activities, (2) degradation of water quality from oil spills or other material spills, (3) collision potential with service vessels, (4) spill-response activities, and (5) trash and debris from structures and service vessels. These impact-producing factors are the same for nonthreatened and nonendangered marine mammal species as well as those listed under the ESA. Chapters 4.2.1.1.5 and 4.2.2.1.5 of the Multisale EIS (USDOI, MMS, 2007) contain a discussion of the impacts from OCS activity and are hereby incorporated by reference into this SEA. The incorporated materials are summarized in the following sections.

Operations

The noise and shadow from helicopter overflights, take-offs, and landings can cause a startle response and can interrupt whales and dolphins while resting, feeding, breeding, or migrating (Richardson et al., 1995). The proposed action is expected to have aircraft, two round trips per day, during installation, development, drilling, and operations. These occurrences would be temporary and pass within seconds. Marine mammals are not expected to be adversely affected by routine helicopter traffic operating at prescribed altitudes.

Atmospheric noise inputs, however, are negligible relative to other sources of noise that are propagated in water (e.g., platform and drill rig operations and vessel traffic). Noise propagated through water may cause a short-term disruption of movement patterns and/or behavior, but such disruptions are unlikely to affect survival or productivity of whale populations in the northern Gulf of Mexico. Further discussion of noise impacts on cetaceans can be found in Chapters 4.2.2.1.5 and 4.5.5 of the Multisale EIS (USDOI, MMS, 2007).

Well completion, workover activities, and operations would produce sounds transmitted to the water at intensities and frequencies that could be heard by whales and dolphins. Noise from structure installation could be intermittent, sudden, and at times high-intensity as one-of-a-kind operations take place. Noise during the production phase of operation is expected to be semi-constant but at low-intensity levels.

The potential effects that water-transmitted noise have on marine mammals include disturbance (subtle changes in behavior, interruption of previous activities, or short- or long-term displacement), masking of sounds (calls from conspecifics, reverberations from own calls, and other natural sounds such as surf or predators), physiological stress, and hearing impairment. Individual marine mammals exposed to recurring disturbance could be stressed or otherwise affected in a negative but inconspicuous way. The behavioral or physiological responses to noise associated with the proposed Cascade-Chinook development, however, are unlikely to affect the long-term survival or productivity of whale or dolphin populations in the northern Gulf of Mexico.

Many types of plastic materials end up as solid waste during drilling and production operations. Some of this material is accidentally lost overboard where whales and dolphins can consume or become ensnared in it. The result of plastic ingestion is certainly deleterious and could be lethal. The probability of a marine mammal encountering trash that appears edible is probably very low. The disposal of solid wastes offshore takes place in covered bins that are warehoused in a secure area on the platform, and the bins are returned to shore by service vessels for disposal. The MMS issued NTL 2003-G11, "Marine Trash and Debris Awareness and Elimination," to help mitigate the potential threat trash and debris pose to marine mammals, fish, sea turtles, and other marine animals.

The primary operational waste discharges generated during offshore oil and gas exploration and development are drilling fluids, drill cuttings, produced water, deck drainage, sanitary wastes, and domestic wastes. During production activities, additional waste streams include produced sand and well treatment, workover, and completion fluids. Minor additional discharges occur from numerous sources; these discharges may include desalination unit discharges, blowout preventer fluids, boiler blowdown discharges, excess cement slurry, and uncontaminated freshwater and saltwater. The USEPA, through general permits issued by the USEPA Region that has jurisdictional oversight, regulates all waste streams generated from offshore oil and gas activities.

Most operational discharges are diluted and dispersed when released in offshore areas and are considered to have sublethal effects (API, 1989; NRC, 1983; Kennicutt, 1995). Any potential impacts from drilling fluids would be indirect, either as a result of impacts to prey species or possibly through ingestion via the food chain (Neff et al., 1989). Contaminants in drilling muds or waste discharge may biomagnify and bioaccumulate in the food web, which may kill or debilitate important prey species of marine mammals or species lower in the marine food web. Trace metals, including mercury, in drilling discharges have been a particular concern. However, Neff et al. (1989) concluded that metals associated with drilling fluid were virtually nonbioavailable to marine organisms. Marine mammals generally are inefficient assimilators of petroleum compounds in prey (Neff, 1990).

Service vessels present a collision hazard to marine mammals. The proposed Cascade-Chinook project is expected to require two roundtrip supply-vessel and three roundtrip crew-vessel trips per week as well as numerous other support vessels onsite during installation and development. As additional projects are pursued by industry in the area, increased ship traffic levels could increase the probability of collisions between ships and marine mammals, resulting in injury or death to some animals. Dolphins may bow-ride vessels that are in transit from a shore base to an offshore location more than 180 mi (290 km) from the nearest shore. The MMS issued NTL 2003-G10, "Vessel Strike Avoidance and Injured/Dead Protected Species Reporting," to help avoid collisions between vessel and marine mammals. The consequence of a vessel collision and a marine mammal is likely to be lethal, but the probability of a collision taking place is low with the current mitigations in place.

Accidental Events

Spills that occur from proposed Cascade-Chinook development activity would be few (if any), volumetrically small, and located near project activities, if they did occur. Oil spills and spill-response activities have the potential to adversely affect whales and dolphins by causing soft tissue irritation, fouling of baleen plates, respiratory stress from inhalation of toxic fumes, food reduction or contamination, direct ingestion of oil and/or tar, and temporary displacement from preferred habitats or migration routes. Some short-term (months) effects of oil may be as follows: (1) changes in cetacean distribution associated with avoidance of aromatic hydrocarbons and surface oil, (2) changes in prey distribution and human disturbance; (3) increased mortality rates from ingestion or inhalation of oil; (4) increased petroleum compounds in tissues; and (5) impaired health (e.g., immunosuppression) (Harvey and Dahlheim, 1994). Potential mechanisms for long-term injury include (1) initial sublethal exposure to oil causing pathological damage; (2) continued exposure to hydrocarbons persisting in the environment, either directly or through ingestion of contaminated prey; and (3) altered availability of prey as a result of the spill (Ballachey et al., 1994). Chronic effects may include (1) change in distribution and abundance because of reduced prey resources or increased mortality rates, (2) change in age structure in the breeding stock because certain year-classes were impacted more by an oil spill, (3) decreased reproductive success, and (4) increased rate of disease or neurological problems from exposure to oil (Harvey and Dahlheim, 1994). It has been speculated that mortalities of killer whales may be linked to the *Exxon Valdez* spill (Matkin et al., 1994). There was no documented evidence to directly link the Gulf War oil spill to marine mammal deaths that occurred at that time (Preen, 1991; Robineau and Fiquet, 1994).

The effects of cleanup activities on cetaceans are unknown. The impacts of dispersant chemicals used on a slick may be as much of an irritant to tissues and sensitive membranes as the oil itself. The increased human presence (e.g., vessels) could add to changes in whale and dolphin behavior and/or distribution, thereby stressing animals further and perhaps making them more vulnerable to various physiologic and toxic effects.

Clearly, the vitality or productivity of some marine mammals can suffer long-term impacts from oil spills if direct contact occurs, but the evidence for cetaceans being among this affected population has not been convincingly established. There is, however, substantial circumstantial evidence based on effects documented in other marine mammals that harmful effects from contact between spilled oil and individual whales or dolphins can be reasonably expected. Contact between marine mammals and spilled oil is unlikely, and the duration of this contact with mobile animals in the open ocean is expected to be very brief. Any impacts to the marine mammal population due to the proposed activities are expected to be sublethal. Effects on marine mammal populations are expected to be insignificant.

Conclusion

The proposed Cascade-Chinook project is expected to have little impact on the vitality of any marine mammal species or productivity of any population endemic to the northern Gulf of Mexico. No deaths would be expected from direct exposure to spilled oil or to chronic long-term effects caused by contact with spilled oil. Although interaction between marine mammals and a weathered oil spill is possible, sublethal effects would be the likely result. Collisions between service vessels and marine mammals would be extremely rare, but they could be lethal or crippling if realized. The MMS's regulations and NTL's are designed to reduce the possibility of collisions. There is no conclusive evidence as to whether or not anthropogenic noise in the water has caused displacements of marine mammal populations or is injurious to the vitality of individuals. Marine mammals could be injured or killed by eating indigestible debris or plastic items originating from the proposed development activities, but the likelihood of such an encounter is very small. Marine mammal populations are not expected to be adversely impacted by routine discharges due to current regulations and guidelines, and rapid dilution.

3.2.2.2.3. Cumulative Analysis

Cumulative impacts on marine mammals include (1) water quality degradation from oil, fuel, and material spills, high nutrient loads, high turbidity, high biochemical oxygen demand (BOD), urban runoff, industrial discharges, pathogens, and upriver contaminants; (2) noise in the water from infrastructure, vessels, and facility removal; (3) vessel traffic and collision hazard; (4) seismic surveying; and (5) trash and debris. Non-OCS activity that contributes to cumulative impacts includes the same impact-producing factors from OCS activity, but which arise from other industrial, commercial, or recreational activity. Also, commercial fishing activity can kill or injure marine mammals by accident. Marine mammal deaths attributable to non-OCS activity, such as commercial fishing, would be much greater than any caused by OCS activity.

Of these effects, the potential for collision between marine mammals and service vessels probably represents the greatest potential for adverse cumulative impacts on marine mammals over the 40-year exploration and production cycle. This judgment is made because collisions between large vessels and cetaceans, though rare events, typically results in crippling injuries or death. The collision hazard from service vessels is expected to decrease because of recent mitigations put into place by MMS, such as observers on vessels who are trained to spot marine mammals and turtles at sea. The potential for collisions with non-OCS vessels remains because requirements applicable to OCS activity do not apply to other industrial or commercial activity. Collisions between marine mammals and freight or cruise ships are not documented. While collision incidents between marine mammal and vessels that result in death attributable to OCS activity decrease or remain the same, the total number of marine mammal deaths resulting from collisions with all vessels associated with non-OCS activity will probably increase or remain the same.

Deaths or serious injuries due to explosive structure-removal operations are not expected or would be extremely rare. Depending on mitigation measures developed during ESA Section 7 consultations and if the removal of subsea production infrastructure is not required in deepwater developments, the chance of harm to marine mammals can be reduced. Noise in the water from platforms or service vessels may (1) disrupt normal activities like feeding, breeding, resting, or deep-dive recovery; (2) cause physiological stress and greater susceptibility to disease or predation; or (3) cause them to avoid these noise sources. There are effective prohibitions on discarding trash or debris from development activity at sea. Marine mammals could be injured or killed from ensnarement in or consumption of marine debris, particularly plastic items, lost from OCS structures and service vessels.

Cumulative impacts on Gulf of Mexico marine mammals include the degradation of water quality resulting from operational discharges, vessel traffic, noise generated at offshore structures, MODU's, helicopters, seismic surveys, explosive structure removals, oil spills, oil-spill-response activities, loss of debris from ocean-going vessels and OCS structures, commercial fishing (capture and removal), pathogens, and negative impacts to prey populations. Cumulative impacts on marine mammals would be expected to result in a number of chronic and sporadic sublethal effects (behavioral effects and nonfatal exposure to or intake of non-OCS and OCS-related contaminants or discarded debris) that may stress and/ or weaken individuals of a local group or population and predispose them to infection from natural or anthropogenic sources. Few deaths would be expected from chance collisions between marine mammals and OCS service vessels, ingestion of debris such as plastic material, and pathogens.

Oil spills and associated slicks of any size are infrequent events, but if they do occur they have a very small potential to contact marine mammals. Sublethal effects could occur with exposure of marine mammals to a weathered oil slick. Disturbance (noise from vessel traffic and drilling operations, etc.)

and/or exposure to platform discharges may cause sublethal effects, may stress animals and weaken their immune systems, and may make them more vulnerable to parasites and diseases.

The net result of any disturbance would be dependent upon the size and percentage of the population affected; ecological importance of the disturbed area; environmental and biological parameters that influence an animal's sensitivity to disturbance and stress; and the accommodation time in response to prolonged disturbance (Geraci and St. Aubin, 1980).

The incremental contribution of the proposed Cascade-Chinook project to the cumulative impacts would be negligible. The effects of the most likely impacts, such as the physical presence and operation of the platform facility, or noise from the platform, helicopters, and service-vessel traffic, would only be expected to modify the behavior of the marine mammals that come into contact with these project facilities.

3.2.2.3. Sea Turtles

3.2.2.3.1. Description

Five species of sea turtle are found in the waters of the Gulf of Mexico: green, leatherback, hawksbill, Kemp's ridley, and loggerhead. All are protected under the ESA, and all except the loggerhead turtle (threatened) are listed as endangered. Sea turtles are long-lived, slow-reproducing animals that spend nearly all of their lives in the water. Females must emerge periodically from the ocean to nest on beaches. It is generally believed that all sea turtle species spend their first few years in pelagic waters, occurring in driftlines and convergence zones (in *Sargassum* rafts) where they find refuge and food in items that accumulate in surface circulation features (Carr and Caldwell, 1956; Carr, 1987). Genetic analysis of sea turtles has revealed in recent years that discrete, non-interbreeding stocks of sea turtles make up "worldwide extensive ranges" of the various species.

Adult turtles are apparently less abundant in the deeper waters of the Gulf than they are in waters less than 27-50 m (80-160 ft) deep (NRC, 1990) and are more abundant in the northeastern Gulf than in the northwestern Gulf (Thompson, 1988). Sea turtle abundance appears to increase dramatically east of Mobile Bay (Davis et al., 2000). Factors such as water depth and turbidity, bottom sediment type, salinity, and prey availability may account for this. In the offshore Gulf, sea turtle distribution has been linked to zones of convergence.

Information on each turtle species can be found in Chapter 3.2.4 of the Multisale EIS (USDOI, MMS, 2007) and is hereby incorporated by reference into this SEA.

3.2.2.3.2. Impact Analysis

The impact-producing factors associated with the exploration and development activites of the proposed Cascade-Chinook project that could affect loggerhead, Kemp's ridley, hawksbill, green, and leatherback turtles (all listed as endangered or threatened species) include (1) noise from helicopter, platform, and vessel traffic; (2) possible collisions with service vessels; (3) brightly-lit structures; (4) project-related trash and debris; (5) oil spills and spill-response activities; and (6) water-quality degradation from platform effluents. Chapters 4.2.1.1.6 and 4.2.2.1.6 of the Multisale EIS (USDOI, MMS, 2007) contain a discussion of impacts from OCS activity and are hereby incorporated by reference into this SEA. The incorporated materials are summarized below.

Operations

The noise from helicopter operation can elicit a startle response and can interrupt sea turtles while resting, feeding, breeding, or migrating. The proposed action is expected to have aircraft, two round trips per day, during installation, development, drilling and operations. These occurrences would be temporary and pass within seconds. There are no published systematic studies about the reactions of sea turtles to aircraft overflights, and anecdotal reports are scarce. Sea turtles spend more than 70 percent of their time underwater, but it is assumed that sea turtles can hear helicopter noise at or near the surface and that unexpected noise may cause animals to alter their activity (Advanced Research Projects Agency, 1995). There is evidence suggesting that turtles may be receptive to low-frequency sounds, which is the level where most industrial noise energy is concentrated. Atmospheric noise inputs, however, are negligible relative to other sources of noise that are propagated in water (e.g., platform or drill rig operations and vessel traffic). It is unlikely that sea turtles would be adversely affected by routine helicopter traffic operating at prescribed altitudes.

Transportation corridors for service vessels will be through areas where sea turtles have been sighted. Noise from service-vessel traffic may elicit a startle and/or avoidance reaction from sea turtles or mask their sound reception. Potential effects on turtles include disturbance (subtle changes in behavior, interruption of behavior), masking of natural sounds (e.g., surf and predators), and stress (physiological). There is the possibility of short-term disruption of movement patterns and behavior, but such disruptions are unlikely to affect survival or productivity. Sea turtles exposed to recurring vessel disturbance could be stressed or otherwise affected in a negative but inconspicuous way. Whether or not persistent noise causes sea turtles to avoid the area is unknown.

Well completion, workover activities, and operations would produce sounds transmitted in the water at intensities and frequencies that could be heard by sea turtles. Noise from structure installation could be intermittent, sudden, and at times high-intensity as one-of-a-kind operations take place. Noise during the production phase of operation is expected to be semi-constant but at low-intensity levels. The industrial noises from platform installation and operation, and vessel traffic would have sublethal effects on sea turtles.

Many types of materials, including plastic wrapping materials, end up as solid waste during exploration and development operations. Some of this material could be accidentally lost overboard where sea turtles can consume it. The result of ingesting materials lost overboard could be lethal. Leatherback turtles are known to mistake plastics for jellyfish and may be more vulnerable to gastrointestinal blockage than other sea turtle species. The probability of a sea turtle encountering trash that appears edible is probably very low. Sea turtles could also become entangled or suffer crippling injuries from debris that is lost by service vessels. Disposal of solid wastes offshore takes place in covered bins that are warehoused in a secure area on the platform, whereupon the bins are returned to shore for landfill disposal by a service vessel for landfill disposal. The MMS issued NTL 2003-G11, "Marine Trash and Debris Awareness and Elimination," to help mitigate the potential threat trash and debris pose to marine mammals, fish, sea turtles, and other marine animals.

The primary operational waste discharges generated during offshore oil and gas exploration and development are drilling fluids, drill cuttings, produced water, deck drainage, sanitary wastes, and domestic wastes. During production activities, additional waste streams include produced sand and well treatment, workover, and completion fluids. Minor additional discharges occur from numerous sources; these discharges may include desalination unit discharges, blowout preventer fluids, boiler blowdown discharges, excess cement slurry, and uncontaminated freshwater and saltwater. The USEPA, through general permits issued by the USEPA Region that has jurisdictional oversight, regulates all waste streams generated from offshore oil and gas activities.

Most operational discharges are diluted and dispersed when released in offshore areas and are considered to have sublethal effects (API, 1989; NRC, 1983; Kennicutt, 1995). Any potential impacts from drilling fluids would be indirect, either as a result of impacts to prey species or possibly through ingestion via the food chain (Neff et al., 1989). Contaminants in drilling muds or waste discharge may biomagnify and bioaccumulate in the food web, which may kill or debilitate important prey species of sea turtles. Produced water is expected to be discharged overboard, after treatment, if required, and is subject to tremendous dilution factors in the offshore environment. The routine discharges from the proposed Cascade-Chinook project would be highly diluted in the open marine environment. These effluents would be within permitted limits and therefore have negligible effects on sea turtles that may come into contact with proposed Cascade-Chinook outfall sources.

Service vessels present a collision hazard to sea turtles. The proposed Cascade-Chinook project is expected to require two roundtrip supply-vessel and three roundtrip crew-vessel trips per week as well as numerous other support vessels onsite during installation and development. As additional projects are pursued by industry in the area, increased ship traffic levels could increase the probability of collisions between ships and sea turtles, resulting in injury or death to some animals. The MMS issued NTL 2003-G10, "Vessel Strike Avoidance and Injured/Dead Protected Species Reporting," to help avoid collisions between vessel and sea turtles. The consequence of a vessel collision and a sea turtle is likely to be lethal, but the probability of a collision taking place is low with the current mitigations in place.

Accidental Events

Spills that occur from proposed Cascade-Chinook development activity would be few (if any), volumetrically small, and located near project activities, if they did occur. When an oil spill occurs, the severity of effects and the extent of damage to sea turtles are affected by (1) geographic location, (2) hydrocarbon type, (3) duration of contact, (4) weathering state of a slick, (5) impact area, (6) oceanographic and meteorological conditions, (7) season, and (8) growth stage of the animal (NRC, 1985). All sea turtle species and life stages are vulnerable to the harmful effects of oil through direct contact or by fouling of their habitats and food.

Contact with spilled oil and consumption of oil (tarballs) and oil-contaminated prey may be lethal or have serious long-term impacts on sea turtles. There is direct evidence that sea turtles, especially hatchlings and juveniles, have been seriously harmed by oil spills. Sea turtles directly exposed to oil or tarballs may suffer inflammatory dermatitis, ventilatory disturbance, salt gland dysfunction or failure, red blood cell disturbances, impaired immune system responses, and digestive disorders or blockages (Vargo et al., 1986; Lutz and Lutcavage, 1989; Lutcavage et al., 1995). Although disturbances may be temporary, long-term effects remain unknown, and chronically ingested oil may accumulate in organs.

No deaths would be expected from direct exposure to spilled oil or to chronic long-term effects. Several potential mechanisms for long-term impacts may be (1) sublethal initial exposure to oil causing pathological damage and weakening of body systems or inhibiting reproductive success; (2) chronic exposure to residual hydrocarbons persisting in the environment or through ingestion of contaminated prey; and (3) altered prey availability as a result of the spill. Turtles may be temporarily displaced from areas impacted by spills. Because sea turtle habitat in the Gulf includes coastal and oceanic waters, as well as numerous beaches in the region, sea turtles could be impacted by accidental spills from vessels supporting the proposed action that are in transit near these environments. Although there is documentation of the harmful effects of acute exposure to spilled oil, the effects of chronic exposure are less certain and are largely inferred. An interaction between sea turtles at sea and spilled oil are unlikely to be realized. Contact between sea turtles and spilled oil is very unlikely, and the duration of this contact with mobile animals in the open ocean would be very brief. Adverse effects on sea turtle populations are expected to be insignificant.

No juvenile deaths or sublethal impacts on young or newly-hatched sea turtles, or nests on nesting beaches and habitats, would be expected because the probability of shoreline impact from an oil spill from the proposed Cascade-Chinook project is extremely small. Further, a slick would be unlikely to survive weathering and sea conditions that would bring it to landfall.

Oil-spill-response activities, such as beach sand removal, can adversely affect sea turtles. Vehicular and vessel traffic during spill-response actions in sensitive habitats during nesting season can occur. Harm to sea turtles is expected to be minimal because of the very low probability of contact between oil and these areas and protective spill remediation procedures. Increased human presence in nesting habitats could alter behavior of turtles, reduce their distribution, or cause them to move to less favorable areas, making them more vulnerable to various physiologic and toxic effects.

Conclusion

The proposed Cascade-Chinook project is expected to have little impact on the vitality of any sea turtle species or productivity of any population endemic to the northern Gulf of Mexico. A sublethal impact to sea turtle individuals exposed to a weathered oil slick is the most likely result. There is no conclusive evidence whether or not anthropogenic noise in the water has caused displacements of sea turtle populations or is injurious to the vitality of individuals. Collisions between service vessels and sea turtles would be rare, but they could be lethal if realized. Sea turtles could be injured or killed by eating indigestible debris or plastic items originating from proposed Cascade-Chinook development activities, but the likelihood of such an encounter is very small.

3.2.2.3.3. Cumulative Analysis

Cumulative impacts on sea turtles and their habitats include (1) water quality degradation from oil, fuel, and other chemical spills, high nutrient loads, high turbidity, urban runoff, industrial discharges, pathogens, and upriver contaminants; (2) habitat loss or degradation; (3) infrastructure and vessel noise, lighting, and removal; (4) vessel traffic and collision hazard; (5) trash and debris; and (6) natural phenomena such as sea-level rise, subsidence, and storms and hurricanes. Non-OCS activity that contributes to cumulative impacts include commercial and recreational fishing that kill or injure turtles by accident, beach lighting, and entrainment in power plant intakes. The cumulative impacts from the major impact-producing factors on sea turtles would be dominantly sublethal, primarily behavioral changes, temporary disturbances, or displacement of localized groups, and rarely lethal. Turtle deaths attributable to non-OCS activity are expected to be greater than any caused by OCS activity.

Of these effects, dislocation from preferred beach-nesting habitats or destruction of these habitats probably represents the greatest potential for adverse cumulative impacts on sea turtles over the 40-year exploration and production cycle. Habitat loss or degradation of preferred nesting beaches can be linked to stresses that act to reduce reproductive success, such as overcrowding on remaining and suitable nesting beaches. Natural influences on habitat displacement or destruction caused by sea-level rise, subsidence of the Mississippi River Delta, and the landfall of hurricanes will greatly eclipse any influences from OCS activity. Natural effects such as subsidence, however, have been accentuated by cumulative changes to the river's flow patterns and sediment load as a result of flood control projects, dams, channelization, and other civil works designed to improve navigation.

Deaths due to explosive structure-removal operations should not take place or should be extremely rare with the explosive removal mitigations required by MMS. The proposed Cascade-Chinook project is far from shoreline nesting habitat, and any bright lighting on the site should have no effect on sea turtle hatchlings. Underwater noise from platforms or service boats may disrupt normal activities and may cause physiological stress, causing turtles to become more susceptible to disease or predation. Collision hazards from service vessels would be expected to decrease because of mitigations put into place by MMS.

There are prohibitions on discarding trash or debris from project activity at sea. Sea turtles could be injured or killed from ensnarement in or consumption of marine debris, particularly plastic items, lost from OCS structures and service vessels.

Oil spills, chemical dispersants, and spill-response activities on sensitive nesting coastlines are potential hazards that may adversely affect sea turtles or the reproductive success of populations. Contact with and consumption of oil and oil-contaminated prey may seriously affect sea turtles. Large spills are extremely rare events and, for this reason, no contact or interaction is expected between turtles and freshly spilled oil. Incidental contact with degraded or weathered oil may be expected between turtles that inhabit or transit through the proposed Cascade-Chinook project area. The effects from contact with spilled oil in a weathered slick would be sublethal behavioral changes.

The incremental contribution of the proposed Cascade-Chinook project to the cumulative impacts would be negligible. The effects of the most likely impacts, such as the physical presence and operation of the platform facility, or noise from the platform, helicopters, and service-vessel traffic, would only be expected to modify the behavior of turtles that come into contact with these project facilities.

3.2.2.4. Essential Fish Habitat and Fish Resources

3.2.2.4.1. Description

Healthy fish resources and fishery stocks depend on essential fish habitat (EFH)—waters and substrate necessary to fish for spawning, breeding, feeding, and growth to maturity. Due to the wide variation of habitat requirements for all life history stages for managed species, EFH was previously identified throughout the Gulf of Mexico, including all coastal and marine waters and substrates from the shoreline to the seaward limit of the Exclusive Economic Zone (200 mi or 322 km from shore). Through analysis in an EIS (GMFMC, 2004), a new approach was adopted with Generic Amendment #3 to all Gulf of Mexico Fishery Management Plans (FMP's). The Generic Amendment to all FMP's (GMFMC, 2005) reduced the extent of EFH relative to the 1998 Generic Amendment by removing EFH description and identification from waters between 100 fathoms (600 ft or 183 m) and the seaward limit of the Exclusive Economic Zone (as deep as 10,499 ft or 3,200 m). However, the habitats most important to managed species (i.e., those shallower than 100 fathoms) will still be designated as EFH, and so the great majority of benefits to the biological environment will remain. The area of the Walker Ridge block complex no longer has a blanket designation as EFH but does retain EFH designation for some specific species, including many highly migratory species such as sharks, tunas, swordfish and sailfish.

The benthic fish populations of the Walker Ridge complex are expected to be very low in density and restricted to the few species that live at water depths below 8,200 ft (2,500 m). Descriptions of other ecological groups of fishes that would occur in the area, including oceanic pelagics and mesopelagics, can be found in Chapter 3.2.8.1 of the Multisale EIS (USDOI, MMS, 2007).

The Magnuson Fishery Conservation and Management Act established the provisions for Fishery Management Councils and FMP's. The only FMP that applies to the Cascade-Chinook area in the Gulf of Mexico region is that for highly migratory species (managed directly by the National Marine Fisheries Service (NMFS)). The Gulf of Mexico FMC's Generic Amendment identifies threats to EFH and makes a number of general and specific habitat preservation recommendations for oil and gas exploration, production, and pipeline activities within State waters and OCS areas. These recommendations can be found in Chapter 3.2.8.2 of the Multisale EIS. In consideration of existing mitigation measures, lease stipulations, and a submitted EFH Assessment document, MMS entered into a Programmatic Consultation agreement with NMFS on July 1, 1999, for petroleum development activities in the CPA and WPA. This agreement was later extended into areas of the Eastern Planning Area including the area known as Lease Sale 181. The NMFS concluded EFH consultation with a letter dated December 21, 2006, on the Multisale EIS and all activities described in the Multisale EIS with no additional conservation recommendations beyond those followed routinely MMS. This consultation also includes all of the blocks in the Cascade-Chinook complex.

It is understood that all previously accepted EFH Conservation Recommendations provided by NMFS in the past will be continued. There have been six additional EFH conservation recommendations provided by NMFS in addition to standard MMS policies (described in Chapter 3.2.8.2 of the Multisale EIS). The MMS has accepted and adopted those six additional EFH conservation recommendations.

3.2.2.4.2. Impact Analysis

The impact-producing factors associated with drilling and production of the Cascade-Chinook project that could affect EFH and fish resources include (1) installation of subsea pumps, manifolds, and flowlines; (2) presence of the FPSO and anchoring of the related turret; (3) anchoring of MODU's and temporary discharge of drilling cuttings and associated drilling fluids; and (4) blowouts or spilled oil. Chapters 4.2.1.1.8, 4.2.2.1.10, and 4.4.10 of the Multisale EIS contain a discussion of the impacts from OCS activity, and they are hereby incorporated by reference (USDOI, MMS, 2007). The incorporated material is summarized below.

The installation of subsea pumps, manifolds, and flow lies will disturb a small area of the seabed and resuspend sediments for a limited time. Benthic fish density is very limited at water depths of 8,200-8,800 ft (2,500-2,683 m). These impacts would be minor and very limited in time and space.

Drilling fluids and cuttings discharged offshore will contribute to localized temporary marine environmental degradation. Drilling operations are restricted in time, and pelagic species in the area could easily avoid discharge plumes. Routine discharges from the FPSO would be highly diluted in the open marine environment. Produced water would influence water quality and could potentially produce sublethal effects in fish over a limited area. Produced water discharged from the FPSO will be treated to meet USEPA standards and is subject to tremendous dilution factors in the offshore environment. Any effects would be local and not significant.

Accidental oil spills or blowouts with associated hydrocarbons also have the potential to affect fish resources and EFH. The MMS initiated and funded a comparative risk analysis to evaluate and compare the relative risks of an FPSO with a fixed platform production hub, a spar, and a tension-leg platform, and their associated oil and natural gas transportation systems (Gilbert et al., 2001). A major conclusion was that there are no significant differences in the oil-spill risks among the four study systems. The expected risks associated with the FPSO are comparable to those for already accepted alternatives for deepwater production, including a spar, a tension-leg platform, and a shallow-water jacket serving as a hub and a host to deepwater production. An additional conclusion of the comparative risk assessment was that the average total volume of oil spilled during the facility lifetime will be dominated by rare, large spills rather than frequent, small spills. Spills that occur from production activity would not be expected, but if they occurred there is no evidence that fish or EFH in the Gulf have been adversely affected on a regional population level by spills or chronic contamination.

An oil-spill risk analysis was performed for the Cascade-Chinook area (**Appendix B**). Spills that potentially could occur from the Cascade-Chinook activity would be few (if any) and, if one occurs, is likely to be volumetrically small and located near project activities. **Table B-8** presents estimates of spill risks to resources due to the facility. The risk of a spill occurring and impacting the coast could be considered to be so low as to approximate zero. Should a blowout or large (≥1,000 bbl) oil spill occur as a result of proposed Cascade-Chinook project activity, the likelihood of contact with shoreline resources remains very small. Smaller spills would be subject to weathering and dispersion and would dissipate before landfall.

Conclusion

The proposed Cascade-Chinook project is expected to have little impact on any coastal or marine fish or EFH in the northern Gulf of Mexico. The subsea structures and FPSO mooring will attract a variety of fish species, some permanently residing on and near to the structures. Impacts on adult fish or EFH are not expected. If a spill occurred, plankton, fish eggs, or larvae would suffer mortality in areas where their numbers are concentrated in the upper few feet or meters of water and where oil concentrations are high enough. There are no significant additional oil-spill risks due to the operation of the FPSO and transfer of hydrocarbons to adjacent tankers. Specific effects from oil spills would depend on several factors, including timing, location, volume and type of oil, environmental conditions, and countermeasures used. Recovery from the spill-related mortality of any fish eggs or larvae would take place rapidly (1 year) from fish populations in adjacent unaffected areas.

3.2.2.4.3. Cumulative Analysis

Principal cumulative impacts on EFH and fish resources include (1) degradation of water quality from oil, fuel, and material spills, high nutrient loads, high turbidity, high BOD, urban runoff, industrial discharges, pathogens, trash and debris, and upriver contaminants; (2) loss of essential habitat important for parts of fish species life cycles, such as healthy estuarine systems, (including wetland loss); and (3) commercial overfishing. Many of these sources would have little to no impact on the deepwater area of the Cascade-Chinook project. Of these, water quality degradation from multiple inputs and sources, not unique to OCS oil and gas activity, represents the greatest potential for cumulative impacts on fish resources and EFH. Cumulative water quality degradation attributable to OCS oil and gas activity, such as large oil spills, can be dramatic and visually striking when it occurs, but historical data show that the probability of occurrence is extremely low. Planktonic fish eggs and larvae are more susceptible than adults to environmental contaminants.

Hurricanes may impact fish resources by destroying both coastal wetlands and offshore live-bottom and reef communities and by changing the physical characteristics of inshore and offshore ecosystems. As a cumulative impacting factor, hurricanes certainly had a substantial impact on Gulf Coast fisheries and EFH in 2005. Contrary to initial fears, however, the majority of significant fishery resource impacts were to the nearshore costal and wetlands areas of Texas, Louisiana, Mississippi, and Alabama. The actual impacts to offshore fish resources and EFH were not significant. Hurricanes have essentially no cumulative impacts in deepwater environments such as the Walker Ridge complex.

There would be no cumulative impacts from commercial fishing in the Walker Ridge complex. There is no commercially viable bottom fishery in the area. Longlining for pelagic species can occur in the vicinity.

The incremental contribution of the proposed action's impacts to the cumulative impact on fish resources and EFH is negligible and likely undetectable among the other cumulative impacts.

3.2.2.5. Gulf Sturgeon

3.2.2.5.1. Description

The description of the biology, life history, distribution and causes for population decline of Gulf sturgeon can be found in Chapter 3.2.7.1 of the Multisale EIS. Designated Gulf sturgeon critical habitat occurs in estuarine and riverine locations along the Gulf Coast east of the Mississippi River in Louisiana, Mississippi, Alabama, and Florida (Chapter 3.2.7.1 of the Multisale EIS). Critical habitat is defined as special geographic areas that are essential for the conservation of a threatened or endangered species and that may require special management and protection. Designated Gulf sturgeon critical habitat is confined to State waters. Most activities related to the proposed action will occur in Federal waters (e.g., structure emplacement, drilling, producing, etc); however, critical habitat may be impacted directly or indirectly. In addition, there has not been any critical habitat designated in coastal or offshore waters west of the Mississippi River. Therefore, there is no critical habitat within the proposed action area due to the distance from shore and the westward proximity to the Mississippi River.

At present, NOAA indicates no changes in critical habitat have occurred, and they are working to develop an estimate of sturgeon habitat loss and a habitat suitability index for the species (Bolden, personal communication, 2007). They also have no data indicating that sturgeons are using the deeper Gulf waters. In general, the mud substrates found in the Gulf waters do not support the appropriate benthic food source for the Gulf sturgeon. The NMFS completed consultation as specified under Section 7 of the Endangered Species Act on the effects of the 2007-2012 5-year OCS Program in the CPA and WPA. A Biological Opinion was rendered on June 29, 2007, agreeing with MMS that the proposed lease sales and related offshore activities would not adversely impact the endangered Gulf sturgeon or its critical habitat and that additional mitigative actions other than those already identified and in place would not be necessary.

No recent information was discovered that would necessitate a reanalysis of the impacts of the proposed action on the Gulf sturgeon. The analysis and potential impacts detailed in the Multisale EIS apply for this proposed action and are summarized below.

Natural phenomenon such as tropical storms and hurricanes occur along the Gulf Coast with varying frequency and intensity between years. Although these are usually localized and sporadic, the 2004-2005 storm seasons brought major and repeated damage to the Gulf Coast area. The effects from Hurricane Katrina (2005) are still being assessed. The impacted area included a large portion of the designated critical habitat and known locations of Gulf sturgeon.

Another unpredictable event that is currently having an effect on some of the Gulf sturgeon habitat in some of the Gulf Coast States are the drought conditions along the upper portions of rivers feeding the lower riverine habitat for the species located in the lower portions of these coastal rivers. Recently, potential threats to the Gulf sturgeon habitat in the Apalachicola River system and the receiving bays have been raised as a consequence of reducing river flow to meet upstream water needs during drought conditions in upper Georgia (Pickard, 2007).

3.2.2.5.2. Impact Analysis

The impact-producing factors that would directly affect the Gulf sturgeon or its critical habitat would be limited to the support activities in the nearshore State waters. Based on numerous observations (Randal, personal communication, 2007; Bolden, personal communication, 2007), there is neither evidence of sturgeon activity, critical habitat, adequate food source, nor proper substrate in the deepwater offshore locations of the proposed Cascade-Chinook project that would attract or sustain the Gulf sturgeon. A detailed impact analysis of the routine, accidental, and cumulative impacts of the proposed action on Gulf sturgeon can be found in Chapters 4.2.2.1.9.1, 4.4.9.1, and 4.5.9.1 of the Multisale EIS (USDOI, MMS, 2007) and Chapters 4.3.9 and 4.4 of the FPSO EIS (USDOI, MMS, 2001). The following information is a summary of the impact analysis incorporated from the Multisale EIS.

Routine activities associated with onshore fabrication and supply activities to support the FPSO may result in maintenance dredging, vessel-related wetland loss, and some potential localized degradation in coastal water quality as a result of discharges from existing processing plants and land-based support facilities. There will be no new navigation channels; dredged material disposal will either be used beneficially for wetland creation, restoration, or placed in existing designated disposal areas. Support vessel traffic will be somewhat increased initially. This vessel traffic will generally only pose a risk to Gulf sturgeon when leaving and returning to port. Major navigation channels are excluded from critical habitat. The Gulf sturgeon's characteristics of bottom-feeding and general avoidance of disturbance make the probability of vessel strike extremely remote.

Impact-producing factors associated with routine exploratory and development activities proposed here could include disturbance of sea bottom with drilling, structure placement, and degradation of estuarine and marine water quality by nonpoint runoff from marine OCS-related facilities, oil or condensate spills associated with well blowout, vessel traffic, and pipeline installation. Due to the distance of the activity from shore (136 mi or 219 km) and the distance from critical habitat, little impact to the Gulf sturgeon is expected.

Coastal inland spills, as opposed to offshore spills, have the greatest potential for damaging Gulf sturgeon or their habitat. Sturgeons are impacted by oil spills through direct ingestion or ingestion of oiled prey or by the absorption of dissolved petroleum products through the gills. Upon any exposure to spilled oil, liver enzymes of adult fish oxidize soluble hydrocarbons into compounds that are easily excreted in the urine (Spies et al., 1982). Behavior studies of other fish species suggest that adult sturgeon are likely to actively avoid an oil spill, thereby limiting the effects and lessening the extent of damage (Baker et al., 1991; Malins et al., 1982; Farr et al., 1995; Nevissi and Nakatani, 1990). Contact with or ingestion/absorption of spilled oil can result in death or nonfatal physiological irritation, especially of gill epithelium and liver function in adult Gulf sturgeon. No long-term effects are expected on the size or productivity of any distinct interbreeding Gulf sturgeon population stock in the Gulf of Mexico.

Conclusion

The proposed Cascade-Chinook project is expected to have little impact on Gulf sturgeon. Based on the recent analysis of spill risk from the Cascade-Chinook FPSO (**Appendix B**), there is a ≤0.5 percent chance of an oil spill reaching coastal waters where Gulf sturgeons or their critical habitat are found. Due to the distance of the exploration and development activities from shore (136 mi or 219 km), any oil reaching those areas would be sufficiently weathered to have the minimal toxic effect on the sturgeon. The greatest danger to the critical habitat and the Gulf sturgeon would be from nearshore, shuttle-tanker collisions or offloading spills (USDOI, MMS, 2001). The historical data from 1985 to 1999 shows no spills from either of these types of operations has occurred (**Appendix B**).

3.2.2.5.3. Cumulative Analysis

The Gulf sturgeon and its critical habitat can be cumulatively impacted by activities such as oil spills, alteration and destruction of habitat, degradation of water quality, channel construction, dredging and filling operations, flood control activities and commercial fishing. In addition, habitat loss as a result of natural forces such as hurricanes has also resulted in temporary displacement of the species within their local range (Paruka, personal communication, 2007). Storm-induced scour and runoff has resulted in the alteration of food source habitats and has temporarily reduced water quality in parent streams.

If the habitat range of the Gulf sturgeon extends west of the Mississippi River Delta, younger sturgeon could suffer physiological stress, irritation, or impaired liver function from coastal spills resulting from the Cascade-Chinook potential shuttle-tanker accidents. However based on the spill risk model there is only a slight probability of this occurring (≤0.5%). The effects from contact with spilled oil will be sublethal and last for less than 1 month. It is expected that the extent and severity of effects from oil spills will be lessened by active avoidance of oil spills by adult sturgeon. Sturgeons are demersal and would forage for benthic prey well below an oil slick on the surface. Adult sturgeon only venture out of the rivers into the marine waters of the Gulf for roughly 3 months during the coolest weather. This reduces the likelihood of sturgeon coming into contact with oil.

Substantial damage to Gulf sturgeon critical habitat is expected from ongoing inshore alteration activities and natural catastrophes. As a result, it is expected that the Gulf sturgeon will experience a decline in population sizes and a displacement from their current distribution that will last more than one generation. Deaths of adult sturgeon are expected to occur from commercial fishing. Natural catastrophes and non-OCS activities such as dredge-and-fill may destroy Gulf sturgeon habitat. Natural catastrophes including storms, floods, droughts, and hurricanes can result in substantial habitat damage. Loss of habitat is expected to have a substantial effect on the reestablishment and growth of Gulf sturgeon populations. Climate changes, such as droughts, that are currently being experienced in some states bordering the Gulf Coast States are having a critical affect on Gulf sturgeon habitat through reducing reservoir releases needed to feed the spawning areas in the coastal spawning streams used by sturgeon. Recently, potential threats to the Gulf sturgeon habitat in the Apalachicola River system and the receiving bays have been raised as a consequence of reducing river flow to meet upstream water needs during drought conditions in upper Georgia (Pickard, 2007).

In summary, since there is no designated critical habitat west of the Mississippi River and the nearest critical habitat to the proposed action is 136 mi (219 km), the current action is not expected to adversely impact the Gulf Sturgeon or its habitat. The incremental contribution of the proposed action to the cumulative impact is negligible because the effect of oil-spill contact with Gulf sturgeon, should exposure occur, would be sublethal and short term (less than 1 month). A biological assessment was prepared by MMS and a Biological Opinion was rendered on June 27, 2007 (as part of consultation on the Multisale EIS) by NMFS, agreeing with MMS that work planned in the CPA and WPA would not adversely affect the Gulf sturgeon or its critical habitat and that no additional mitigation was required. The incremental contribution of the proposed action to the cumulative impact on Gulf sturgeon is negligible and likely undetectable among the other cumulative impacts.

3.2.2.6. Coastal and Marine Birds

3.2.2.6.1. Description

The distributions and populations of birds in offshore waters (i.e., outer continental shelf, slope, and abyssal areas) of the Central and Western Gulf of Mexico are not well known. The offshore waters, coastal beaches, and contiguous wetlands of the northeastern Gulf of Mexico are populated by both resident and migratory species of coastal and marine birds. The area is seasonally traversed by a diverse and sizeable array of migratory coastal bird and landbird species. There are six major aquatic groups: (1) seabirds; (2) shorebirds; (3) marsh and wading birds; (4) waterfowl; (5) raptors; and (6) diving birds. Information on coastal and marine birds can be found in Chapter 3.2.6 of the Multisale EIS (USDOI, MMS, 2007) and Chapter 3.2.5 of the FPSO EIS (USDOI, MMS, 2001). This information is hereby incorporated by reference and is summarized in the following sections.

Seabirds

Generally, offshore waters are inhabited by seabird species, both resident and migratory. Many species are mostly pelagic and are rarely sighted nearshore. Three taxonomic orders of seabirds (defined as species that spend a large portion of their lives on or over seawater) are found in the offshore waters of the northern Gulf of Mexico: (1) Procellariiformes (albatrosses, petrels, shearwaters, and storm-petrels); (2) Pelecaniformes (frigatebirds, tropicbirds, gannets, and boobies); and (3) Charadriiformes (phalaropes, skuas and jaegers, gulls, and terns) (Clapp et al., 1982a-c; Harrison, 1983; Warham, 1990; Olsen and Larsson, 1995 and 1997; Peake et al., 1995; Harrison, 1996; National Geographic Society, 1999).

Seabirds are a diverse group of birds that spend much of their lives on or over saltwater. Collectively, they live far from land most of the year, roosting on the water surface, except at breeding time when they return to nesting areas along coastlines (Terres, 1991). Seabirds typically aggregate in social nesting groups called colonies; the degree of colony formation varies between species (Parnell et al., 1988). They also tend to associate with various oceanic conditions including specific sea-surface temperatures, salinities, areas of high planktonic productivity, or current activity. Seabirds obtain their food from the sea with a variety of behaviors including piracy, scavenging, dipping, plunging, and surface seizing.

Systematic survey data collected during the MMS-funded GulfCet I and II studies represent the most recent contributions toward the understanding of seabird distributions and abundances in offshore waters of the Gulf of Mexico (Davis et al., 1998 and 2000). GulfCet I surveys were conducted between the Alabama-Florida and Texas-Mexico borders, between the 100- and 2,000-m (328- and 6,562-ft) isobaths. GulfCet II surveyed the oceanic northern Gulf, the previous GulfCet I survey area, and the continental slope of the Eastern Gulf. Fourteen species represented over 99 percent of the total sightings made during the GulfCet survey program.

Shorebirds

Shorebirds are those members of the order Charadriiformes generally restricted to coastline margins (beaches, mudflats, etc.). Gulf of Mexico shorebirds comprise five taxonomic families—Jacanidae (jacanas), Haematopodidae (oystercatchers), Recurvirostridae (stilts and avocets), Charadriidae (plovers), and Scolopacidae (sandpipers, snipes, and allies) (Hayman et al., 1986). An important characteristic of almost all shorebird species is their strongly developed migratory behavior, with some shorebirds migrating from nesting places in the far north to the southern part of South America (Terres, 1991). Both spring and fall migrations take place in a series of "hops" to staging areas where birds spend time feeding heavily to store up fat for the sustained flight to the next staging area; many coastal habitats along the GOM are critical for such purposes. Along the Gulf Coast, observers have recorded 44 species of shorebirds. Six species nest in the area; the remaining species are wintering residents and/or "staging" transients (Pashley, 1991). Although variations occur between species, most shorebirds begin breeding at 1-2 years of age and generally lay 3-4 eggs per year. They feed on plants and a variety of marine and freshwater invertebrates and fish.

Marsh and Wading Birds

"Wading bird" is a collective term referring to birds that have adapted to living in marshes and shallow water. These birds have long legs for wading in shallow water, while they use their usually long necks and long bills to probe underwater or to make long swift strokes to seize fish, frogs, aquatic insects, crustaceans, and other prey (Terres, 1991). These families have representatives in the northern Gulf: Ardeidae (herons, bitterns, and egrets), Ciconiidae (storks), Threskiornithidae (ibises and spoonbills), and Gruidae (cranes).

Seventeen species of wading birds in the Order Ciconiiformes currently nest in the U.S., and all except the wood stork nest in the northern Gulf coastal region (Martin, 1991). Louisiana supports the majority of nesting wading birds. Great egrets are the most widespread nesting species in the Gulf region; they often occupy urban canals (Martin, 1991). Members of the Rallidae family (rails, moorhens, gallinules, and coots) are elusive marsh birds, rarely seen within the low vegetation of fresh and saline marshes, swamps, and rice fields (Bent, 1926; National Geographic Society, 1983; Ripley and Beehler, 1985).

Waterfowl

Waterfowl belong to the taxonomic order Anseriformes and include swans, geese, and ducks. A total of 27 species are regularly reported along the north-central and western Gulf Coast. Among these are 1 swan, 4 geese, 7 surface-feeding (dabbling) ducks and teal, 4 diving ducks (pochards), and 11 others (including the wood duck, whistling duck, sea ducks, ruddy duck, and mergansers) (Clapp et al., 1982a-c; National Geographic Society, 1983; Madge and Burn, 1988). Many species usually migrate from wintering grounds along the Gulf Coast to summer nesting grounds in the northern United States. Waterfowl migration pathways have traditionally been divided into four parallel north-south paths, or "flyways," across the North American continent. The Gulf Coast serves as the southern terminus of the Mississippi (Louisiana, Mississippi, and Alabama) flyway. Waterfowl are social and have a diverse array of feeding adaptations related to their habitat (Johnsgard, 1975).

Raptors

The American peregrine falcon was removed from the endangered species list on August 20, 1999. The species is still protected under the Migratory Bird Treaty Act. The FWS will continue to monitor the falcon's status for 13 years to ensure that recovery is established.

Diving Birds

There are three main groups of diving birds: cormorants and anhingas; loons; and grebes. Of the two pelican species in North America, only the brown pelican is listed as endangered under the ESA.

Threatened and Endangered Species

Most species of coastal and marine birds that are in the Gulf of Mexico, and that are currently listed as endangered or threatened, inhabit or frequent coastal areas or waters of the inner continental shelf. These include whooping crane (*Grus americanus*), piping plover (*Charadrius melodus*), and brown pelican (*Pelecanus occidentalis*) (USDOI, FWS, 1998). Because of their normal coastal or inner continental shelf ranges, these species are not expected in deep water, which is where the proposed FPSO will be installed.

3.2.2.6.2. Impact Analysis

Impacts can result from installation, routine operations, and decommissioning. Impact-producing factors include discharges from OCS service and construction vessels from additional drilling and downhole workover operations subsequent to installation; disturbance from helicopter and OCS vessel (service vessel and shuttle tanker) traffic across or within coastal and nearshore habitats; and ingestion of, or entanglement in, debris that has been accidentally lost overboard.

Major operational discharges include sanitary and domestic wastes and limited operational wastes (e.g., bilge water). All operational wastes will be treated or monitored for relative levels of contaminants prior to discharge, and plumes of released wastes mix rapidly with ambient seawater and are thus diluted.

For drilling and completion operations (taking about 18 months), the following support vessels will be used: a DP drilling rig (onsite 6 months); a moored drilling rig (onsite 12 months); and an anchor handling tug for moored rig moves. For the same operations and also for production operations (taking 6-8 years), the following vessels and aircraft will be used: crewboats/fast suppliers (3 round trips per week); offshore service vessels (2 round trips per week); and helicopters (2 round trips per day). A field service tug will be onsite all of the time for production operations, for offloading, and for general marine support. For FPSO installation operations, the following vessels and aircraft will be used (duration of trips in days are in parentheses): a DP pipelay barge for Chinook flowlines (30 days); a DP pipelay barge for Cascade flowlines and gas export (60 days); three DP construction vessels, respectively, for FSHR's (40 days), flexible jumpers and flying leads (30 days), and subsea heavy lifts (30 days); an offshore service vessel for multiple work scopes (180 days); an anchor-handling tug for the FPSO mooring system and various piles (45 days); a tug with a barge to support the Chinook flowlines (9 days); and a helicopter to support all installation work scopes (180 days).

The bilge water within FPSO-related vessels may contain some quantity of machinery waste oil. Fluid wastes, when permitted, will be released on site and diluted and dispersed rapidly. All sanitary and domestic wastes will either be treated or monitored for relative levels of contaminants prior to discharge. Wastes include produced waters, produced sand, workover fluids deck drainage, miscellaneous well fluids (e.g., cement); sanitary and domestic wastes; gas and oil processing wastes; ballast water; and storage displacement water. Most waste fluids are treated and/or monitored for relative levels of oil and grease, and priority contaminants, prior to discharge. Produced solids are not discharged.

Discharged fluids may have sublethal effects on seabirds under certain circumstances. These effects may be indirect, as a result of the impact of the discharges on prey species (reduction in prey) or direct, through prolonged exposure to the discharge or through the ingestion of the affected prey species (Kennicutt, 1995; API, 1989; NRC, 1983). However, because of the low concentrations of contaminants discharged, the rapid dilution of discharged fluid plumes in offshore waters, and the short-term duration of drilling operations, impacts on seabirds associated with the release of operational discharges are expected to be adverse but not significant. Discharges are not expected to contact and possibly impact coastal or continental shelf bird species, which will be far from the FPSO site.

Helicopter and service-vessel traffic related to the installment of a FPSO system could, on occasion, disturb individual or groups of coastal or marine birds. These disturbances would pertain to helicopter or service-vessel traffic within or across sensitive coastal habitats such as wetlands, which may support feeding, resting, or breeding birds. A detailed discussion of the impacts of helicopter and vessel traffic and the legal guidelines including Federal Aviation Administration requirements, is provided in Chapter 4.1.1.8 of the Multisale EIS (USDOI, MMS, 2007). With guidelines in effect, traffic associated with installation, routine operations, and decommissioning of an FPSO is expected to have only negligible impacts on coastal and marine birds.

Debris that has been accidentally lost overboard may entangle coastal and marine birds or they may ingest the debris. Entanglement with debris can lead to damaged or lost limbs, entrapment, or the prevention or hindrance of flight or swimming. Ingested debris may irritate or block the digestive tract, impair digestion of food in the tract, or release toxins. Currently, the discharge or disposal of solid debris from both OCS structures and vessels is prohibited by MMS NTL's (30 CFR 250.40) and by the Coast Guard (MARPOL, Annex V, Public Law 100-220 (101 Statute 14580)). Therefore, debris lost overboard from FPSO installation, routine operations, and decommissioning is expected to have only negligible impacts on coastal and marine birds.

Oil-Spill Impacts

Bird use of the sea surface and intertidal zone, where spilled oil tends to accumulate, makes them vulnerable to exposure to oil following a spill. Although the chances of an oil spill from the FPSO or shuttle tankers are unlikely, oil spills from the FPSO vessel pose the greatest potential direct and indirect impacts to coastal and marine birds. Birds that are heavily oiled are usually killed. If physical oiling of individuals or local groups of birds occurs, some degree of both acute and chronic physiological stress associated with direct and secondary uptake of oil would be expected. Lightly oiled birds can sustain tissue and organ damage from oil ingested during feeding and grooming or from oil that is inhaled. Such birds may appear healthy at first but may be affected by stress that does not occur until much later. Stress, trauma, and shock enhance the effects of exposure and poisoning. Low levels of oil could stress birds by interfering with food detection, feeding impulses, predator avoidance, territory definition, homing of migratory species, susceptibility to physiological disorders, disease resistance, growth rates, reproduction, and respiration. Reproductive success can be affected by the toxins in oil. Indirect effects occur by fouling of nesting habitat, and displacement of individuals, breeding pairs, or populations to less favorable habitats. Competition may exclude refugee seabirds from all habitats. The combined probability of an oil spill occurring and contacting coastal bird resources within 30 days is <0.5 percent for all coastal counties or parishes analyzed. Therefore, impacts on coastal birds are considered negligible. However, the occurrence of seabirds in offshore waters is not known and needs study.

New research, experience, and testing will help the efficacy of rehabilitation of oiled birds and probably improve scare methods that will keep birds away from an oil slick. Rehabilitation can be significant to the survival of threatened and endangered bird species.

Dispersants used in spill cleanup activity can have toxic effects similar to oil on the reproductive success of coastal and marine birds. The, air, vehicle, and foot traffic that takes place during shoreline clean up activity can disturb nesting populations and degrade or destroy habitat if not properly regulated.

Conclusion

Discharges in the area of the proposed action are monitored for contaminants prior to discharge and will be rapidly diluted. Impacts on birds are expected to be negligible. With aircraft and service-vessel guidelines in effect, helicopter flights and vessel trips are expected to have negligible impacts on bird resources. With regulations in effect and enforced, impacts of trash and debris on birds in the area of the proposed action are expected to be negligible. The probability of an oil spill occurring and contacting coastal birds is <0.5 percent. Because of this and with adequate use of dispersants, cleanup operations, and rehabilitation of oiled birds, impacts of oil spills on birds due to the proposed action are expected to be negligible.

3.2.2.6.3. Cumulative Analysis

Cumulative impacts may include OCS activities; State oil and gas activities; crude oil imports transported by tanker; and other commercial, military, recreational offshore, and coastal activities. Sources of potential adverse impacts include air emissions; oil spills and spill-response activities; degradation of water quality; aircraft and vessel traffic and noise, including OCS helicopters and service vessels; habitat loss and modification resulting from coastal construction and beached trash and debris. It is expected that the majority of effects from the major impact-producing factors on coastal and marine birds are sublethal (behavioral effects and nonfatal exposure to or intake of contaminants or discarded debris) and will cause primarily temporary disturbances and displacement of localized inshore groups. Chronic sublethal stress is often undetectable in birds, but it can weaken individuals (especially serious for migratory species) and expose them to infection and disease. Lethal effects, resulting primarily from uncontained coastal oil spills and associated spill-response activities in wetlands and other biologically sensitive coastal habitats, are expected to remove a number of individuals from any or all groups through primary effects from physical oiling and the ingestion of oil and secondary effects resulting from the ingestion of oiled prey. Recruitment of birds through successful reproduction is expected to take many years, depending upon the species and existing conditions. The net effect of habitat loss from oil spills, new construction, and maintenance and use of pipeline corridors and navigation waterways will alter species composition and reduce the overall carrying capacity of disturbed areas in general.

The cumulative impact on coastal and marine birds, which will result from net decreases in preferred and/or critical habitats, is expected to result in discernible declines in the number of birds that form localized groups or populations, with associated changes in species composition and distribution. Based on historic census data, some of these changes are expected to be permanent. The incremental contribution of the proposed action to the cumulative impact on marine and coastal birds is expected to be negligible. It is expected that there will be little interaction between OCS-related oil spills and coastal and marine birds.

3.3. SOCIOECONOMIC AND HUMAN RESOURCES

Description of and impacts to the socioeconomic and human resources in the Gulf of Mexico region are characterized in the Deepwater EA (USDOI, MMS, 2000a), FPSO EIS (USDOI, MMS, 2001), and Multisale EIS (USDOI, MMS, 2007) and are hereby incorporated by reference into this SEA. Summaries of these resources follow.

3.3.1. Socioeconomic Resources

Socioeconomic resources in the Gulf of Mexico region are characterized in Chapter 3.3 of the Multisale EIS (USDOI, MMS, 2007). Summaries of these resources follow and include (1) the socioeconomic impact area for the proposed Cascade-Chinook project, (2) commercial fisheries, (3) recreational resources, and (4) archaeological resources.

3.3.1.1. Socioeconomic Impact Area

The MMS defines the Gulf of Mexico impact area for population, labor, and employment as that portion of the Gulf of Mexico coastal zone whose social and economic well-being (population, labor, and employment) is directly or indirectly affected by the OCS oil and gas industry. For this analysis, the coastal impact area consists of 132 counties and parishes along the U.S. portion of the Gulf of Mexico. This area includes 42 counties in Texas, 32 parishes in Louisiana, 7 counties in Mississippi, 8 counties in Alabama, and 43 counties in Florida, which are listed in Table 3-17 and illustrated in Figure 3-12 of the Multisale EIS (USDOI, MMS, 2007). Thirteen economic impact areas (EIA's) divide the impact area for analysis purposes and are considered in Chapters 3.3.1 and 3.3.2 of the Multisale EIS (USDOI, MMS, 2007) as the economic impact area for the proposed Cascade-Chinook project.

The criteria for including counties and parishes in this impact area are explained in Chapter 3.3.5.1 of the Multisale EIS (USDOI, MMS, 2007). This impact area is based on sets of counties (and parishes in Louisiana) that have been grouped on the basis of intercounty commuting patterns. The labor market areas identified by this grouping are commuting zones, as identified by Tolbert and Sizer (1996). In their research, Tolbert and Sizer (1996) used journey-to-work data from the 1990 census to construct matrices of commuting flows from county to county. A statistical procedure known as hierarchical cluster analysis was employed to identify counties that were strongly linked by commuting flows. The researchers identified 741 of these commuting zones for the U.S. Twenty-three of these labor market areas span the Gulf Coast, from the southern tip of Texas to Miami and the Florida Keys, and comprise the 13 MMS-defined EIA's for the Gulf.

The socioeconomic resources evaluated in this SEA are limited to that portion of the Gulf of Mexico's coastal zone directly or indirectly affected by activities associated with the Cascade-Chinook project.

3.3.1.2. Commercial Fisheries

3.3.1.2.1. Description

The most recent, complete information on landings and value of fisheries for the U.S. was compiled by NMFS for 2006. During 2006, commercial landings of all fisheries in the Gulf of Mexico totaled nearly 1.35 billion pounds, valued at over $684 million (USDOC, NMFS, 2007b). The Gulf of Mexico provides over 33 percent of the commercial fish landings in the continental U.S. (excluding Alaska) on an annual basis. Menhaden, with landings of about 1.02 billion pounds and valued at $44.9 million, was the most important Gulf of Mexico species in terms of quantity landed during 2006. Shrimp, with landings of nearly 257 million pounds and valued at about $367 million, was the most important Gulf of Mexico species in terms of value landed during 2006.

Commercial fishing in deeper waters, i.e., >200 m (>656 ft), of the Gulf of Mexico is characterized by fewer species and lower landed weights and values than the fisheries on the continental shelf. Historically, the deepwater offshore fishery contributes less than 1 percent to the regional total weight and value (USDOI, MMS, 2001). Target species can be classified into three groups: (1) epipelagic (open water) fishes; (2) reef fishes; and (3) invertebrates. The FPSO development and the Cascade-Chinook project area are beyond the normal depth range of commercial reef fishes and invertebrates. While it is possible that new species of demersal fish or invertebrates may be pursued in the future, if other fisheries fail, it appears unlikely at present because of the high cost and risk of fishing in extreme water depths and the general lack of commercially viable densities or biomass in very deep Gulf waters. In addition, considerable time, effort, and finances would have to be expended to develop markets for new species. Thus, if new fisheries develop in the deepwater Gulf, the most likely target species would be the epipelagic fishes, normally fished using surface longlines.

Epipelagic commercial fishes include dolphin, silky and tiger sharks (many other species of shark are now protected and harvest is prohibited), snake mackerels (escolar and oilfish), swordfish, tunas (bigeye, blackfin, bluefin, and yellowfin), and wahoo (USDOI, MMS, 2001). These species are widespread in the Gulf and assuredly occur in Walker Ridge. Oceanic pelagic fishes were not landed in high quantities relative to other finfish groups.

3.3.1.2.2. Impact Analysis

The impact-producing factors associated with the FPSO project in Walker Ridge that could affect commercial fishing include (1) coastal and marine environmental degradation, (2) space-use conflicts, (3) temporary discharge of drilling cuttings (4) longer-term discharge of produced water and permitted effluents, and (5) blowouts or oil spills. Chapters 4.2.1.1.9, 4.2.2.1.11, and 4.4.10 of the Multisale EIS (USDOI, MMS, 2007) contain a discussion of impacts from OCS activity and are incorporated by reference into this document. The incorporated material is summarized below.

Some area previously available to longline fishing will be eliminated by the installation of the FPSO facility. There is a slight possibility of pelagic longlines becoming entangled in the offshore structures; however, longline fishers use radar and generally are aware of offshore structures when placing their sets. Therefore, little or no impact on pelagic longlining is expected.

Virtually all commercial trawling in the Gulf of Mexico is performed in water depths <200 m (656 ft). Longline fishing is performed in water depths >100 m (328 ft) and usually beyond 300 m (984 ft). Either activity is carried out in water depths that are substantially shallower than the bottom locations of potential obstructions from the Cascade-Chinook project. Subsea production infrastructure would be located in water depths of approximately 8,200 ft (2,500 m). Because these subsea facilities (i.e., boosting systems, umbilicals, and flowlines) are in water depths >800 m (2,624 ft), they could be left in place without the requirement to sever and remove the equipment to a depth of 5 m (16 ft) below the mudline with MMS authorization.

Routine discharges from the production facility would be highly diluted in the open marine environment. Produced water discharged is expected to be treated, if required, and is subject to tremendous dilution factors in the offshore environment.

Spills that could occur from the FPSO would be few (if any), and located near project activities if they did occur. A blowout or large oil spill (≥1,000 bbl) from the FPSO would be recovered offshore, and what is not recovered would arrive inshore in a highly weathered and degraded state. Adult fish must become exposed to crude oil for some time, probably on the order of several months, to sustain a dose that causes biological damage (Payne et al., 1988). Adult fish also possess some capability for metabolizing oil (Spies et al., 1982). Farr et al. (1995) documented an avoidance reaction by fish to waters containing dissolved hydrocarbon, and analogous behavior can be expected of commercially important fish.

Besides the risk of contact from an offshore spill, coastal waters could experience a spill along vessel transit corridors and near ports that support offshore operations (shuttle tankers). Most of the commercially important fish and shellfish in the Gulf of Mexico are estuary-related during at least part of their life cycles. They usually remain in coastal waters where most of the fishery is concentrated. Spills that contact coastal bays and estuaries of the OCS when pelagic eggs and fish larvae are present have the greatest potential to affect commercial fishery resources by killing large numbers of fish eggs and larvae. If a spill contacts nearshore waters during specific times of the year, commercially important migratory species, such as mackerel, cobia, and crevalle, could be impacted, as would more localized populations, such as menhaden, shrimp, blue crabs, or oysters. Although the quantity of commercial landings of migratory species in the Gulf of Mexico is comparatively small, these species can be of high value.

Tainting (oily-tasting fish), public perception of tainting, or the potential of tainting commercial catches will prevent fishermen (either voluntarily or imposed by state regulatory agencies) from operating in a spill area. Restrictions on catch could decrease landings and/or value for several months. Because the ranges of commercially important fish resources are large, Gulf fishermen do not fish in one locale and have responded to past petroleum spills by moving elsewhere for a few months without substantial loss of catch or income. The effect of oil spills on commercial fishing is expected to cause a minimal decrease in commercial fishing efforts, landings, or value of those landings. Any affected commercial fishing activity would recover quickly. Potential effects caused by the level of activity of the FPSO would be indistinguishable from variations due to natural causes.

Conclusion

There may be some unavoidable loss of fishing space because of the physical presence of the development that could otherwise have been used for pelagic fishing such as longlining. This impact is not considered to be significant because the overall footprint of the development is very small compared with the total space available in the Gulf, and the FPSO will be the only surface structure in the Cascade-Chinook project area. A large oil spill might have commercial implications but, for the most part, the Gulf fishing fleets are highly mobile and cover a wide area. In addition, there are no commercially important demersal species at the water depth of this proposed action.

The proposed FPSO is expected to have little impact on the productivity of any commercial fisheries endemic to the northern Gulf of Mexico. There are no commercial fisheries that are restricted exclusively to the Walker Ridge area, nor is the FPSO project uniquely located to impact a commercial fishery that includes the Walker Ridge Blocks 206, 249, and 425 area or adjacent grids. Bottom obstructions are not expected to be an issue because of extreme water depths and the lack of commercially important species. Desirable pelagic fish species may also be attracted to the structure and could potentially improve commercial catches using fishing techniques other than longlining. A large oil spill might adversely affect commercial resources, but populations recover quickly and Gulf fishing fleets can respond by temporarily moving the location of their operations.

3.3.1.2.3. Cumulative Analysis

Cumulative impacts on commercial fisheries are the same as on fish resources in general and on EFH. These impacts include (1) degradation of water quality (i.e., from oil, fuel, and material spills; high nutrient loads; high turbidity; high BOD; urban runoff; industrial discharges; pathogens; trash and debris; and upriver contaminants); (2) loss of essential habitat important for parts of a fishery's life cycle, such as healthy estuarine systems (including wetland loss); and (3) overfishing.

Impact-producing factors of the cumulative scenario that are expected to substantially affect commercial fishing include commercial and recreational fishing techniques or practices, hurricanes, installation of other production platforms in the foreseeable future, additional underwater OCS obstructions, seismic surveys, petroleum spills, subsurface blowouts, and offshore discharges of drilling muds and produced waters. At the estimated level of cumulative impact, the resultant influence on commercial fishing, landings, and value of those landings is not expected to be substantial due to the remote location of and extreme water depths.

The incremental contribution of the proposed action's impacts to the cumulative impact on commercial fishing is negligible and likely undetectable among the other cumulative impacts.

3.3.1.3. Recreational Resources

3.3.1.3.1. Description

The northern Gulf of Mexico coastal zone is one of the major recreational regions of the U.S., particularly for beach-related activities. The shorefronts along the Gulf Coasts of Florida, Alabama, Mississippi, Louisiana, and Texas offer a diversity of natural and developed landscapes and seascapes. Chapter 3.3.3 of the Multisale EIS (USDOI, MMS, 2007) contains a more detailed description of recreational resources and use and is hereby incorporated by reference into this SEA. Chapter 4.3 of the FPSO EIS (USDOI, MMS, 2001) also describes recreational resources and use and analyzes possible impact-causing factors that may be associated with the proposed Cascade-Chinook project and is hereby incorporated by reference into this SEA. The incorporated material is summarized in the following sections.

Residents of the Gulf South and tourists from throughout the Nation and foreign countries extensively and intensively use the coastal beaches, barrier islands, estuarine bays and sounds, river deltas, and tidal marshes for recreational activity. Coastal recreational resources include recreation areas (e.g., national seashores, parks, beaches, wildlife lands) and designated preservation areas (e.g., historic and natural sites, landmarks, wilderness areas, wildlife sanctuaries, scenic rivers), as well as resorts, marinas, amusement parks, and ornamental gardens. The millions of annual visitors attracted to the coastal beaches in the Gulf of Mexico region add thousands of local jobs and billions of dollars to local economies. The recreational activities occurring along shorelines include beach use, boating and marinas, camping, water sports, and bird watching.

3.3.1.3.2. Impact Analysis

The impact-producing factors associated with the exploration and development activities of the proposed Cascade-Chinook project that could affect recreational resources include trash and debris, boat and helicopter traffic, blowouts, and spilled oil. Chapter 4.2.1.1.1.1 of the Multisale EIS (USDOI, MMS, 2007) discusses possible impacts from OCS activity on recreational resources and is incorporated by reference into this SEA. The incorporated material is summarized below. The location of the proposed Cascade-Chinook project is more than 150 mi (241 km) from the nearest shore, which precludes any visual impacts on people engaged in activity along the shoreline or in coastal waters.

The oil and gas industry is not the main source for trash and debris that litter shorelines along the Gulf. People engaged in recreational activities along the coast are primary sources of this litter, as well as trash and debris originating onshore but ending up in the sea through deliberate or careless acts. The U.S. National Park Service documented the origins of trash and debris on South Padre Island in Texas. About 13 percent of the 63,000+ items collected were attributable to the offshore oil and gas industry (Miller and Echols, 1996). Other sources of trash and debris include (1) accidental loss from staffed structures in State and Federal waters where hydrocarbons are produced, (2) commercial shrimping and fishing, (3) runoff from storm drains, (4) antiquated storm and sewage systems in older cities, and (5) commercial and recreational fishermen who discard plastics. While some accidental loss of solid wastes may occur from the proposed Cascade-Chinook project or service vessels, existing mitigations and regulations that control the handling of offshore trash and debris are expected to largely limit these inputs. Therefore, they are expected to have a negligible impact on recreational resources.

Spills that potentially could occur from the Cascade-Chinook activity would be few (if any) and, if one occurs, is likely to be volumetrically small and located near project activities (**Appendix B**). **Table B-8** presents estimates of spill risks to resources due to the facility. The risk of a spill occurring and impacting the coast could be considered to be so low as to approximate zero. Should a blowout or large oil spill ≥1,000 bbl occur as a result of proposed Cascade-Chinook project activity, the likelihood of contact with shoreline resources remains very small. Should one make landfall, it could present aesthetic impacts, but it is likely to be in a degraded state. Recreational beaches may be temporarily closed during cleanup and displace and inconvenience recreational users for up to 1 year. Smaller spills would be subject to weathering and dispersion and would dissipate before landfall.

Conclusion

The proposed Cascade-Chinook project is likely to have little impact on recreational resources. While some accidental loss of solid wastes may occur from the proposed Cascade-Chinook project or service vessels, existing mitigations and regulations that control the handling of offshore trash and debris are expected to limit these inputs so that they will have a negligible impact on recreational resources. The risk of a large oil spill occurring because of the proposed development operations is very small. The displacements, inconvenience, or closure of recreational resources caused by an oil spill is below the level of social and economic concern.

3.3.1.3.3. Cumulative Analysis

Under the cumulative case, debris and litter derived from both offshore and onshore sources are expected to diminish the tourist potential of beaches and to degrade the ambience of shoreline recreational activities, thereby affecting the enjoyment of recreational beaches throughout the area. However, the incremental beach trash resulting from the proposed Cascade-Chinook project is expected to be minimal when compared with other sources.

Under the cumulative case, platforms and drilling rigs operating nearshore are expected to affect the ambience of recreational beaches, especially beach wilderness areas. The sound, wakes, and sight of

OCS-related and non-OCS-related vessels, as well as OCS helicopter and other light aircraft traffic, are occasional distractions that are noticed by some beach users. However, the incremental contributions to sound and wake resulting from the proposed Cascade-Chinook project are expected to be minimal because the project will not be in sight of beaches.

Oil that contacts the coast may preclude short-term recreational use of one or more Gulf Coast beaches at the park or community levels. Displacement of recreational use from impacted areas will occur, and a short-term decline in tourism may result. Beach use at the regional level is unlikely to change from normal patterns; however, closure of specific beaches or parks directly impacted by a large oil spill is likely during cleanup operations. However, the chances of an oil spill occurring and reaching recreational areas of the Gulf Coast is unlikely. The incremental contribution of the proposed action's impact to the cumulative impacts on recreational resources is minimal.

3.3.1.4. Archaeological Resources

3.3.1.4.1. Description

Archaeological resources are any material remains of human life or activity that are at least 50 years old and that are of archaeological interest. The archaeological resources regulation (30 CFR 250.194) provides specific authority to each MMS Regional Director to require archaeological resource surveys, analyses, and reports. Surveys are required prior to any exploration or development activities proposed on leases within the high-probability areas (NTL 2005-G07 and NTL 2006-G07). A complete description of the prehistoric and historic archaeological resources can be found in Chapter 3.3.4 of the Multisale EIS (USDOI, MMS, 2007).

The description of prehistoric and historic archaeological resources in the Gulf of Mexico region can be found in Chapter 3.3.4. of the FPSO EIS and Chapter 3.3.4.1 of the Multisale EIS (USDOI, MMS, 2001; USDOI, MMS, 2007, respectively). The following information is a summary of the description incorporated by reference from the FPSO EIS and Multisale EIS.

Walker Ridge Blocks 205, 206, 249, 250, 425, 426, 469, and 470 are not located within either of MMS's designated high-probability areas for the occurrence of prehistoric or historic archaeological resources. No impacts on prehistoric or historic resources are expected from the proposed action. Prehistoric archaeological resources are precluded from the area due to the water depth. The high-probability area for prehistoric resources is shoreward of the 60-m (197-ft) isobath.

There are areas of the northern Gulf of Mexico that are considered by MMS to have a high probability for historic period shipwrecks (Garrison et al., 1989; Pearson et al., 2003). Statistical analysis of the shipwreck location data identified two specific types of high-probability areas: (1) within 10 km (6 mi) of the shoreline and (2) proximal to historic ports, barrier islands, and other loss traps. Additionally, MMS has created high-probability search polygons associated with individual shipwrecks to afford protection to wrecks located outside the two high-probability areas.

According to Garrison et al. (1989) and Pearson et al. (2003), the shipwreck database lists no known shipwrecks that lie, or are presumed to lie, in Walker Ridge Blocks 205, 206, 249, 250, 425, 426, 469, and 470. However, recent research on historic shipping routes suggests that the ultra-deep water areas of the Gulf of Mexico, including parts of Walker Ridge, were located along the historic Spanish trade route, which therefore increases the probability that an historic shipwreck could be located in this area (Lugo-Fernandez et al., 2007). The specific locations of archaeological sites cannot be known without first conducting a high-resolution, remote-sensing survey of the seabed and near-surface sediments. Regular reporting of shipwrecks did not occur until late in the 19th century, and losses of several classes of vessel, such as small fishing boats, were largely unreported in official records. Aside from acts of war, hurricanes cause the greatest number of wrecks in the Gulf. Wrecks occurring in deeper water on the Federal OCS would have a moderate to high preservation potential because they lie beyond the influence of storm currents and waves. Additionally, temperature at the seafloor in deep water is extremely cold, which slows the oxidation of ferrous metals and helps to preserve wood structures and features. The cold water would also eliminate the wood-boring shipworm *Terredo navalis* (Anuskiewicz, 1989). Shipwrecks occurring in shallow water nearer to shore are more likely to have been reworked and disturbed by storms. Historic research indicates that shipwrecks occur less frequently in Federal waters, where they are likely to be better preserved, less disturbed, and, therefore, more likely to be eligible for nomination to the National Register of Historic Places than are wrecks in shallower State waters.

The MMS approved the latest revision of NTL 2005-G07, "Archaeological Resource Surveys and Reports," on July 1, 2005. This revised NTL (1) continues to require a 50-m (164-ft) line-spacing density for historic shipwreck remote-sensing surveys in water depths <200 m (656 ft) and a 300-m (984-ft) line-spacing density for historic shipwreck remote-sensing surveys in water depths >200 m (656 ft), (2) increases the number of historic shipwreck blocks along the deepwater approach to the Mississippi River, (3) issues a reminder to operators of their requirement to notify MMS within 48 hours of the discovery of any potential archaeological site, and (4) updates some of the reporting requirements for archaeological assessments.

3.3.1.4.2. Impact Analysis

A detailed impact analysis of the routine, accidental, and cumulative impacts of the proposed development activities on historic archeological resources can be found in Chapters 4.3.13, 4.4.4.12, 4.5.3.13, and 4.5.3.14 of the FPSO EIS (USDOI, MMS, 2001) and Chapters 4.2.1.1.12.1, 4.2.2.1.14.1, 4.4.13.1, and 4.5.14.1 of the Multisale EIS (USDOI, MMS, 2007). The following information is a summary of the impact analysis incorporated by reference from the FPSO EIS and Multisale EIS.

The impact-producing factors associated with exploration and development activities within the Cascade/Chinook project areas in Walker Ridge that could affect archaeological resources include (1) direct contact or disturbance by the installation rig, (2) ferromagnetic structures or debris on the seabed, (3) onshore development in support of the project, and (4) oil spills.

The MMS's operational regulation at 30 CFR 250.194 requires that an archaeological survey be conducted prior to development of leases within the high-probability zones for historic and prehistoric archaeological resources. Walker Ridge Blocks 205, 206, 249, 250, 425, 426, 469, and 470 are not located within MMS's designated high-probability areas for the occurrence of historic archaeological resources. There is a low probablibility of potential impacts to historic shipwrecks in Walker Ridge Blocks 205, 206, 249, 250, 425, 426, 469, and 470.

Direct physical contact with a shipwreck site could destroy fragile remains, such as the hull and wooden or ceramic artifacts, and could disturb the site context. The result would be the loss of archaeological data on ship construction, cargo, and the social organization of the vessel's crew, as well as the loss of information on maritime culture for the time period from which the ship dates.

Offshore operations can introduce tons of ferromagnetic structures, components, and debris onto water that if dropped or accidentally lost without recovery have the potential to mask the magnetic signatures of historic shipwrecks. However, the use of a marine magnetometer for archaeological survey is not required in Walker Ridge due to the extreme water depth. Therefore, the task of locating historic resources via an archaeological survey would not be made more difficult as a result of operational practices that leave ferromagnetic debris from OCS activity on the seabed.

Conclusion

The Cascade-Chinook project is expected to have no direct or indirect impact on the inventory of known or unknown historical shipwrecks located in Walker Ridge Blocks 205, 206, 249, 250, 425, 426, 469, and 470. There is a low probability of impacting historic shipwrecks by the proposed development activities, however, as stated in 30 CFR 250.194(c) and 30 CFR 250.1010(c), if Petrobras discovers man-made debris that appears to indicate the presence of a shipwreck, Petrobras must immediately halt operations, take steps to ensure that the site is not disturbed in any way, and contact the Regional Supervisor, Leasing and Environment, within 48 hours of its discovery.

3.3.1.4.3. Cumulative Analysis

Prehistoric archaeological resources are precluded from the area due to the water depth. Cumulative impacts on historic archeological resources include the sources identified in Chapter 3.3.4.1 of the Multisale EIS (USDOI, MMS, 2007). According to Garrison et al. (1989) and Pearson et al. (2003), the shipwreck database lists no known historic shipwrecks within Walker Ridge Blocks 205, 206, 249, 250, 425, 426, 469, and 470.

No offshore historic properties have been identified in Walker Ridge Blocks 205, 206, 249, 250, 425, 426, 469, and 470.. Onshore historic properties include locations such as historic buildings, forts, lighthouses, homesteads, cemeteries, and battlefields. Sites already listed on the National Register of

Historic Places and those considered eligible for the National Register have already been evaluated as being able to make a unique or significant contribution to science. At present, unidentified historic sites may contain unique historic information and would have to be assessed after discovery to determine their importance. The incremental contribution of the proposed action's impacts to the cumulative impact on archeological resources is negligible if the attached mitigation is followed.

3.3.2. Human Resources and Land Use

Human resources and land use in the Gulf of Mexico economic impact area are characterized in Chapter 3.3.5 of the Multisale EIS (USDOI, MMS, 2007) and are hereby incorporated by reference into this SEA. Summaries of these resources follow and include (1) population and education, (2) infrastructure and land use, (3) navigation and port use, (4) employment, (5) current economic baseline data, and (6) environmental justice.

The impacts on human resources and economic activity including (1) population and education, (2) infrastructure and land use, (3) navigation and port use, (4) employment and economic activity, and (5) environmental justice are discussed in the following sections. Chapters 4.2.1.1.13 and 4.2.2.1.15 of the Multisale EIS (USDOI, MMS, 2007) contain a discussion of impacts on land use, coastal infrastructure, demographics, economic factors, and environmental justice from OCS activity and are incorporated by reference into this SEA. The resources described in the Multisale EIS are summarized in the sections below.

The human resources and economic activity evaluated in this SEA are limited to that portion of the Gulf of Mexico's coastal zone directly or indirectly affected by activities related to the described Cascade-Chinook development scenario. This economic impact area is concentrated primarily in Texas and Louisiana; however, multiplier effects extend into the other Gulf Coast States as well. The impacts that result from industry activity on the Federal OCS are taking place in the midst of dynamic commercial and industrial enterprises that move goods and services on Gulf waters and that cause some of the same impact-producing factors as OCS activity.

3.3.2.1. Population

3.3.2.1.1. Description

A detailed description of the population and demographics of the Gulf Coast can be found in Chapter 3.3.5.4 of the Multisale EIS (USDOI, MMS, 2007). Table 3-35 of the Multisale EIS contains the analysis area's baseline population projections by MMS-defined EIA. These projections are based on the Woods & Poole's *Complete Economic and Demographic Data Source* (Woods & Poole Economics, Inc., 2006) and assume the continuation of existing social, economic, and technological trends at the time of the forecast. Therefore, the projections include population associated with the continuation of current patterns in OCS leasing activity as well as the continuation of trends in other industries important to the region. These projections also include Woods & Poole's assumptions regarding Hurricanes Katrina and Rita's impact on the Southeast.

The 2007 Woods & Poole data became available in late August 2007 and contains their revised estimates regarding the economic and demographic impacts of the 2005 hurricanes on the Gulf region (Woods & Poole Economics, Inc., 2007). In the new data, population, income, and employment estimates declined from 2005 to 2006 by 76 percent in St. Bernard Parish, Louisiana; 51 percent in Orleans Parish, Louisiana; 22 percent in Plaquemines Parish, Louisiana; 19 percent in Cameron Parish; Louisiana; 13 percent in Hancock County, Mississippi; and 11 percent in Harrison County, Mississippi. In each case, these losses were less than those that were predicted in the Woods & Poole 2006 data. The 2007 data also has revised assumptions regarding counties and parishes that experienced population and employment gains because of Hurricane Katrina displacement: 9 percent in Pearl River County, Mississippi; 7 percent in Tangipahoa Parish, Louisiana; 5 percent in St. John the Baptist Parish, Louisiana; 5 percent in East Baton Rouge Parish, Louisiana; and 4 percent in St. Charles Parish, Louisiana from 2005 to 2006. In each case, these gains were less than those that were predicted in the 2006 data.

3.3.2.1.2. Impact Analysis

Projected population changes reflect the number of people dependent on income from the OCS-related employment for their livelihood (e.g., family members of oil and gas workers), which is based on the ratio of population to employment in the analysis area over the life of a proposed lease sale. Thus, population impacts from the Cascade-Chinook project mirror the employment impacts discussed in Chapter 3.3.2.4.2 of the Multisale EIS. The project is expected to have minimal impacts on population throughout all 13 of the EIA's identified above in **Chapter 3.3.1.1**. The majority of population impacts resulting from the proposed project are expected to occur in EIA's in Louisiana and Texas because of the location of the project and because the oil and gas industry is well established in these areas. Even assuming that all 1,500 jobs would occur in any single EIA in Louisiana or Texas (a highly unrealistic assumption used to evaluate maximum possible impacts), the population does not exceed 1 percent of the total baseline population projections for any given EIA. Employment demand for the project is expected to be met primarily with the existing available labor force. The MMS does expect some employment will be met through in-migration; however, this level is projected to be small and localized.

The employment impacts from accidental events are discussed in Chapter 3.3.2.4.2 of the Multisale EIS. Given that the net employment impacts of an accidental event are expected to be minimal, the resulting population and demographic impacts are also expected to be minimal.

Conclusion

The proposed Cascade-Chinook project is expected to have minimal impacts on population and demographics in the Texas, Louisiana, Mississippi, Alabama, and Florida EIA's. The project is expected to generate less than a 1 percent increase in population in any of these subareas.

3.3.2.1.3. Cumulative Analysis

Much of the cumulative analysis for demographics presented in Chapter 4.5.15.2 of the Multisale EIS (USDOI, MMS, 2007) is applicable to this cumulative analysis and is hereby incorporated by reference into this SEA. The cumulative analysis considers the effects of OCS-related, impact-producing as well as non-OCS-related factors on demographics. The OCS-related factors consist of population and employment from prior, current, and future OCS lease sales. Non-OCS factors include fluctuations in workforce, net migration, relative income, oil and gas activity in State waters, and offshore LNG activity. Most approaches to analyzing cumulative effects begin by assembling a list of "other likely projects and actions" that will be included with the proposed action for analysis. However, no such list of future projects and actions could be assembled that would be sufficiently current and comprehensive to support a cumulative analysis for all 132 of the coastal counties and parishes in the analysis area over the time period of analysis. Instead of an assemblage of future possible projects and actions, this analysis employs the baseline employment projections used above in **Chapter 3.3.2.1.1** to define the contributions of other likely projects, actions, and trends to the cumulative case. These projections represent a more comprehensive and accurate appraisal of cumulative conditions than could be generated using the traditional list of possible projects actions.

The incremental contribution of the Cascade-Chinook project to the cumulative population impacts are expected to be minor. The employment (and resulting population impacts) from the Cascade-Chinook project is expected to be considerably less than the impacts associated with the Thunder Horse project, the largest project on the OCS to date. Even for a project comparable in size and complexity to Thunder Horse, population impacts in any given subarea for any given year would still not be expected to exceed 1 percent of the baseline population for any subarea. Thus, population impacts in any given subarea for any given year would not be expected to exceed 1 percent of the baseline population for any subarea from the Cascade-Chinook project.

Employment demand will continue to be met primarily with the existing population and available labor force in most EIA's. The MMS does expect some employment will be met through in-migration; however, this level is projected to be small and localized.

3.3.2.2. *Infrastructure and Land Use*

3.3.2.2.1. Description

The Gulf of Mexico OCS has one of the highest concentrations of oil and gas activity in the world. The offshore oil and gas industry has experienced dramatic changes over the past two decades. Most of this activity has been concentrated on the continental shelf off the coasts of Texas and Louisiana. Future activity is expected to extend into progressively deeper waters and further east where only exploration activities have taken place to date. The high level of offshore oil and gas activity in the Gulf of Mexico is accompanied by an extensive development of onshore service and support facilities. The major types of onshore infrastructure are described in Chapter 3.3.5.8 of the Multisale EIS (USDOI, MMS, 2007) and include service bases, gas processing plants, navigation channels, oil refineries, pipelines and pipeline landfalls, pipecoating and storage yards, platform fabrication yards, service bases, terminals, and other industry-related installations such as landfills and disposal sites for drilling and production wastes. The vast majority of this infrastructure also supports oil and gas activities in State waters and onshore.

A service base is a community of businesses that load, store, and supply equipment, supplies, and personnel needed at offshore work sites. Although a service base may primarily serve the OCS planning area and subarea in which it is located, it may also provide significant services for the other OCS planning areas and subareas. As OCS operations have progressively moved into deeper waters, larger vessels with deeper drafts (>27 ft or 8 m) have been phased into service mainly for their greater range of travel, greater speed of travel, and larger carrying capacity. Service bases with the greatest appeal for deepwater activity have several common characteristics: (1) a strong and reliable transportation system; (2) adequate depth and width of navigation channels; (3) adequate port facilities; (4) existing petroleum industry support infrastructure; (5) location central to OCS deepwater activities; (6) adequate worker population within commuting distance; and (7) insightful and strong leadership.

A large number of potential ports between Corpus Christi, Texas, and Mobile, Alabama, may be utilized during the proposed activities. Ports considered for offloading of shuttle tankers require deeper channels and the infrastructure necessary to support the offloading, transporting, and refining of the crude. Descriptions of navigation channels and ports potentially impacted by the proposed activity are further described in Chapter 4.1.2.1 of the Multisale EIS (USDOI, MMS, 2007).

Land use in the impact area varies from state to state. Louisiana's coastal impact area is mostly vast areas of wetlands and small communities and industrial areas that extend inland. The coasts of Texas and Florida are a mixture of urban, industrial, recreational beach, wetland, forest, and agricultural areas. Alabama's coastal impact area is predominantly recreational beaches and small residential and fishing communities. Mississippi's coast consists of barrier islands, some wetlands, recreational beaches, and urban areas.

3.3.2.2.2. Impact Analysis

Oil transportation to market from the Cascade-Chinook project will be achieved through the use of dedicated, chartered shuttle vessels. Shuttle vessels will either be shuttle tankers or articulated tug barges. After production ramp up, the FPSO will offload oil to a shuttle vessel approximately once a week and the shuttle vessel will transport the product to the terminals of choice along the Gulf of Mexico, potentially including terminals in Texas, Louisiana, Mississippi, and Alabama. The utilization of shuttle vessels for a transportation system will provide a high level of flexibility over the life of the development regarding the terminals to be utilized. Although a number of terminals across the Gulf Coast may be utilized over the life of the development due to real-time market considerations (e.g., commercial terms, available capacity of terminals), MMS does anticipate that the bulk of the product will be transported to several select terminals. However, the project operator has not yet determined which specific terminals will be used or otherwise which terminals are most likely to be utilized. The regions where potential terminals of choice are located include Mobile, Pascagoula, Lower Mississippi River (e.g., Norco, Chalmette, and Belle Chasse), Baton Rouge, Lake Charles, Port Arthur/Beaumont, Houston/Galveston, and Corpus Christi. Given the level of current shuttle-tanker operations in the Gulf of Mexico, the incremental impact of the FPSO-related tanker traffic will represent a small percentage of total tanker levels for Gulf ports (Table 4-4 of the Multisale EIS and Chapter 4.3.1.1 of the FPSO EIS).

The existing oil and gas infrastructure in the region is expected to be sufficient to handle activities associated with the proposed Cascade-Chinook project. The primary onshore support base for operations will be the existing facilities at Port Fourchon, Louisiana. Port Fourchon has a longstanding history servicing offshore oil and gas and is capable of providing the services necessary for the project. It is unlikely that there will be any significant expansions at any existing infrastructure facilities as a result of the proposed activity. No new navigation channels will be required by, and current navigation channels will not change as a result of, the Cascade-Chinook project.

Changes in land use throughout the region as a result of the proposed activity would be contained and minimal. While land use in the impact area will change over time, the majority of this change is estimated as general regional growth. Increased OCS deepwater activity is expected to impact Port Fourchon and other OCS ports with deepwater capability.

Activities associated with the Cascade-Chinook project are not expected to significantly impact forms of social infrastructure (e.g., schools, hospitals, social services, etc.) in Fourchon or elsewhere in the region due to the minimal population increase expected as a result of the project (**Chapter 3.3.2.1.2**).

Since the oil-spill risk of occurrence for shuttle vessels is less than that for pipeline transport, there is no greater risk of spill occurrence based upon unique FPSO transport. Spill impact analysis for nearshore spills will, therefore, be generically addressed in this document. The FPSO EIS provides additional information on spills and potential impacts. Spills that occur from Cascade-Chinook exploration and development activities would be few (if any), volumetrically small, and located near project activities if they did occur. Should a blowout or large oil spill occur as a result of Cascade-Chinook project activity, the likelihood of contact with shoreline resources is very small. Smaller spills would be subject to weathering and dispersion and would likely dissipate before landfall.

Conclusion

The proposed Cascade-Chinook project is expected to have minimal impact on the region's existing infrastructure or land-use patterns. The existing oil and gas infrastructure is expected to be sufficient to handle development associated with the proposed activities. Accidental events such as oil spills and blowouts would have no effects on land use.

3.3.2.2.3. Cumulative Analysis

Much of the cumulative analysis for land use and coastal infrastructure presented in Chapter 4.5.15.1 of the Multisale EIS (USDOI, MMS, 2007) is applicable to the cumulative analysis of the proposed Cascade-Chinook project and is incorporated by reference into this SEA. The incorporated material is summarized below.

Land use in the analysis area will evolve over time. The majority of this change is estimated as general regional growth rather than activities associated with the OCS Program and State oil and gas activities. Except for the projected new gas processing plants (up to 14 assuming average retirement and no expansions and/or the addition of new capacity to replace what is physically depreciating at all existing facilities) and the 4-6 pipeline shore facilities, the OCS Program will require no new oil and gas coastal infrastructure. There may be some expansion at current facilities, but the land in the analysis area is sufficient to handle development. There is also sufficient land to construct the projected new gas processing plants and pipeline shore facilities in the analysis area. While it is possible that up to 14 new, greenfield gas processing facilities could be developed, it is much more likely that a large share of the natural gas processing capacity that is needed in the industry will be located at existing facilities, using future investments for expansions and/or to replace depreciated capital equipment. New facilities and expansions would also support State oil and gas production. Thus, the results of OCS and State oil and gas activities are expected to minimally alter the current land use of the area.

Shore-based OCS and State servicing should also increase slightly in the ports of Galveston, Texas; Port Fourchon, Louisiana; and Mobile, Alabama. There is sufficient land designated in commercial and industrial parks and adjacent to the Galveston and Mobile area ports to minimize disruption to current residential and business use patterns. Port Fourchon, though, has limited land available; operators have had to create land on adjacent wetland areas. Any changes in the infrastructure at Port Fourchon that lead to increases in Louisiana Highway 1 (LA Hwy 1) usage will contribute to the increasing deterioration of the highway. On January 6, 2006, the Louisiana Department of Transportation and Development announced that it accepted a bid for the first of three phases on a new LA Hwy 1 toll road and bridge in lower Lafourche and Jefferson Parishes. Phase 1A, construction of the two-lane elevated highway from the new Leeville Overpass to Port Fourchon, is underway and is expected to be complete in 2011. Phase

1B and 1C, the overpass at Bayou Lafourche in Leeville and its on- and off-ramps, is underway and expected to be complete in early 2009. Phase 1D, the Customer Service Center and Tolling System, is scheduled to go out to bid in January 2008 and to open in 2009 along with the Leeville Overpass. The toll will be $2.50 for cars and light trucks, and $1.25 per additional axle. A large portion of the tolls paid to finance the construction of this project will be paid by transportation activities associated with OCS oil- and gas-related activities. Traffic counts on LA Hwy 1 have continued to increase with over 7,000 cars, trucks and industrial vehicles having traveled along LA Hwy 1 during October 2007. In the absence of the planned expansions, LA Hwy 1 would not be able to handle future OCS and State activities. Additional OCS activity will further strain Lafourche Parish's social infrastructure as well, such as local schools and the water system.

Other ports in the analysis area that have sufficient available land plan to make infrastructure changes. Since the State of Florida and many of its residents reject any mineral extraction activities off their coastline, oil and gas businesses are not expected to be located there.

The incremental contribution of the Cascade-Chinook project to the cumulative impacts on land use and coastal infrastructure are expected to be minor. Of the new coastal infrastructure projected as a result of the OCS Program, none are expected to be constructed as a result of the proposed project. The proposed project would contribute to a very small percentage of the projected OCS-related activity at Port Fourchon.

3.3.2.3. Employment

3.3.2.3.1. Description

Table 3-41 of the Multisale EIS (USDOI, MMS, 2007) contains the analysis area's baseline employment projections by MMS-defined EIA. These projections are based on the Woods & Poole's *Complete Economic and Demographic Data Source* (Woods & Poole Economics, Inc., 2006) and assume the continuation of existing social, economic, and technological trends at the time of the forecast. Therefore, the projections include employment associated with the continuation of current patterns in OCS leasing activity as well as the continuation of trends in other industries important to the region. These projections also include Woods & Poole's assumptions regarding Hurricanes Katrina and Rita's impact on the Southeast.

Average annual employment growth projected from 2005 through 2030 ranges from a low of 1.22 percent for EIA LA-4 to a high of 2.50 percent for EIA FL-1 in the western panhandle of Florida. Over the same time period, employment for the United States is expected to grow at about 1.57 percent per year, while the Gulf of Mexico economic impact analysis area is expected to grow at about 1.73 percent per year. As described above, this represents growth in general employment for the EIA's.

The industrial composition for the EIA's adjacent to the CPA and WPA are similar. In 2005, the top three ranking sectors in terms of employment in all EIA's in the analysis area, except FL-4, were the services, retail trade, and State and local government sectors—with the service industry ranking number one in all EIA's and retail trade ranking second in all EIA's, except FL-2, where State and local government is second. In FL-4, the top three rankings sectors were services; retail trade; and finance, insurances and real estate, in that order, with State and local government a close fourth. In EIA's TX-1, LA-1, LA-3, and FL-2, construction ranks fourth; in EIA's AL-1, MS-1, and TX-2, manufacturing ranks fourth; in EIA's LA-4, TX-3, and FL-3, finance, insurance, and real estate ranks fourth; and in EIA LA-2, mining ranks fourth.

In the Multisale EIS, MMS used data from Woods & Poole's *Complete Economic and Demographic Data Source* (Woods & Poole Economics, Inc., 2006) for baseline population and employment estimates over the 40-year life of a typical proposed WPA lease sale. The 2007 Woods & Poole data became available in late August 2007 and contains their revised estimates regarding the economic and demographic impacts of the 2005 hurricanes on the Gulf region (Woods & Poole Economics, Inc., 2007). In the new data, population, income, and employment were assumed to decline from 2005 to 2006 by 76 percent in St. Bernard Parish, Louisiana; 51 percent in Orleans Parish, Louisiana; 22 percent in Plaquemines Parish, Louisiana; 19 percent in Cameron Parish; Louisiana; 13 percent in Hancock County, Mississippi; and 11 percent in Harrison County, Mississippi. In each case, these losses were less than those that were assumed in the Woods & Poole 2006 data. The 2007 data also have revised assumptions regarding counties and parishes that experienced population and employment gains because of Hurricane Katrina displacement: 9 percent in Pearl River County, Mississippi; 7 percent in Tangipahoa Parish,

Louisiana; 5 percent in St. John the Baptist Parish, Louisiana; 5 percent in East Baton Rouge Parish, Louisiana; and 4 percent in St. Charles Parish, Louisiana from 2005 to 2006. In each case, these gains were less than those that were assumed in the 2006 data.

More than 2 years after Hurricanes Katrina and Rita, the recovery remains uneven throughout the areas originally affected. Areas where the most severe problems remain are Orleans and St. Bernard Parishes, Louisiana, and Hancock County, Mississippi. Affordable housing continues to be a problem in these areas, particularly in New Orleans. Adding to the problem is the high cost of insurance and building materials, causing many prospective developers to postpone projects until these issues are better resolved. Recovery is well underway in Jefferson and Calcasieu Parishes, Louisiana, as well as in Biloxi, Gulfport, and Pascagoula, Mississippi; and Bayou La Batre, Alabama. Recovery is driving expansion in East Baton Rouge and St. Tammany Parishes in Louisiana; Jackson, Hattiesburg, and Laurel, Mississippi; and in Gulf Shores and Mobile, Alabama. The measures of recovery are the functions of local government, population, crime, economic and fiscal effects, local government budgets, housing, and labor (Rowley, 2007).

Researchers continue to study the employment impacts of the 2005 hurricane season. The Bureau of Labor Statistics did a special review of the employment impacts of Hurricane Katrina and found that St. Bernard, Orleans, and Jefferson Parishes had the largest percent declines in employment between September 2004 and September 2006 (38%, 27%, and 24.5%, respectively). In the 2S months following Hurricane Katrina, nonfarm payroll employment in Louisiana fell by 241,000, a decline of 12 percent; in the New Orleans metro area, employment declined by 215,000, or 35 percent. In the New Orleans metro area in June 2006, it was 30 percent below the level a year earlier. Total nonfarm employment in Louisiana decreased by 184,600 jobs or 9.6 percent from September 2004 to September 2005, and in May 2006, the year-to-year loss was 177,700 jobs or 9.1 percent (U.S. Dept. of Labor, Bureau of Labor Statistics, 2006; pages 2, 4, 6, 8, 27, and 28). However, more recent data show nonfarm payroll employment in Louisiana increasing 3.8 percent between April 2006 and April 2007 (one of the largest over-the-year percentage gains in employment for a State), or an increase of 69,500 from 1,835,700 to 1,905,200 (U.S. Dept. of Labor, Bureau of Labor Statistics, 2007).

Estimating employment data has proven more difficult post-Katrina, and some previous estimates are being revised as data-gathering limitations are addressed. For example, the Atlanta Federal Reserve Bank announced a revision to their employment estimates for Louisiana from 1,766,400 to 1,844,300 (an increase of 77,900 or 4.4%) between March 2005 and March 2006. Much of the revision was to account for job growth in the State's construction industry that had been underestimated due to survey sampling issues (such as identifying and sampling new construction businesses). Professional and business services is another industry where employment in Louisiana appears to have been originally underestimated (Federal Reserve Bank of Atlanta, 2006).

Researchers also continue to examine the impacts of the 2005 hurricane season on businesses in the region. For example, a Louisiana State University report on the hurricanes' effect on businesses comparing the second quarter of 2005 with the second quarter of 2006 concludes that, after a decline of over 5,000 in the number of employers (5.3%), the entire State of Louisiana had 2,270 fewer employers (2.3%) one year after the hurricanes (Terrell and Bilbo, 2007). The business failure rate in the year after the storms was 11.7 percent for the State as a whole compared with 26.5 percent for the five-parish southeast region.

3.3.2.3.2. Impact Analysis

Chapter 4.3.11 of the FPSO EIS (USDOI, MMS, 2001) discusses the estimated employment impacts from an FPSO project and is hereby incorporated by reference into this SEA. The incorporated material is summarized below.

The greatest potential employment impacts of an FPSO project are related to the construction and outfitting of an FPSO and possible associated shuttle tankers. However, the proposed Cascade-Chinook project scenario indicates that the vessel(s) will not be built in a Gulf port; the FPSO hull will be a converted foreign flag tanker. The base-case employment scenario in the FPSO EIS indicates that an FPSO vessel would have a standard staffing of 40 persons. While others would be employed in shuttle transport, the employment impacts would still be considered negligible (i.e., less than several hundred jobs) during normal operations.

The importance of the oil and gas industry to the coastal communities of the Gulf of Mexico is significant, particularly in Louisiana, eastern Texas, and coastal Alabama. This economic analysis focuses on the potential direct, indirect, and induced impacts of the OCS oil and gas industry on the population and employment of the counties and parishes in the impact region. Peak-year direct, indirect, and induced employment associated with development activities proposed for Thunder Horse, the largest development plan proposed to date on the OCS, was projected at about 1,500 jobs (USDOI, MMS, 2002b). Total peak-year employment projections for activities resulting from the Marco Polo project were comparable with Thunder Horse, 1,565 jobs per year throughout all subareas: 795 direct, 350 indirect, and 420 induced (USDOI, MMS, 2003c). The total peak-year employment from the Cascade-Chinook project is not expected to exceed these projects, but rather be considerably smaller.

The Cascade-Chinook project is expected to have minimal impacts on employment throughout all 13 of the EIA's identified above in **Chapter 3.3.1.1**. The majority of employment resulting from the proposed project is expected to occur in EIA's in Louisiana and Texas because of the location of the project and because the oil and gas industry is well established in these areas. Even assuming that all 1,500 jobs would occur in any single EIA in Louisiana or Texas, a highly unrealistic assumption but one used to evaluate maximum possible impacts, employment does not exceed 1 percent of the total baseline employment projections for any given EIA. Employment demand for the project is expected to be met primarily with the existing available labor force.

Since the oil-spill risk of occurrence for shuttle vessels is less than that for pipeline transport, there is no greater risk of spill occurrence based upon unique FPSO transport. Spill impact analysis for near shore spills will, therefore, be generically addressed in this document. The FPSO EIS provides additional information on spills and potential impacts. Spills that occur from Cascade-Chinook exploration and development activities would be few (if any), volumetrically small, and located near project activities if they did occur. Should a blowout or large oil spill occur as a result of Cascade-Chinook project activity, the likelihood of contact with shoreline resources is very small. Smaller spills would be subject to weathering and dispersion, and the spills would likely dissipate before landfall. The potential positive and negative employment impacts of an oil spill are characterized in Chapter 4.4.14.3 of the Multisale EIS (USDOI, MMS, 2007) and are hereby incorporated by reference into this SEA. The net employment impacts of a spill, as discussed in the Multisale EIS, are expected to be minimal.

Conclusion

The proposed Cascade-Chinook project is expected to have minimal impacts on employment in the Texas, Louisiana, Mississippi, Alabama, and Florida EIA's. The project is expected to generate less than a 1 percent increase in employment in any of these subareas.

3.3.2.3.3. Cumulative Analysis

Much of the cumulative analysis for economic factors presented in Chapter 4.5.15.3 of the Multisale EIS (USDOI, MMS, 2007) is applicable to this cumulative employment analysis and is incorporated by reference into this SEA. The incorporated material is summarized below.

This cumulative employment analysis focuses on the potential direct, indirect, and induced employment impacts from activities associated with the Cascade-Chinook project, together with those of other likely future projects (including those under the OCS Program), and trends in the region. Most approaches to analyzing cumulative effects begin by assembling a list of "other likely projects and actions" that will be included with the proposed action for analysis. However, no such list of future projects and actions could be assembled that would be sufficiently current and comprehensive to support a cumulative analysis for all 132 of the coastal counties and parishes in the analysis area over the time period of analysis. Instead of an arbitrary assemblage of future possible projects and actions, this analysis employs the baseline employment projections used above in **Chapter 3.3.2.3.2** to define the contributions of other likely projects, actions, and trends to the cumulative case. These projections represent a more comprehensive and accurate appraisal of cumulative conditions than could be generated using the traditional list of possible projects actions.

The incremental contribution of the Cascade-Chinook project to the cumulative employment impacts are expected to be minor. The employment from the Cascade-Chinook project is expected to be considerably less than the employment impacts associated with Thunder Horse, the largest project on the OCS to date. Even for a project comparable in size and complexity with Thunder Horse, employment impacts in any given subarea for any given year would still not be expected to exceed 1 percent of the baseline employment for any subarea (see **Chapter 3.3.2.3.2** above). Thus, employment impacts in any given subarea for any given year would not be expected to exceed 1 percent of the baseline employment for any subarea from the Cascade-Chinook project.

Employment demand will continue to be met primarily with the existing population and available labor force in most EIA's. The MMS does expect some employment will be met through in-migration; however, this level is projected to be small and localized. Port Fourchon is experiencing full employment, housing shortages, and stresses on local infrastructure—roads (LA Hwy 1), water supply, schools, hospitals, etc. Port Fourchon is a focal point for OCS development, especially deepwater OCS operations. The Port (and the surrounding community and infrastructure) is experiencing increased activity as a result of the 2005 hurricane season. Any additional employment, particularly new residential employment, and the resultant strain on infrastructure, are expected to have a significant impact on the area. In addition, ports throughout the Gulf are experiencing labor shortages for higher skilled positions as electricians, fitters, crane operators, and boat captains, an issue that existed prior to the 2005 hurricane season. This may lead to additional in-migration to these areas to fill these positions.

3.3.2.4. *Current Economic Baseline Data*

Oil and natural gas prices are used to evaluate the oil and gas industry's ability to economically develop resources. Current oil and natural gas prices are above the economically viable threshold for drilling in the Gulf of Mexico. As of November 30, 2007, the West Texas Intermediate price was $88.72/bbl and the Henry Hub natural gas price was $7.280/MMBtu in the U.S. spot market (Oilnergy, 2007). On December 4, 2007, the NYMEX January contract for benchmark U.S. light sweet crude was $88.32/bbl (*Oil and Gas Journal*, 2007).

Drilling rig use is employed by the industry as another barometer of economic activity. Rig utilization rates in the Gulf of Mexico were 72.9 percent in the end of November 2007, the lowest level since the early 1990's, and down from 80.0 percent a year ago (Greenberg, 2007; One Offshore, 2007). Average day rates for semisubmersibles operating in the Gulf of Mexico have experienced a decline since the summer; semi day rates averaged $432,500 during August and September 2007. In October, the average day rate for semisubmersibles fell to $346,875 (One Offshore, 2007). Most of the drop in the contracted rig count can be attributed to the jackup market, which was reeling from low natural gas prices during the summer. Drilling contractors could see a slight increase in jackup activity following the hurricane season, which ended on November 30th.

Lesser activity in the offshore rig market has also meant lower average day rates and utilization for offshore service vessels. The September 2007 average day rates were as follows: anchor-handling towing/supply (AHTS) vessels averaged $75,000 for over 8,000-horsepower (hp) vessels; supply boats ranged from $8,450 for boats up to 200 ft (61 m) and $17,125 for boats 200 ft (61 m) and over; and crewboats ranged from $4,250 for boats under 125 ft (38 m) to $6,718 for boats 125 ft (38 m) and over (Greenberg, 2007). In comparison, the September 2006 average day rates were as follows: AHTS vessels averaged $70,000 for over 8,000-hp vessels; supply boats ranged from $13,000 for boats up to 200 ft (61 m) and $20,333 for boats 200 ft (61 m) and over; and crewboats ranged from $6,500 for boats under 125 ft (38 m) to $7,533 for boats 125 ft (38 m) and over (Greenberg, 2007).

Lease sales are another indicator of the offshore oil and gas industry. Sales over the last several years have resulted in a relative increase in the number of blocks leased. Lease Sale 200, which was held in August 2006, garnered close to $341 million in high bids from 62 companies. The total of all 541 bids on 381 tracts was nearly $463 million, a 38 percent increase over the Western Gulf sale held in August 2005. Interest in deepwater oil and gas production continues to grow, with 67 percent of all tracts receiving bids in water depths greater than 400 m (1,312 ft). The increased number of tracts receiving bids in shallow water indicates ongoing industry interest in deep gas in shallow waters as well.

Western Gulf of Mexico Lease Sale 204, held on August 22, 2007, garnered 358 bids totaling $289.95 million in high bids from 47 companies on 282 tracts. The MMS accepted $287.08 million in high bids and awarded 274 leases to the successful high bidders after the bid evaluation process, and rejected high bids totaling $2.87 million on eight tracts as insufficient for fair-market value. The highest bid accepted on a tract was $37,588,800 submitted by Statoil Gulf of Mexico LLC for Alaminos Canyon Block 810.

Central Gulf of Mexico Lease Sale 205, held on October 3, 2007, attracted $2.9 billion in high bids, the second highest total of high bids in U.S. leasing history. The sale underscores the Gulf's continuing importance as a vital source of domestic energy production for the Nation. A total of 1,428 bids on 723 tracts were received from 84 companies. The sum of all bids received – losing as well as winning bids –

was $5.25 billion. Approximately 40 percent of the tracts receiving bids are in ultra-deep water, more than 5,249 ft or 1,600 m. The deepest tract to receive a bid is Amery Terrace Block 206 in 11,148 ft or 3,398 m of water. The highest bid received on a block was $90,488,445 submitted by Shell Offshore Inc. for Walker Ridge Block 7.

3.3.2.5. Environmental Justice

3.3.2.5.1. Description

On February 11, 1994, President William J. Clinton issued Executive Order 12898, *Federal Actions to Address Environmental Justice in Minority Populations and Low-Income Populations*, which directs Federal agencies to assess whether their actions have disproportionate environmental effects on people of ethnic or racial minorities or people with low incomes. Those environmental effects encompass human health, social, and economic consequences. There are no environmental justice issues in the actual offshore Gulf of Mexico OCS planning areas; however, environmental justice concerns may be related to nearshore and onshore activities in support of the proposed Cascade-Chinook project. Environmental justice issues are in two categories—those related to routine operations and those related to accidental events. Issues related to routine operations center on increases in onshore activity (such as employment, migration, commuter traffic, and truck traffic) and on additions to or expansions of the infrastructure supporting this activity (such as fabrication yards, supply ports, and onshore disposal sites for offshore waste). Issues related to accidents focus on oil spills.

3.3.2.5.2. Impact Analysis

Routine operations related to the Cascade-Chinook project will have few effects on the environment and health of people of ethnic or racial minorities. The existing onshore facilities that can support the proposed Cascade-Chinook project are well established along the Gulf Coast. There will be no new infrastructure that might affect ethnic or racial minorities, and the nature of the operations of current facilities should not change. For these reasons, the proposal will not have disproportionate impacts on ethnic or racial minorities or people with low incomes.

Conclusion

The proposed Cascade-Chinook project will not have disproportionate impacts on ethnic or racial minorities or people with low incomes.

3.3.2.5.3. Cumulative Analysis

Chapter 4.5.15.4 of the Multisale EIS (USDOI, MMS, 2007) discusses the cumulative environmental justice effects in Lafourche Parish, Louisiana. Future years may bring expansion or upgrading of existing onshore facilities that support OCS activities, but entirely new development is unlikely. The existing coastal support facilities are well established and their continued operation will have disproportionate effects on ethnic or racial minorities or people with low income. In the Gulf of Mexico coastal area, the contribution of the proposed Cascade-Chinook project to the cumulative effects on environmental justice is expected to be negligible to minor.

4. CONSULTATION AND COORDINATION

The Coastal Zone Management Act places requirements on any applicant for an OCS plan that describes in detail Federal license or permit activities affecting any coastal use or resource, in or outside of a State's coastal zone. The applicant must provide in the OCS plan submitted to MMS a certification and necessary data and information for the State to determine that the proposed activities comply with the enforceable policies of the State's approved program, and that such activities will be conducted in a manner consistent with the program (16 U.S.C. 1456(c)(3)(A) and 15 CFR 930.76.).

The States of Texas, Louisiana, Mississippi, and Alabama, affected States for activities proposed in this OCS plan, have approved CZM programs. Therefore, certificates of coastal zone consistency from the operator were required for the proposed activities. The MMS and the affected States revised CZM consistency information for OCS plans, permits, and licenses to conform to the revised CZM regulations that were effective January 8, 2001, and updated on January 5, 2006, and have also incorporated streamlining improvements into the latest NTL's (NTL's 2006-G14 and 2007-G11). The affected States require an adequate description, objective, and schedule for the project; site-specific information on the onshore support base, support vessels, shallow hazards, oil-spill response, wastes and discharges, transportation activities, and air emissions; and a Federal consistency certification, assessment, and findings. The States' requirements for Federal consistency review of OCS plans are based specifically on DOI's regulations at 30 CFR 250, 30 CFR 254, 30 CFR 250 256, and NOAA's Federal consistency regulations at 15 CFR 930.

In accordance with the requirements of 15 CFR 930.76, the MMS Gulf of Mexico OCS Region sends copies of an OCS plan, including the consistency certification and other necessary information, to the designated State CZM agency by receipted mail or other approved communication. If no State-agency objection is submitted by the end of the consistency review period, MMS shall presume consistency concurrence by the State (15 CFR 930.78 (b)). The MMS can require modification of a plan if the operator has agreed to certain requirements requested by the State.

If MMS receives a written consistency objection from the State, MMS will not approve any activity described in the OCS plan unless (1) the operator amends the OCS plan to accommodate the objection, concurrence is subsequently received or conclusively presumed; (2) upon appeal, the Secretary of Commerce, in accordance with 15 CFR 930 Subpart H, finds that the OCS plan is consistent with the objectives or purposes of the Coastal Zone Management Act or is necessary in the interest of national security; or (3) the original objection is declared invalid by the courts.

The MMS published a Notice of Preparation of an Environmental Assessment for the Cascade-Chinook project in the *Morgan City Newspaper* on November 6, 2007, and in *The Times-Picayune* on November 7, 2007. The notice described the activities Petrobras proposes for the Cascade-Chinook project. The notice requested that interested parties submit comments to MMS on issues that should be addressed in the SEA. The 30-day comment period ended on December 19, 2007; no comments were received during this period.

5. REFERENCES

Advanced Research Projects Agency. 1995. Final environmental impact statement/environmental impact report (EIS/EIR) for the California Acoustic Thermometry of Ocean Climate (ATOC) Project and its associated Marine Mammal Research Program (MMRP) (Scientific Research Permit Application [P557A]), Vol. 1.

Aharon, P., D. Van Gent, B. Fu, and L.M. Scott. 2001. Fate and effects of barium and radium-rich fluid emissions from hydrocarbon seeps on the benthic habitats of the Gulf of Mexico offshore Louisiana. U.S. Dept. of the Interior, Minerals Management Service, Gulf of Mexico OCS Region, New Orleans, LA. OCS Study MMS 2001-004. 142 pp.

Alexander, S.K. and J.W. Webb. 1983. Effects of oil on growth and decomposition of *Spartina alterniflora*. In: Proceedings, 1983 Oil Spill Conference, February 28-March 3, 1983, San Antonio, TX. Washington, DC: American Petroleum Institute. Pp. 529-532.

Alexander, S.K. and J.W. Webb. 1987. Relationship of *Spartina alterniflora* growth to sediment oil content following an oil spill. In: Proceedings, 1987 Oil Spill Conference, April 6-9, 1988, Baltimore, MD. Washington, DC: American Petroleum Institute. Pp. 445-450.

American Petroleum Institute (API). 1989. Effects of offshore petroleum operations on cold water marine mammals: A literature review. Washington, DC: American Petroleum Institute. 385 pp.

Anderson, C.M. and R.P. LaBelle. 2000. Update of comparative occurrence rates for offshore oil spills. Spill Science and Technology Bulletin 6(5/6):302-321.

Anton, A., J. Cebrian, D. Foster, K. Sheehan, and M. Miller. 2006. The effects of Hurricane Katrina on the ecological services provided by seagrass (*Halodule wrightii* and *Ruppia maritima*) meadows. Poster, Ocean Sciences Conference, 2006.

Anuskiewicz, R.J. 1989. A study of maritime and nautical sites associated with St. Catherines Island, Georgia. Ph.D. dissertation presented to the University of Tennessee, Knoxville, TN. 90 pp.

Avanti Corporation. 1993. Environmental analysis of the final effluent guideline, offshore subcategory, oil and gas industry. Volume II. Prepared for the U.S. Environmental Protection Agency, Water Management Division, Region VI. USEPA Contract No. 68-C9-0009.

Baker, J.M., R.B. Clark, and P.F. Kingston. 1991. Two years after the spill: Environmental recovery in Prince William Sound and the Gulf of Alaska. Institute of Offshore Engineering, Heriot-Watt University, Edinburgh, EH14 4AS, Scotland. 31 pp.

Ballachey, B.E., J.L. Bodkin, and A.R. DeGange. 1994. An overview of sea otter studies. In: Loughlin, T.R., ed. Marine mammals and the *Exxon Valdez*. San Diego, CA: Academic Press. Pp. 47-59.

Barbour, H. 2006. One year after Katrina – progress report on recovery, rebuilding and renewal. Office of Governor Haley Barbour. August 29, 2006.

Barras, J.A. 2006. Land area change in coastal Louisiana after the 2005 hurricanes: A series of three maps. U.S. Dept. of the Interior, Geological Survey. Open-File Report 06-1274. Internet website: http://pubs.usgs.gov/of/2006/1274/.

Barras, J.A. 2007. Land area changes in coastal Louisiana after Hurricanes Katrina and Rita. In: Farris, G.S., G.J. Smith, M.P. Crane, C.R. Demas, L.L. Robbins, and D.L. Lavoie, eds. Science and the storms: The USGS response to the hurricanes of 2005. U.S. Dept. of the Interior, Geological Survey. Geological Survey Circular 1306. Pp. 97-112. Internet website: http://pubs.usgs.gov/circ/1306/pdf/c1306_ch5_b.pdf.

Barras, J.A., S. Beville, D. Britsch, S. Hartley, S. Hawes, J. Johnston, P. Kemp, Q. Kinler, A. Martucci, J. Porthouse, D. Reed, K. Roy, S. Sapkota, and J. Suhayda. 2003. Historical and projected coastal Louisiana land changes: 1978-2050. U.S. Dept. of the Interior, Geological Survey. Open File Report 03-334.

Barry A. Vittor & Associates, Inc. 2004. Mapping of submerged aquatic vegetation in Mobile Bay and adjacent waters of coastal Alabama in 2002. Prepared for the Mobile Bay National Estuary Program. Internet website: http://www.mobilebaynep.com/site/news_pubs/Publications/MBNEP_SAVrpt.pdf. 63 pp. (To access online map for SAV from the 2002 study, with links to low-resolution Ortho images, go to http://gis.disl.org/savmbnep02.htm.

Barry A. Vittor and Associates, Inc. 2006. Characterization of vegetation and wildlife on Isle Aux Herbes. Prepared for the Mobile Bay National Estuary Program. Internet website: http://www.mobilebaynep.com/site/news_pubs/news/Documents/Characterization%20Reports/Isle%20aux%20Herbes%20report.pdf

Basan, P.B., C.K. Chamberlain, R.W. Frey, J.D. Howard, A. Seilacher and J.E. Warme. 1978. Trace fossil concepts. Society of Economic Paleontologists and Mineralogists, Short Course No. 5, Tulsa, OK. 181 pp. U.S. Dept. of the Interior, Interagency Archaeological Services, Office of Archaeology and Historic Preservation.

Bent, A.C. 1926. Life histories of North American marsh birds. New York: Dover Publications.

Boesch, D.F., L. Shabman, L.G. Antle, J.W. Day, R.G. Dean, G.E. Galloway, C.G. Groat, S.B. Laska, R.A. Luettich, W.J. Mitsch, N.N. Rabalais, D.J. Reed, C.A. Simenstad, B.J. Streever, R.B. Taylor, R.R. Twilley, C.C. Watson, J.T. Wells, and D.F. Whigham. 2006. A new framework for planning the future of coastal Louisiana after the hurricanes of 2005. Working Group for Post-Hurricane Planning for the Louisiana Coast. Internet website: http://www.umces.edu/la-restore/New%20Framework%20Final.pdf.

Bolden, S. 2007. Personal communication. Information concerning the critical habitat and damage assessments of the Gulf sturgeon. U.S. Dept. of Commerce, National Marine Fisheries Service. May 9.

Boyd, P.W. and S. Penland. 1988. A geomorphic model for Mississippi Delta evolution. In: Transactions—Gulf Coast Association of Geological Societies. Volume XXXVII.

Brooks, J.M., C. Fisher, H. Roberts, B. Bernard, I. MacDonald, R. Carney, S. Joye, E. Cordes, G. Wolff, and E. Goehring. In press. Investigations of chemosynthetic communities on the lower continental slope of the Gulf of Mexico: Interim report. U.S. Dept. of the Interior, Minerals Management Service, Gulf of Mexico OCS Region, New Orleans, LA.

Brown, Jr, L.F., J.H. McGowen, T.J. Evans, C.S. Groat, and W.L. Fisher. 1977. Environmental geological atlas of the Texas coastal zone: Kingsville area. Austin, TX: The University of Texas at Austin, Bureau of Economic Geology.

Byron, D. and K.L. Heck, Jr. 2006. Hurricane effects on seagrasses along Alabama's Gulf Coast. Estuaries and Coasts 29(6A):939-942. Internet website: http://estuariesandcoasts.org/journal/ESTU2006/ESTU2006_29_6A_939_942.pdf.

Carr, A. 1987. Impact of nondegradable marine debris on the ecology and survival outlook of sea turtles. Marine Pollution Bulletin 18:352-356.

Carr, A. and D.K. Caldwell. 1956. The ecology and migration of sea turtles. I. Results of field work in Florida, 1955. Amer. Mus. Novit. 1793:1-23.

Clapp, R.B., R.C. Banks, D. Morgan-Jacobs, and W.A. Hoffman. 1982a. Marine birds of the southeastern United States and Gulf of Mexico. Part I. Gaviiformes and Pelecaniformes. U.S. Dept. of the Interior, Fish and Wildlife Service, Office of Biological Services, Washington, DC. FWS/OBS-82/01.

Clapp, R.B., R.C. Banks, D. Morgan-Jacobs, and W.A. Hoffman. 1982b. Marine birds of the southeastern United States and Gulf of Mexico. Part II. Anseriformes. U.S. Dept. of the Interior, Fish and Wildlife Service, Office of Biological Services, Washington, DC. FWS/OBS-82/01.

Clapp, R.B., R.C. Banks, D. Morgan-Jacobs, and W.A. Hoffman. 1982c. Marine birds of the southeastern United States and Gulf of Mexico. Part III. Charadriiformes. U.S. Dept. of the Interior, Fish and Wildlife Service, Office of Biological Services, Washington, DC. FWS/OBS-82/01.

Clark, T. 2006. Personal communication. Co-chair of the Industry Taskforce on Offshore Lightering (ITOL) Group, Houston, TX. Telephone interview with Jeff Hammond, Ecology and Environment, Inc., Buffalo, NY, August 8, 2006.

Continental Shelf Associates, Inc. (CSA). 1997. Gulf of Mexico produced water bioaccumulation study: Definitive component technical report. Prepared for Offshore Operators Committee. 258 pp.

Continental Shelf Associates, Inc. (CSA). 2006. Effects of oil and gas exploration and development at selected continental slope sites in the Gulf of Mexico. Volume II: Technical report. U.S. Dept. of the Interior, Minerals Management Service, Gulf of Mexico OCS Region, New Orleans, LA. OCS Study MMS 2006-045. 636 pp.

Corliss, J.B., J. Dymond, L.I. Gordon, J.M. Edmond, R.P. von Herzen, R.D. Ballard, K. Green, D. Williams, A. Bainbridge, K. Crane, and T.H. van Andel. 1979. Submarine thermal springs on the Galapagos Rift. Science 203:1073-1083.

Dahl, T.E. 1990. Wetlands losses in the United States 1780's to 1980's. U.S. Dept. of the Interior, Fish and Wildlife Service, Washington, DC. 21 pp.

Davis, R.W. and G.S. Fargion, eds. 1996. Distribution and abundance of cetaceans in the north-central western Gulf of Mexico: Final report. Volume II: Technical report. U.S. Dept. of the Interior, Minerals Management Service, Gulf of Mexico OCS Region, New Orleans, LA. OCS Study MMS 96-0027. 355 pp.

Davis, R.W., G.S. Fargion, N. May, T.D. Leming, M. Baumgartner, W.E. Evans, L.J. Hansen, and K. Mullin. 1998. Physical habitat of cetaceans along the continental slope in the north-central and western Gulf of Mexico. Mar. Mamm. Sci. 14:490-507.

Davis, R.W., W.E. Evans, and B. Würsig, eds. 2000. Cetaceans, sea turtles, and seabirds in the northern Gulf of Mexico: Distribution, abundance and habitat associations. Volume I: Executive summary. U.S. Dept. of the Interior, Geological Survey, Biological Resources Division, USGS/BRD/CR-1999-0006 and Minerals Management Service, Gulf of Mexico OCS Region, New Orleans, LA. OCS Study MMS 2000-002. 40 pp.

Delaune, R.D., W.H. Patrick, and R.J. Bureh. 1979. Effect of crude oil on a Louisiana *Spartina alterniflora* salt marsh. Environ. Poll. 20:21-31.

Doering, F., I.W. Duedall, and J.M. Williams. 1994. Florida hurricanes and tropical storms 1871-1993: An historical survey. Florida Institute of Technology, Division of Marine and Environmental Systems, Florida Sea Grant Program, Gainesville, FL. Tech. Paper 71. 118 pp.

Duke, T. and W.L. Kruszynski, eds. 1992. Report on the status and trends of emergent and submerged vegetated habitats of Gulf of Mexico coastal waters, U.S.A. Gulf of Mexico Program, Habitat Degradation Subcommittee. U.S. Environmental Protection Agency, John S. Stennis Space Center, MS. EPA 800-R-92-003. 161 pp.

Eadie, B.J., J.A. Robbins, P. Blackwelder, S. Metz, J.H. Trefry, B. McKee, and T.A. Nelson. 1992. A retrospective analysis of nutrient enhanced coastal ocean productivity in sediments from the Louisiana continental shelf. In: Nutrient Enhanced Coastal Ocean Productivity Workshop Proceedings, TAMU-SG-92-109, Technical Report. Pp. 7-14.

Eckdale, A.A., R.G. Bromley and S.G. Pemberton. 1984. Ichnology; the use of trace fossils in sedimentology and stratigraphy. Society of Economic Paleontologists and Mineralogists, Short Course No. 15. Tulsa, OK. 317 pp.

Ehrhart, L.M. 1978. Choctawhatchee beach mouse. In: Layne, J.N., ed. Rare and endangered biota of Florida. Volume I: Mammals. Gainesville, FL: University Presses of Florida. Pp. 18-19.

Farr, A.J., C.C. Chabot, and D.H. Taylor. 1995. Behavioral avoidance of flurothene by flathead minnows (*Pimephales promelas*). Neurotoxicology and Teratology 17(3):265-271.

Federal Reserve Bank of Atlanta. 2006. Louisiana continues to march toward recovery—Louisiana employment: Better than the data suggest. EconSouth 8(4), fourth quarter 2006. Internet website: http://www.frbatlanta.org/invoke.cfm?objectid=A6993158-5056-9F12-12433D9D81C1D2AC&method=display_body. Accessed June 14, 2007.

Figueiredo, M.W., Kuchpil, C., and E.F. Caetano. 2006. Application of subsea processing and boosting in Campos Basin. In: Proceedings, 2006 Offshore Technology Conference, 1-4 May 2006, Houston, TX. Washington, DC: American Petroleum Institute. 8 pp. Red Hook, NY: Curran Associates, Inc. OTC Paper 18198.

Fischel, M., W. Grip, and I.A. Mendelssohn. 1989. Study to determine the recovery of a Louisiana marsh from an oil spill. In: Proceedings, 1989 Oil Spill Conference, February 13-16, 1989, San Antonio, TX. Washington, DC: American Petroleum Institute. Pp. 383-387.

Fisher, W.L., J.H. McGowen, L.F. Brown, Jr., and C.G. Groat. 1972. Environmental geologic atlas of the Texas coastal zone: Galveston-Houston area. Austin, TX: The University of Texas at Austin, Bureau of Economic Geology.

Fisher, C.R. 1990. Chemoautotrophic and methanotrophic symbioses in marine invertebrates. Reviews in Aquatic Sciences 2:399-436.

Florida A&M University. 1988. Meteorological database and synthesis for the Gulf of Mexico. U.S. Dept. of the Interior, Minerals Management Service, Gulf of Mexico OCS Region, New Orleans, LA. OCS Study MMS 88-0064. 486 pp.

Frey, R.W. 1975. The study of trace fossils; a synthesis of principles, problems, and procedures in ichnology. New York, NY: Springer-Verlag. 562 pp.

Fu, B. and P. Aharon. 1998. Sources of hydrocarbon-rich fluids advecting on the seafloor in the northern Gulf of Mexico. Gulf Coast Association of Geological Societies Transactions 48:73-81.

Gallaway, B.J. and M.C. Kennicutt II. 1988. Northern Gulf of Mexico Continental Slope Study, Final Report: Year 4. Vol. III: Appendices. U.S. Dept. of the Interior, Minerals Management Service, Gulf of Mexico OCS Region, New Orleans, LA. OCS Study MMS 88-0054. Pp. 2-1 to 2-45.

Gallaway, B.J., L.R. Martin, and R.L. Howard, eds. 1988a. Northern Gulf of Mexico continental slope study: Annual report, year 3. Volume I: Executive summary. U.S. Dept. of the Interior, Minerals

Management Service, Gulf of Mexico OCS Region, New Orleans, LA. OCS Study MMS 87-0059. 154 pp.

Gallaway, B.J., L.R. Martin, and R.L. Howard, eds. 1988b. Northern Gulf of Mexico continental slope study, annual report: Year 3. Volume II: Technical narrative. U.S. Dept. of the Interior, Minerals Management Service, Gulf of Mexico OCS Region, New Orleans, LA. OCS Study MMS 87-0060. 586 pp.

Gallaway, B.J., J.G. Cole, and R.G. Fechhelm. 2003. Selected aspects of the ecology of the continental slope fauna of the Gulf of Mexico: A synopsis of the northern Gulf of Mexico continental slope study, 1983-1988. U.S. Dept of the Interior, Minerals Management Service, Gulf of Mexico OCS Region, New Orleans, LA. OCS Study MMS 2003-072. 38 pp. + app.

Garrison, E.G., C.P. Giammona, F.J. Kelly, A.R. Tripp, and G.A. Wolf. 1989. Historic shipwrecks and magnetic anomalies of the northern Gulf of Mexico: Reevaluation of archaeological resource management zone 1. U.S. Dept. of the Interior, Minerals Management Service, Gulf of Mexico OCS Region, New Orleans, LA. OCS Study MMS 89-0024. 241 pp.

Geraci, J.R. and D.J. St. Aubin. 1980. Offshore petroleum resource development and marine mammals: A review and research recommendations. Marine Fisheries Review 42:1-12.

Gilbert, R.B., E.G. Ward, A.J. Wolford. 2001. Comprehensive risk analysis for deepwater production systems: Final report. Prepared by Offshore Technology Research Center for the U.S. Dept. of the Interior, Minerals Management Service. 368 pp.

Greenberg, J. 2007. OSV day rates. Workboat. Internet website: http://www.workboat.com. Accessed December 5, 2007.

Gulf of Mexico Alliance. 2005. Improving and protecting water quality white paper. Internet website: http://www.dep.state.fl.us/gulf/files/files/waterquality.pdf. Last updated 2005. Accessed February 1, 2008.

Gulf of Mexico Fishery Management Council (GMFMC). 2004. Final environmental impact statement for the generic essential fish habitat amendment to the following fishery management plans of the Gulf of Mexico: Shrimp fishery of the Gulf of Mexico, red drum fishery of the Gulf of Mexico, reef fish fishery of the Gulf of Mexico, stone crab fishery of the Gulf of Mexico, coral and coral reef fishery of the Gulf of Mexico, spiny lobster fishery of the Gulf of Mexico and south Atlantic, coastal migratory pelagic resources of the Gulf of Mexico and south Atlantic. Internet website: http://www.gulfcouncil.org/.

Gulf of Mexico Fishery Management Council (GMFMC). 2005. Generic amendment number 3 for addressing essential fish habitat requirements, habitat areas of particular concern, and adverse effects of fishing in the following fishery management plans of the Gulf of Mexico: Shrimp fishery of the Gulf of Mexico, United States waters red drum fishery of the Gulf of Mexico, reef fish fishery of the Gulf of Mexico, coastal migratory pelagic resources (mackerels) in the Gulf of Mexico and South Atlantic, stone crab fishery of the Gulf of Mexico, spiny lobster in the Gulf of Mexico and South Atlantic,,coral and coral reefs of the Gulf of Mexico. Gulf of Mexico Fishery Management Council, Tampa, FL.

Hardegree, B. 2007. Texas seagrass: Status, statewide issues, and restoration. Gulf of Mexico Alliance Regional Restoration Coordination Team Workshop, Galveston, TX. Internet website: http://www2.nos.noaa.gov/gomex/restoration/workshops/workshops.html.

Harrison, P. 1983. Seabirds: An identification guide. Boston, MA: Houghton Mifflin Co. 448 pp.

Harrison, P. 1996. Seabirds of the world. Princeton, NJ: Princeton University Press, Princeton, NJ. 317 pp.

Harvey, J.T. and M.E. Dahlheim. 1994. Cetaceans in oil. In: Loughlin, T.R., ed. Marine mammals and the *Exxon Valdez*. San Diego, CA: Academic Press. Pp. 257-264.

Hayman, P., J. Marchant, and T. Prater. 1986. Shorebirds: An identification guide to the waders of the world. Boston, MA: Houghton Mifflin Co. 412 pp.

Heck, K.L., Jr., and D. Byron. 2006. Post Hurricane Ivan damage assessment of seagrass resources of coastal Alabama. Mobile Bay National Esturary Program. Internet website: http://www.mobilebaynep.com/news/Documents/Heck%20and%20Byron--ADCNR_SeagrassSurvey_finalreport.pdf.

Henfer, L.M., B.O. Wilen, T.E. Dahl, and W.E. Frayer. 1994. Southeast wetlands: Status and trends, mid-1970's to mid-1980's. U.S. Dept. of the Interior, Fish and Wildlife Service, Atlanta, GA. 32 pp.

Herold, P. and J. McCombs. 2007. Personal communication. U.S. Dept. of Commerce, NOAA, Coastal Services Center, Charleston, SC. As referenced in USDOC, NMFS, 2007a of this document.

Jochens, A., D. Biggs, K. Benoit-Bird, D. Engelhardt, J. Gordon, C. Hu, N. Jaquet, M. Johnson, R. Leben, B. Mate, P. Miller, J. Ortega-Ortiz, A. Thode, P. Tyack, and B. Würsig. In press. Sperm whale seismic study in the Gulf of Mexico: Synthesis report. U.S. Dept. of the Interior, Minerals Management Service, Gulf of Mexico OCS Region, New Orleans, LA. OCS EIS/EA MMS 2008-006.

Johansen, O., H. Rye, and C. Cooper. 2001. DeepSpill JIP—Field study of simulated oil and gas blowouts in deep water. In: Proceedings from the Fifth International Marine Environment Modeling Seminar, October 9-11, 2001, New Orleans, LA. 377 pp.

Johnsgard, P.A. 1975. Waterfowl of North America. Bloomington, IN: Indiana University Press. 575 pp.

Kennicutt, M.C., J. Sericano, T. Wade, F. Alcazar, and J.M. Brooks. 1987. High-molecular weight hydrocarbons in the Gulf of Mexico continental slope sediment. Deep-Sea Research 34:403-424.

Kennicutt II, M.C., ed. 1995. Gulf of Mexico offshore operations monitoring experiment, Phase I: Sublethal responses to contaminant exposure, final report. U.S. Dept. of the Interior, Minerals Management Service, Gulf of Mexico OCS Region, New Orleans, LA. OCS Study MMS 95-0045. 709 pp.

Kwik, K.H. 1992. A system for optimal management of canal ship traffic: Bulletin de l'Association Internationale Permanente des Congres de Navigation 76:105-114.

Louisiana Dept. of Wildlife and Fisheries, Fur and Refuge Division, and the U.S. Dept. of the Interior, Geological Survey, Biological Resources Division. 1997. Louisiana coastal marsh vegetative type map (database). Louisiana Dept. of Wildlife and Fisheries, Baton Rouge, LA.

Lousiana Sea Grant. 2005. Louisiana hurricane resources: Barrier islands and wetlands. Internet website: http://www.laseagrant.org/hurricane/archive/wetlands.htm

Lugo-Fernández, A., D.A. Ball, M. Gravois, C. Horrell, J.B. Irion. 2007. Analysis of the Gulf of Mexico's Veracruz-Havana route of *La Flota de la Nueva España*. Journal of Maritime Archaeology 2:24-47. June 2007.

Lutcavage, M.E., P.L. Lutz, G.D. Bossart, and D.M. Hudson. 1995. Physiologic and clinicopathologic effects of crude oil on loggerhead sea turtles. Arch. Environ. Contam. Toxicol. 28:417-422.

Lutz, P.L. and M. Lutcavage. 1989. The effects of petroleum on sea turtles: Applicability to Kemp's ridley. In: Caillouet, C.W., Jr. and A.M. Landry, Jr., eds. Proceedings of the First International Symposium on Kemp's Ridley Sea Turtle Biology, Conservation and Management. Texas A&M University Sea Grant College Program, Galveston. TAMU-SG-89-105. Pp. 52-54.

Lytle, J.S. 1975. Fate and effects of crude oil on an estuarine pond. In: Proceedings, Conference on Prevention and Control of Oil Pollution, San Francisco, CA. Pp. 595-600.

MacDonald, I.R., ed. 1992. Chemosynthetic ecosystems study literature review and data synthesis: Volumes I-III. U.S. Dept. of the Interior, Minerals Management Service, Gulf of Mexico OCS Region, New Orleans, LA. OCS Study MMS 92-0033 through 92-0035. 25, 218, and 263 pp., respectively.

Madge, S. and H. Burn. 1988. Waterfowl: An identification guide to the ducks, geese, and swans of the world. Boston, MA: Houghton Mifflin. 298 pp.

Maiaro, J.L. 2007. Disturbance effects on nekton communities of seagrasses and bare substrates in Biloxi Marsh, Louisiana. Master's thesis, Louisiana State University, Baton Rouge, LA. 78 pp. Internet website: http://etd.lsu.edu/docs/available/etd-07032007-101237/unrestricted/Maiaro_thesis.pdf.

Malins, D.C., S. Chan, H.O. Hodgins, U. Varanasi, D.D. Weber, and D.W. Brown. 1982. The nature and biological effects of weathered petroleum. Environmental Conservation Division, Northwest and Alaska Fisheries Center, National Marine Fisheries Service, Seattle, WA. 43 pp.

Martin, R.P. 1991. Regional overview of wading birds in Louisiana, Mississippi, and Alabama. In: Proceedings of the Coastal Nongame Workshop. U.S. Dept. of the Interior, Fish and Wildlife Service, Region 4 and the Florida Game and Fresh Water Fish Commission. Pp. 22-33.

Matkin, C.O., G.M. Ellis, M.E. Dahlheim, and J. Zeh. 1994. Status of killer whales in Prince William Sound, 1985-1992. In: Loughlin, T.R., ed. Marine mammals and the *Exxon Valdez*. San Diego, CA: Academic Press. Pp. 141-162.

May, C.A. 2007. Distribution, status, and trends of seagrasses in Mississippi. Gulf of Mexico Alliance Regional Restoration Coordination Team Workshop, March 6-9, 2007, Spanish Fort, AL. 15 pp. Internet website: http://www2.nos.noaa.gov/gomex/restoration/workshops/workshops.html.

Michot, T.C. and C.J. Wells. 2005. Hurricane Katrina photographs, August 30, 2005. U.S. Dept. of the Interior, Geological Survey, National Wetlands Research Center. Internet website: http://www.nwrc.usgs.gov/hurricane/post-hurricane-katrina-photos.htm.

Miller, J.E. and D.L. Echols. 1996. Marine debris point source investigation: Padre Island National Seashore, March 1994-September 1995. U.S. Dept. of the Interior, Minerals Management Service, Gulf of Mexico OCS Region, New Orleans, LA. OCS Study MMS 96-0023. 35 pp.

Mitchell, R. 2000. Scientists find that tons of oil seep into the Gulf of Mexico each year. U.S. Dept. of Commerce, National Atmospheric and Science Administration, Earth Observatory. Internet website: http://earthobservatory.nasa.gov/Newsroom/MediaAlerts/2000/200001261633.html. Accessed January 26, 2002.

Mississippi Dept. of Marine Resources. 2005. Preliminary assessment of Mississippi marine resources. Mississippi Dept. of Marine Resources, Office of Marine Fisheries, Biloxi, MS.

Moyers, J.E. 1996. Food habits of Gulf Coast subspecies of beach mice (*Peromyscus polionotus* spp.). M.S. Thesis, Auburn University, AL. 84 pp.

Murray, S.P. 1998. An observational study of the Mississippi/Atchafalaya coastal plume: Final report, U.S. Dept. of the Interior, Minerals Management Service, Gulf of Mexico OCS Region, New Orleans, LA. OCS Study MMS 98-0040. 513 pp.

National Geographic Society. 1983. Field guide to the birds of North America. Washington, DC: National Geographic Society. 464 pp.

National Geographic Society. 1999. Field guide to the birds of North America, third edition. Washington, DC: National Geographic Society. 480 pp.

National Research Council (NRC). 1983. Drilling discharges in the marine environment. Panel on Assessment of Fates and Effects of Drilling Fluids and Cuttings in the Marine Environment. Marine Board, Commission on Engineering and Technical Systems, National Research Council. Washington, DC: National Academy Press.

National Research Council (NRC). 1985. Oil in the sea – inputs, fates and effects. Washington, DC: National Academy Press. 601 pp.

National Research Council (NRC). 1990. The decline of sea turtles: Causes and prevention. Washington, DC: National Academy Press. 183 pp.

National Research Council (NRC). 2003. Oil in the sea III: Inputs, fates, and effects. Washington, DC: National Academy Press. 265 pp.

Neff, J.M. 1990. Composition and fate of petroleum and spill-treating agents in the marine environment. In: Geraci, J.R. and D.J. St. Aubin, eds. Sea mammals and oil: confronting the risks. San Diego, CA: Academic Press, Inc. Pp. 1-33.

Neff, J.M., T.C. Sauer, and N. Maciolek. 1989. Fate and effects of produced water discharges in nearshore marine waters. Prepared for the American Petroleum Institute, Washington, DC.

Neff, M.J. 1997. Metals and organic chemicals associated with oil and gas well produced water: Bioaccumulation, fates, and effects in the marine environment. Report prepared for Continental Shelf Associates, Inc., Jupiter, FL, to Offshore Operators Committee, New Orleans, LA. April 14, 1997.

Neumann, C.J., B.R. Jarvinen, and J.D. Elms. 1993. Tropical cyclones of the north Atlantic Ocean, 1871-1992. U.S. Dept. of Commerce, National Oceanic and Atmospheric Administration, Asheville, NC. 193 pp.

Nevissi, A.E. and R.E. Nakatani. 1990. Effect of Prudhoe Bay oil on the homing of Coho salmon in marine waters. Journal of Fish Biology 34:621-629.

Nowlin, W.D., Jr. 1972. Winter circulation patterns and property distributions. In: Capurro, L.R.A. and J.L. Reid, eds. Contributions on the physical oceanography of the Gulf of Mexico. Texas A&M University Oceanographic Studies, Vol. 2. Houston, TX: Gulf Publishing Co. Pp. 3-51.

Nowlin, W.D., Jr., A.E. Jochens, R.O. Reid, and S.F. DiMarco. 1998. Texas-Louisiana shelf circulation and transport processes study: Synthesis report. Volume II: Appendices. U.S. Dept. of the Interior, Minerals Management Services, Gulf of Mexico OCS Region, New Orleans, LA. OCS Study MMS 98-0036. 288 pp.

Oil and Gas Journal. 2007. Market watch. Internet website: http://www.ogj.com. Accessed December 5, 2007.

Oilnergy. 2007. Cash petroleum spot prices. Internet website: http://www.oilnergy.com. Accessed December 5, 2007.

Olds, W.T., Jr. 1984. In: U.S. Congress, House Committee on Merchant Marine Fisheries, Offshore Oil and Gas Activity and Its Socioeconomic and Environmental Influences, 98th Cong., 2d sess., 1984. Pp. 54-55.

Olsen, K.M. and H. Larsson. 1995. Terns of Europe and North America. Princeton, NJ: Princeton University Press. 175 pp.

Olsen, K.M. and H. Larsson. 1997. Skuas and jaegers. New Haven, CT: Yale University Press. 190 pp.

One Offshore. 2007. Gulf of Mexico Newsletter. ODS-Petrodata 22(7).

Paruka, F. 2007. Personal communication. Information concerning the critical habitat, sampling programs, and damage assessments of the Gulf sturgeon. U.S. Dept. of the Interior, Fish and Wildlife Service, Ecological Services, Fisheries Resource Office, Panama City, FL. May 29.

Pashley, D.N. 1991. Shorebirds, gulls, and terns: Louisiana, Mississippi, Alabama. In: Proceedings of the Coastal Nongame Workshop. U.S. Dept. of the Interior, Fish and Wildlife Service, Region 4 and Florida Game and Fresh Water Fish Commission. Pp. 79-83.

Payne, J.F., J. Kiceniuk, L.L. Fancey, U. Williams, G.L. Fletcher, A. Rahimtula, and B. Fowler. 1988. What is a safe level of polycyclic aromatic hydrocarbons for fish: Subchronic toxicity study on winter flounder (*Pseudopleuronectes americanus*). Can. J. Fish. Aquat. Sci. 45:1983-1993.

Peake, D., G. Fargion, K. Mullen, and R. Pitman. 1995. Seabirds of the northwestern and central Gulf of Mexico. In: Abstracts of the Joint Meeting of the Wilson Ornithological Society and Virginia Society of Ornithology, Virginia, 4-7 May, 1995.

Pearson, C.E., S.R. James, Jr., M.C. Krivor, and S.D. El Darragi. 2003. Refining and revising the Gulf of Mexico outer continental shelf region high-probability model for historic shipwrecks: Final report. 3 vols. U.S. Dept. of the Interior, Minerals Management Service, Gulf of Mexico OCS Region, New Orleans, LA. OCS Study MMS 2003-060 through 2003-062. 13, 338, and 138 pp., respectively.

Pequegnat, W.E. 1983. The ecological communities of the continental slope and adjacent regimes of the northern Gulf of Mexico. Prepared by TerEco Corp. for the U.S. Dept. of the Interior, Minerals Management Service, New Orleans, LA. Contract no. AA851-CT1-12. 398 pp.

Petrobras America Inc. 2007. Initial development operations coordination document for Walker Ridge Block 206 Unit and Walker Ridge Block 425 Unit, OCS Federal waters, Gulf of Mexico, offshore, Louisiana. Plan Control No. N-9015.

Pickard, M. 2007. Sturgeon need water below the dam. Article printed from staff reporter for Channel 11 News, Mobile, AL. Internet website: http://www.11alive.com/news/ article_news.aspx?storyid=105741. Accessed November 1, 2007.

Porrier, M.A. and J. Cho. 2002. Biological resources: Submersed aquatic vegetation. In: Penland, S., A. Beall, and J. Kindinger, eds. Environmental Atlas of the Lake Pontchartrain Basin. U.S. Dept. of the Interior, Geological Survey. Open File Report 02-206. Internet website: http://pubs.usgs.gov/of/2002/of02-206/biology/sav.html.

Preen, A. 1991. Report on the die-off of marine mammals associated with the Gulf War oil spill. Report prepared for The National Commission for Wildlife Conservation and Development. 8 pp.

Pulich, W., Jr. 1998. Seagrass conservation plan for Texas. Texas Parks and Wildlife Department, Austin, TX.

Quammen, M.L. and C.P. Onuf. 1993. Laguna Madre seagrass changes continue decades after salinity reduction. Estuaries 16:302-310.

Randal, M. 2007. Personal communication at the Annual Gulf Science and Management Conference, Spanish Fort, AL, November 7, 2007. U.S. Dept. of the Interior, Geological Survey, Florida Intergrated Science Center, Gainesville, FL.

Regg, J.B., comp. 1998. Floating production, storage, and offloading systems in the Gulf of Mexico – proceedings of a workshop, Houston, April 16, 1997. U.S. Dept. of the Interior, Minerals Management Service, Gulf of Mexico OCS Region, New Orleans, LA. OCS Report MMS 98-0019. 305 pp.

Renger, E. and K. Bednarczyk. 1986. Sediment transport by ship traffic in offshore channels. Kueste 44:89-132.

Richardson, W.J., C.R. Greene, C.I. Mame, and D.H. Thomson. 1995. Marine mammals and noise. San Diego, CA: Academic Press Inc.

Ripley, S.D. and B.M. Beechler. 1985. Rails of the world, a compilation of new information, 1975-1983, (Aves: Rallidae). Smithsonian Contributions to Zoology, No. 417. Washington, DC: Smithsonian Institute Press.

Robineau, D. and P. Fiquet. 1994. Cetaceans of Dawhat ad-Dafi and Dawhat al-Musallamiya (Saudi Arabia) one year after the Gulf War oil spill. In: Abuzinada, A.H. and F. Krupp, eds. The status of coastal and marine habitats two years after the Gulf War oil spill. Courier Forschung Institut Senckenberg Special Publication 166:76-80.

Rodrigues, R., R. Soares, J.S. de Matos, C.A.G. Pereira, and G.S. Ribeiro. 2005. A new approach for subsea boosting – pumping module on the seabed. In: Proceedings, 2005 Offshore Technology Conference, 2-5 May 2005, Reliant Center, Houston, TX. Baltimore, MD: Port City Press. OTC Paper 17398. 8 pp. Internet website: http://202.120.57.205/cdbook/otc-2005/pdfs/otc17398.pdf.

Roland, G.R. 2007. Personal communication. Petrobras America Inc. October 15, 2007.

Rowe, G.T. and M.C. Kennicutt II. 2002. Deepwater program: Northern Gulf of Mexico continental slope habitat and benthic ecology. Year 2: Interim report. U.S. Dept. of the Interior, Minerals Management Service, Gulf of Mexico OCS Region, New Orleans, Louisiana. OCS Study MMS 2002-063. 158 pp.

Rowley K. 2007. GulfGov reports: A year and a half after Katrina and Rita, an uneven recovery. Nelson A. Rockefeller Institute of Government, Albany, NY, and Public Affairs Research Council of

Louisiana, Baton Rouge, LA. 73 pp. Internet website: http://www.rockinst.org/WorkArea/showcontent.aspx?id=9920.

Sassen, R., J.M. Brooks, M.C. Kennicutt II, I.R. MacDonald, and N.L. Guinasso, Jr. 1993a. How oil seeps, discoveries relate in deepwater Gulf of Mexico. Oil and Gas Journal 91(16):64-69.

Sassen, R., H.H. Roberts, P. Aharon, J. Larkin, E.W. Chinn, and R. Carney. 1993b. Chemosynthetic bacterial mats at cold hydrocarbon seeps, Gulf of Mexico continental slope. Organic Geochemistry 20(1):77-89.

Silvestro, R.D. 2006. Natural acts: When hurricanes hit habitat. National Wildlife Federation, National Wildlife, Aug/Sep 2006, 44:5. Internet website: http://www.nwf.org/nationalwildlife/article.cfm?issueID=109&articleId=1378.

Smith, G.J. 2005. Biological impacts of Hurricane Katrina on the Gulf Coast. Geological Society of America, Annual Meeting and Exposition, October 16-19, 2005, Salt Lake City, UT. U.S. Dept. of the Interior, Geological Survey, Lafayette, LA. Internet website: http://gsa.confex.com/gsa/2005AM/finalprogram/abstract_98476.htm.

Spalding, E.A. and M.W. Hester. 2007. Interactive effects of hydrology and salinity on oligohaline plant species productivity: Implications of relative sea-level rise. Estuaries and Coasts 30(2):214-225. Internet website: http://erf.org/cesn/vol30n2r4.html.

Spies, R.B., J.S. Felton, and L. Dillard. 1982. Hepatic mixed-function oxidases in California flatfishes are increased in contaminated environments and by oil and PCB ingestion. Mar. Biol. 70:117-127.

Terrell, D. and R. Bilbo. 2007. A report on the impact of Hurricanes Katrina and Rita on Louisiana businesses: 2005Q2-2006Q2. Louisiana State University, Division of Economic Development, Baton Rouge, LA. 41 pp. Internet website: http://www.bus.lsu.edu/centers/ded/. Accessed March 2007.

Terres, J.K. 1991. The Audubon Society encyclopedia of North American birds. New York: Wing Books. 1,109 pp.

Thompson, N.B. 1988. The status of loggerhead, *Caretta caretta*; Kemp's ridley, *Lepidochelys kempi*; and green, *Chelonia mydas*, sea turtles in U.S. waters. Marine Fisheries Review 50(3):16-23.

Tiner, R.W. 1984. Wetlands of the United States: Current status and recent trends. U.S. Dept. of the Interior, Fish and Wildlife Service. 59 pp.

Tolbert, C.M. and M. Sizer. 1996. U.S. commuting zones and labor market areas: 1990 update. U.S. Dept. of Agriculture, Economic Research Service, Rural Economy Division. Staff Paper No. AGES-9614.

U.S. Dept. of Commerce. National Marine Fisheries Service. 2007a. Impact of Hurricanes Katrina, Rita, and Wilma on commercial and recreational fishery habitat of Alabama, Florida, Louisiana, Mississippi, and Texas. Internet website: http://www.nmfs.noaa.gov/msa2007/docs/HurricaneImpactsHabitat_080707_1200.pdf. Accessed September 2007.

U.S. Dept. of Commerce. National Marine Fisheries Service. 2007b. Fisheries of the United States 2005. Current fishery statistics. Internet website: http://www.st.nmfs.noaa.gov/st1/fus/fus05/fus_2005.pdf.

U.S. Dept. of Commerce. National Oceanic and Atmospheric Administration. 1992. Oil spill case histories 1967-1991: Summaries of significant U.S. and international spills. U.S. Dept. of Commerce, National Oceanic and Atmospheric Administration, Hazardous Materials Response and Assessment Division, Seattle, WA. Report No. HMRAD-92-11. Internet website: http://www.response.restoration.noaa.gov/oilaids/spilldb.pdf

U.S. Dept. of Commerce. National Oceanic and Atmospheric Administration. National Hurricane Center. 2006. U.S. mainland hurricane strikes by state, 1851-2004. Internet website: http://www.nhc.noaa.gov/paststate.shtml. Accessed October 24, 2006.

U.S. Dept. of Labor. Bureau of Labor Statistics. 2006. Review: Special issue – Hurricane Katrina. Monthly Labor Review 129(8):78 pp. August 2006. Internet website: http://www.stats.bls.gov/opub/mlr/2006/08/contents.htm. Accessed June 1, 2007.

U.S. Dept. of Labor. Bureau of Labor Statistics. 2007. News – Regional and state employment and unemployment: April 2007. U.S. Dept. of Labor, Bureau of Labor Statistics, Washington, DC. USDL 07-0713. Internet website: http://www.bls.gov/news.release/archives/laus_09252007.pdf.

U.S. Dept. of the Interior. Fish and Wildlife Service. 1998. Endangered and threatened wildlife and plants. 50 CFR 17.11 and 17.12, December 31, 1998. 56 pp.

U.S. Dept. of Interior. Fish and Wildlife Service. 2005. Press release: Conducting initial damage assessments to wildlife and national wildlife refuges, September 9, 2005. U.S. Dept. of the Interior, Fish and Wildlife Service, Southeast Region.

U.S. Dept. of the Interior. Geological Survey. 1988. Report to Congress: Coastal barrier resource system. Recommendations for additions to or deletions from the Coastal Barrier Resource System. Vol. 18, Louisiana.

U.S. Dept. of the Interior. Geological Survey. 1998. Chandeleur Islands, La. – 1992 submerged aquatic vegetation. Geospatial data presentation form: Map. Maintained by the U.S. Dept. of the Interior, Geological Survey, National Wetlands Research Center, Lafayette, Louisiana.

U.S. Dept. of the Interior. Geological Survey. 2005. Post Hurricane Katrina flights over Louisiana's barrier islands. Internet website: http://www.nwrc.usgs.gov/hurricane/katrina-post-hurricane-flights.htm. Accessed September 2007.

U.S. Dept. of the Interior. Minerals Management Service. 2000a. Gulf of Mexico deepwater operations and activities: Environmental assessment. U.S. Dept. of the Interior, Minerals Management Service, Gulf of Mexico OCS Region, New Orleans, LA. OCS EIS/EA MMS 2000-001. 264 pp.

U.S. Dept. of the Interior. Minerals Management Service. 2000b. Marine riser failure: Safety alert no. 186. U.S. Dept. of the Interior, Minerals Management Service, Gulf of Mexico OCS Region, New Orleans, LA. March 3, 2000.

U.S. Dept. of the Interior, Minerals Management Service. 2001. Proposed use of floating production, storage, and offloading systems on the Gulf of Mexico Outer Continental Shelf, Western and Central Planning Areas—final environmental impact statement. U.S. Dept. of the Interior, Minerals Management Service, Gulf of Mexico OCS Region, New Orleans, LA. OCS EIS/EA MMS 2000-090. 782 pp.

U.S. Dept. of the Interior. Minerals Management Service. 2002a. Gulf of Mexico OCS oil and gas lease sales: 2003-2007; Central Planning Area Sales 185, 190, 194, 198, and 201; Western Planning Area Sales 187, 192, 196, and 200—final environmental impact statement. 2 vols. U.S. Dept. of the Interior, Minerals Management Service, Gulf of Mexico OCS Region, New Orleans, LA. OCS EIS/EA MMS 2002-052.

U.S. Dept. of the Interior. Minerals Management Service. 2002b. Programmatic environmental assessment for Grid 16: Site-specific evaluation of BP Exploration and Production, Inc.'s initial development operations coordination document, N-7459; Thunder Horse Project, Mississippi Canyon Block 777 Unit (Blocks 775, 776, 777, 778, 819, 820, 821, and 822). U.S. Dept. of the Interior, Minerals Management Service, Gulf of Mexico OCS Region, New Orleans, LA. OCS EIS/EA MMS 2002-081. 165 pp.

U.S. Dept. of the Interior. Minerals Management Service. 2003a. Exploration activities in the Eastern sale area: Eastern Planning Area, Gulf of Mexico OCS—programmatic environmental assessment. U.S. Dept. of the Interior, Minerals Management Service, Gulf of Mexico OCS Region, New Orleans, LA. OCS EIS/EA MMS 2003-008. 202 pp.

U.S. Dept. of the Interior. Minerals Management Service. 2003b. Marine riser failure. Safety Alert no. 213. U.S. Dept. of the Interior, Minerals Management Service, Gulf of Mexico OCS Region, New Orleans, LA. June 11, 2003.

U.S. Dept. of the Interior. Minerals Management Service. 2003c. Programmatic environmental assessment for Grid 13: Site-specific evaluation of Anadarko Petroleum Corporation's initial development operations coordination document, N-7753; Marco Polo Project, Green Canyon Block 608. U.S. Dept. of the Interior, Minerals Management Service, Gulf of Mexico OCS Region, New Orleans, LA. OCS EIS/EA MMS 2003-067. 115 pp.

U.S. Dept. of the Interior. Minerals Management Service. 2007. Gulf of Mexico OCS oil and gas lease sales: 2007-2012; Western Planning Area Sales 204, 207, 210, 215,and 218; Central Planning Area Sales 205, 206, 208, 213, 216, and 222—final environmental impact statement. 2 vols. U.S. Dept. of the Interior, Minerals Management Service, Gulf of Mexico OCS Region, New Orleans, LA. OCS EIS/EA MMS 2007-018.

U.S. Environmental Protection Agency. 2005. Mississippi River basin and Gulf of Mexico hypoxia reassessment 2005. Internet website: http://www.epa.gov/msbasin/taskforce/peer_review.htm. Accessed March 1, 2005 (last updated February 22, 2006).

U.S. Environmental Protection Agency. 2007. National Estuary Program Coastal Condition Report. U.S. Environmental Protection Agency, Office of Water, Office of Research and Development, Washington DC. EPA-842/B-06/001. Internet website: http://www.epa.gov/owow/oceans/nepccr/index.html. Accessed February 1, 2008.

Vargo, S., P. Lutz, D. Odell, E. Van Vleet, and G. Bossart. 1986. Study of the effects of oil on marine turtles, a final report. Volume II: Technical report. 3 vols. U.S. Dept. of the Interior, Minerals Management Service, Atlantic OCS Region, Washington, DC. OCS Study MMS 86-0070. 181 pp.

Warham, J. 1990. The petrels: their ecology and breeding systems. San Diego, CA: Academic Press. 440 pp.

Webb, J.W., G.T. Tanner, and B.H. Koerth. 1981. Oil spill effects on smooth cordgrass in Galveston Bay, Texas. Contributions in Marine Science 24:107-114.

Webb, J.W., S.K. Alexander, and J.K. Winters. 1985. Effects of autumn application of oil on *Spartina alterniflora* in a Texas salt marsh. Environ. Poll., Series A 38(4):321-337.

Webb, J.W. 1988. Establishment of vegetation on oil-contaminated dunes. Shore and Beach, October. Pp. 20-23.

White, W.A., T.R. Calnan, R.A. Morton, R.S. Kimble, T.G. Littleton, J.H. McGowen, H.S. Nance, and K.E. Schmedes. 1986. Submerged lands of Texas, Brownsville-Harlingen area. University of Texas at Austin, Bureau of Economic Geology, Austin, TX.

Williams, J.H. and I.W. Duedall. 1997. Florida hurricanes and tropical storms; revised edition. Gainesville, FL: The University of Florida Press. 146 pp.

Woods & Poole Economics, Inc. 2006. The 2006 Complete Economic and Demographic Data Source (CEDDS) on CD-ROM.

Woods & Poole Economics, Inc. 2007. The 2007 Complete Economic and Demographic Data Source (CEEDS) on CD-ROM.

Zieman, J.C. and R.T. Zieman. 1989. The ecology of the seagrass meadows of the west coast of Florida: A community profile. U.S. Dept. of the Interior, Fish and Wildlife Service. Biological Report 85(7.25). 155 pp. Internet website: http://www.gomr.mms.gov/PI/PDFImages/ESPIS/3/3752.pdf.

6. PREPARERS

NEPA Coordinators

| Greg Kozlowski | Environmental Scientist |
| G. Ed Richardson | Senior Environmental Scientist |

Contributors

Patrick H. Adkins	Information Management Specialist
David Ball	Archaeologist—Archaeological Issues
Richard Bennet	Biologist—Chemosyntheitc Communities Issues
Greg Boland	Biologist—Fisheries, Benthic Issues
Darice Breeding	Physical Scientist—Hydrocarbon Spill Issues
Tre W. Glenn	Biologist—Marine Mammal and Sea Turtle Issues
Larry Hartzog	Biologist—Coastal Environments and Gulf Sturgeon
Bonnie Johnson	Environmental Scientist—Coastal Zone Management Issues
Harry Luton	Sociologist—Socioeconomic Issues
Stacie Merritt-Hendon	Physical Scientist—Air Quality Issues
Margaret Metcalf	Physical Scientist—Water Quality Issues
Deborah Miller	Technical Publications Editor
David P. Moran	Environmental Scientist—Beach Mice and Bird Issues
Catherine Rosa	Environmental Assessment Program Specialist
James Sinclair	Marine Biologist—Seagrasses
Kristen Strellec	Economist—Socioeconomic Issues
Wilfred Times	GIS/Visual Information Specialist

Reviewers and Supervisors

| Gary Goeke | Supervisor, NEPA/CZM Coordination Unit |
| Dennis Chew | Chief, Environmental Assessment Section |

7. APPENDICES

Appendix A. Offshore Discharges and Waste Disposal
Appendix B. Accidental Oil-Spill Review

Appendix A

Offshore Discharges and Waste Disposal

APPENDIX A.   OFFSHORE DISCHARGES AND WASTE DISPOSAL

The discharge of wastes into offshore waters is regulated by USEPA under the authority of the Clean Water Act. No wastes generated during oil and gas operations can be discharged overboard unless they meet the standards required within an NPDES permit. All of the waste types generated from the proposed phased drilling, completion, and production activities for the Cascade Chinook project will be either (1) discharged overboard in compliance with NPDES requirements or (2) transported to shore for disposal in permitted or licensed commercial facilities or for recycling. The wastes for overboard discharge and transport to shore for recycling or disposal are summarized in **Tables A-1 and A-2**, respectively.

Wastes generated during the various activities of the Cascade-Chinook project consist of (1) drill fluids; (2) drill cuttings (water-based fluid and SBF); (3) deck drainage; (4) sanitary and domestic wastes; (5) uncontaminated seawater used for cooling, desalinization, and ballast; (6) well completion fluids; (7) bilge water; (8) chemically treated seawater or freshwater; (9) used SBF; (10) used oil; and (11) solid trash and debris.

Routine sanitary and domestic wastes necessarily arise from people working offshore on drilling rigs, production platforms, and support vessels. Petrobras estimated that 30 gal/person/day of sanitary waste and 50 gal/person/day of domestic waste would be discharged from the semisubmersible drill rig, Diamond's *Ocean Endeavor*, the FPSO, and the shuttle tanker or ATB.

Deck drainage effluent is primarily rainwater containing residual oil and grease from equipment washwater and rainwater. The overboard discharge of deck drainage is governed by the NPDES permit requirement for no visible oil sheen.

Table A-1

Projected Ocean Discharges from the Cascade-Chinook Project
(drilling and completion, production, and shuttle-vessel operations)

Type of Waste	Total Amount Discharged	Discharge Rate	Discharge Method
Water-based mud	16,000 bbl/well	500 bbl/hr	Overboard
Cuttings containing synthetic-based mud	7,200 bbl/well	15 bbl/hr	Overboard
Drill cuttings associated with water-based drilling fluids	6,000 bbl/well	15 bbl/hr	Overboard
Muds, cuttings at the seafloor	35,000 bbl/well	400 bbl/hr	Discharged at seabed
Sanitary waste	126,000 [a] bbl/mo 36,000 [b] bbl/mo 22,500 [c] bbl/mo	30 gal/person/day	Chlorinate and discharge
Domestic waste	210,000 [a] bbl/mo 60,000 [b] bbl/mo 37,500 [c] bbl/mo	50 gal/person/day	Remove floating solids and discharge
Desalination unit brine water	145,000 [a] bbl/mo 900 [b] bbl/mo 900 [c] bbl/mo	30-100 bbl/day	Discharge overboard
Deck drainage	3,000 bbl/mo 17,000 bbl/mo 17,000 bbl/mo	100-560 bbl/day	Treat for oil and grease and discharge; dependent upon rainfall
Completion fluids (Well test)	9,000 bbl well	200 bbl/hr	Oily water treatment and then discharge overboard
Uncontaminated fresh or seawater	90,000 [a] bbl/mo 3,600 [b] bbl/mo 3,600 [c] bbl/mo	125 bbl/hr 120 bbl/day 120 bbl/day	Discharge overboard
Ballast water	45,000 [a] bbl/mo 1,410,000 [b] bbl/mo 1,410,000 [c] bbl/mo	1,000 bbl/hr 47,000 bbl/day 47,000 bbl/day	Discharged overboard; no free oil
Bilge water	2,000 [a] bbl/mo 3,300 [b] bbl/mo 3,300 [c] bbl/mo	10 [a] bbl/hr 110 [b] bbl/day 110 [c] bbl/day	Discharged overboard; no free oil

[a] drilling and completion operations.
[b] production operations.
[c] shuttle-vessel operations.

Table A-2

Wastes for Transport to Shore on the Proposed Cascade-Chinook Project

Type of Waste—Approximate Composition	Amount	Name/Location of Disposal Facility	Treatment and/or Storage, Transport, and Disposal Method
Synthetic-based drilling mud	2,500 bbl	U.S. Liquids, Newpark Services, or CCT	Transport to shore base for recycling
Trash and Debris	4 [a, b, c] standard containers per month	Solid Waste Disposal or Gagliano Waste [a, b] To be determined [c]	Transport to shore base for pickup and disposal
Hazardous Liquid - Used oil	50 bbl	L &L [a, b] To be determined [c]	Transport to shore base for recycling

[a] drilling and completion operations.
[b] production operations.
[c] shuttle-vessel operations.

Appendix B

Accidental Oil-Spill Review

ANALYSIS OF THE POTENTIAL FOR AN ACCIDENTAL OIL SPILL AND THE POTENTIAL FOR IMPACTS FROM THE CASCADE-CHINOOK FPSO PROJECT, WALKER RIDGE BLOCKS 206, 249, AND 469 – N-9015

Introduction

The NEPA requires Federal agencies to consider potential environmental impacts (direct, indirect, and cumulative) of proposed actions as part of agency planning and decisionmaking. The NEPA analyses address many issues relating to potential impacts, including issues that may have a very low probability of occurrence, but which the public considers important or for which the environmental consequences could be significant.

The past several decades of spill data show that accidental oil spills ($\geq$1,000 bbl) associated with oil and gas exploration and development are low probability events in Federal OCS waters of the Gulf of Mexico, yet the issue of oil spills is important to the public. Further, the risk of spills unique to FPSO operations in the Gulf of Mexico is low (USDOI, MMS, 2001). This appendix summarizes key information about the probability of accidental spills from offshore oil and gas and FPSO activity in the Gulf of Mexico.

Proposed Action

The development activities associated with this DOCD reflect simultaneous first oil production from the Cascade and Chinook Units. This analysis will cover Phase I of the development plan since additional phases are dependent upon the results of Phase I. If future phases of the development plan are desired, Petrobras will be required to supplement their proposed plan as appropriate. This new information will undergo additional environmental analysis when this information is submitted. Phase I will consist of the drilling and completion of three wells. The produced fluids from the three wells will be transported to a common FPSO in Walker Ridge Block 249 through flowlines and four production FSHR's. The subsea architecture is consistent with existing technology in the Gulf of Mexico with the exception of the subsea booster pumps, which will be used to enhance production when reservoir pressures decrease over time. Produced oil will be separated, treated, measured, and temporarily stored on the FPSO prior to transportation to market. The usable capacity of the cargo tanks on the FPSO will be approximately 600,000 bbl. The FPSO will have a disconnectible mooring system that will allow it to disconnect and motor away from named storms and hurricanes under its own power, returning for reconnection when it is safe to do so. Oil transportation to market will be achieved through the use of dedicated chartered shuttle vessels. Shuttle vessels will either be shuttle tankers or articulated tug barges. After production ramp up, the FPSO will offload oil to a shuttle vessel approximately once a week, and the shuttle vessel will transport the product to the terminals of choice along the Gulf of Mexico. Gas that is not used to power equipment on the FPSO will be exported to market via a gas export FSHR and a gas export pipeline that will be tied into an existing facility in Green Canyon. The proposed action includes the activity listed in **Tables B-1 and B-2**. The estimated worst-case discharge volumes for the proposed action is listed in **Table B-3** and discussed below.

Table B-1

Proposed Production Wells and FPSO

	Name	Block	Surface Structure
1	FPSO	WR 249	Yes
2	Cascade West Well # 3	WR 249	No
3	Cascade East Well # 4	WR 206	No
4	Chinook Well # 2	WR 469	No

FPSO – floating, production, storage, and offloading.
WR – Walker Ridge.

Table B-2

Proposed Pipelines

	Type	Size (in)	Length (ft)	From	To
1	Lease term	9 5/8	13,578	Cascade East – WR 206	Cascade West – WR 249
2	Lease term	9 5/8	22,252	Cascade West – WR 249	FPSO riser base – WR 249
3	ROW	Not given	Not given	Chinook – WR 469	FPSO – WR 249

FPSO – floating, production, storage, and offloading.
ROW – right-of-way.
WR – Walker Ridge.

Spill Prevention

The MMS has comprehensive, pollution-prevention requirements for drilling and production that include redundant levels of safety devices, as well as inspection and testing requirements to confirm that these devices work. Many of these requirements have been in place since about 1980. Spill trends analysis for the Gulf of Mexico OCS show that spills from facilities have decreased over time, indicating that MMS engineering and safety requirements have minimized the potential for spill occurrence and associated impacts.

Primary responsibility for the enforcement of U.S. Maritime laws and regulations in Gulf of Mexico waters falls upon the USCG. The Coast Guard's responsibilities for regulating activities on the OCS, the continental shelf, and in ports or harbors, as applicable to the proposed action are presented in 33 CFR 1-199, 43 U.S.C. 1331, 46 U.S.C. 21-47 (Parts A and B), and OPA 90. The USCG is responsible for managing and regulating provisions for safe navigation of vessels in U.S. waters, as well as the enforcement of environmental and pollution-prevention regulations.

Table B-3

Estimated Worst-Case Discharge Volumes for the Project Components

Component Name	Blocks	Blowout Volume (bbl/day)	Total Worst-Case Discharge
1) FPSO – MMS-regulated production facilities	WR 249	N/A	10,120 bbl
2) FPSO cargo under USCG jurisdiction*	WR 249	N/A	600,000 bbl**
3) Cascade West Well # 3	WR 249 – subsea location no tanks	12.284	12,284 bbl/day
4) Cascade East Well # 4	WR206 – subsea location no tanks	12.284	12,284 bbl/day
5) Chinook Well # 2	WR 469 – subsea location no tanks	12.284	12,284 bbl/day
6) 9 5/8 inch pipeline	From Cascade East WR 206 to Cascade West WR 249	N/A	1,055 bbl
7) 9 5/8 inch pipeline	From Cascade West WR 249 to FPSO riser base WR 249	N/A	1,055 bbl
8) ROW Pipeline	From Chinook WR 469 to FPSO WR 249	N/A	7,100 bbl
9) Shuttle vessel*	Range from WR 249 FPSO site to terminals throughout the Gulf of Mexico	N/A	185,000-500,000 bbl

*Cargo and fuel tank storage on the FPSO and the shuttle vessel fall under USCG jurisdiction and are covered in a vessel response plan submitted to USCG.

**Based on USCG calculation requirements for the FPSO cargo volume, the estimated maximum most probable discharge is 2,500 bbl and the average most probable discharge is 50 bbl.

FPSO – floating, production, storage, and offloading.
ROW – right-of-way.
WR – Walker Ridge.

Spills in the Past

This summary presents data for the period 1985-1999 of past OCS spills from drilling, production, and pipeline activity. The 1985-1999 time period was chosen to reflect more modern engineering and regulatory requirements and because OCS spill rates are available for this period. For the period 1985-1999, there were no spills $\geq$1,000 bbl from OCS platforms, eight spills $\geq$1,000 bbl from OCS pipelines, and no spills $\geq$1,000 bbl from OCS blowouts (**Tables B-4 through B-7**). It should be noted that past OCS spills (**Tables B-4 through B-7**), some of which are considerably >1,000 bbl, have not resulted in any documented significant impacts to shorelines or other resources.

Past spills from FPSO's are discussed in the FPSO EIS (USDOI, MMS, 2001). Since this is the first FPSO system proposed for the Gulf of Mexico, none of the spills assessed in this document occurred on the Gulf of Mexico OCS.

Table B-4

Historical Record of OCS Spills ≥1,000 Barrels from OCS Facilities, 1985-1999

Spill Date	Area and Block (water depth and distance from shore)	Volume Spilled (barrels)	Cause of Spill

No OCS facility spills ≥1,000 bbl during the period 1985-1999.

Table B-5

Historical Record of OCS Spills ≥1,000 Barrels from OCS Pipelines, 1985-1999

Spill Date	Area and Block (water depth and distance from shore)	Volume Spilled (barrels)	Cause of Spill
February 7, 1988	South Pass 60 (75 ft, 3.4 mi)	15,576	Service vessel's anchor damaged pipeline
January 24, 1990	Ship Shoal 281 (197 ft, 60 mi)	14,423*	Anchor drag, flange and valve broke off
May 6, 1990	Eugene Island 314 (230 ft, 78 mi)	4,569	Trawl drag pulled off valve
August 31, 1992	South Pelto 8 (30 ft, 6 mi)	2,000	Hurricane Andrew, loose drilling rig's anchor drag damaged pipeline
November 22, 1994	Ship Shoal 281 (197 ft, 60 mi)	4,533*	Trawl drag
January 26, 1998	East Cameron 334 (264 ft, 105 mi)	1,211*	Service vessel's anchor drag damaged pipeline during rescue operation
September 29, 1988	South Pass 38 (110 ft, 6 mi)	8,212	Hurricane Georges, mudslide parted pipeline
July 23, 1999	Ship Shoal 241 (133 ft, 50 mi)	3,189	Jack-up barge sat on pipeline

*condensate

Table B-6

Historical Record of OCS Spills ≥1,000 Barrels from OCS Blowouts, 1985-1999

Spill Date	Area and Block (water depth and distance from shore)	Volume Spilled (barrels)	Cause of Spill

No OCS blowout spills ≥1,000 bbl during the period 1985-1999.

Table B-7

Spill Rates Used to Estimate the Future Potential for Spills

Spill Source	Volume of Oil Handled in Billions of Barrels	Number of Wells Drilled	No. of Spills ≥1,000 Barrels	Risk of Spill from Facilities Pipelines, Shuttle Tankers, or FPSO's per Billion Barrels	Risk of Spill from Drilling Blowout per Well
Facilities	7.41[a]	Not Applicable	1[a]	>0 to <0.13[c]	Not Applicable
Pipelines	5.81	Not Applicable	8	1.38	Not Applicable
Drilling	Not Applicable	14,067	1[b]	Not Applicable	>0 to <0.00007
Shuttle Tanker[d]	Not Available	Not Applicable	Not Available	1.2	Not Applicable
FPSO[d]	Not Available	Not Applicable	Not Available	0.37	Not Applicable

[a] There were actually zero spills ≥1,000 bbl from facilities during the period 1985-1999. The data shown represent 1980-1999. The spill period for facility spills was expanded to 1980 to include a spill for facilities to result in a non-zero risk

[b] There have been no spills ≥1,000 bbl from blowouts during the period 1985-1999. One spill was "assigned" to provide a non-zero spill rate.

[c] There were no facility or blowout spills ≥1,000 bbl for the period 1985-1999; however, a non-zero spill rate was calculated by expanding the facility period to 1980 and by "assigning" a blowout spill. Therefore, the spill rates for these categories are presented as greater than zero but below the rates calculated by expanding the data period and assigning a spill.

[d] USDOI, MMS, 2001.

Estimating Future Potential Spills

The MMS estimates the risk of future potential spills by multiplying variables to result in a numerical expression of risk. These variables include the potential of a spill occurring based on historical spill rates and a variable for the potential for a spill to be transported to environmental resources based on trajectory modeling. The following subsections describe the spill occurrence and transport variables used to estimate risk and the risk calculation for the proposed action.

Spill Occurrence Variable (SOV) Representing the Potential for a Spill

The SOV is derived based on past spill frequency. That is, data from past spills are used to estimate future potential spills. The MMS has estimated spill rates for spills from the following sources: facilities, pipelines, blowouts, FPSO's, and shuttle tankers.

Spill rates for facilities and pipelines have been developed for several time periods and an analysis of trends for spills is presented in *Update of Comparative Occurrence Rates for Offshore Oil Spills* (Anderson and LaBelle, 2000). Spill rates for the most recent period analyzed, 1985-1999, are presented here. Data for this recent period should reflect more modern spill-prevention requirements.

Spill rates for facilities and pipelines are based on the number of spills per volume of oil handled. Spill rates for the period 1985-1999 are shown in **Table B-7**. It should be noted that there were no platform or blowout spills ≥1,000 bbl for the period 1985-1999. The use of "zero" spills would result in a zero spill rate. To allow for conservative future predictions of spill occurrence, a spill number of one was "assigned" to provide a non-zero spill rate for blowouts. The spill period was expanded to 1980 to include a spill for facilities. While there were no facility or blowout spills during the 1985-1999 period for which data are available, spills could occur in the future. In fact, pipeline spills ≥1,000 bbl were reported subsequent to this period, so it is reasonable to include a spill to provide a non-zero spill rate.

Spill rates for an FPSO unique oil release is also based upon on the number of spills per volume of oil produced. Spill rates for shuttle-tanker-related failures are based upon the number of spills per volume of oil transported. The spill rates for FPSO's and shuttle tankers were calculated as part of the FPSO EIS analyses (USDOI, MMS, 2001). As evident in **Table B-7**, the oil-spill risk for shuttle tanker transport is comparable with and slightly less than that of pipeline transport.

Spill rates are combined with site-specific data on production or pipeline volumes, pipeline and reservoir lifetime, volume transported, or number of wells being drilled to result in a site-specific SOV.

Transport Variable (TV) Representing the Potential for a Spill to be Transported to Important Environmental Resources

The TV is derived using an oil-spill trajectory model. This model predicts the direction that winds and currents would transport spills. The model uses an extensive database of observed and theoretically computed ocean currents and fields that represent a statistical estimate of winds and currents that would occur over the life of an oil and gas project, which may span several decades. This model produces the TV that can be combined with other variables, such as the SOV, to estimate the risk of future potential spills and impacts.

Risk Calculation for the Proposed Action

Tables B-8 through B-11 present an estimate of spill risk to resources using two variables—the SOV and the TV. The coastal counties and international boundary lines that could be impacted/contacted are indicated in these tables. The final column in these tables presents the result of combining the SOV's and TV's.

The SOV for the FPSO was determined using a spill rate of 0.37 from **Table B-7**, the estimated production to be handled at the FPSO and the estimated maximum duration of the Phase I wells. The SOV for the shuttle tanker activity at the FPSO location was determined using a spill rate of 1.2 from **Table B-7**, the estimated production to be transported and the estimated maximum duration of the Phase I wells (USDOI, MMS, 2001). The SOV for the production activity was determined using a spill rate of 0.13 from **Table B-7**, the estimated production rate for each facility and the estimated life years of the reserves proposed to be produced. The SOV for the associated pipelines was determined using a spill rate of 1.38 from **Table B-7**, the volume of oil proposed to be transported, and the estimated design life of the pipeline.

Combined risk was not determined for shuttle vessels at each potential terminal site in the Gulf of Mexico because the operator indicated that they might utilize terminals throughout most of the Gulf of Mexico, ranging from Corpus Christi, Texas, to Mobile, Alabama, and because the oil-spill risk of occurrence (SOV) for shuttle tanker transport is comparable with and slightly less than that for the typical mode of crude transport, pipeline transport. Since the oil spill risk of occurrence for shuttle vessels is less than that for pipeline transport, there is no greater risk of spill occurrence based upon unique FPSO transport. Spill impact analysis for near shore spills will, therefore, be generically addressed in this document. The most recent Final EIS's provides additional information on spills and potential impacts.

Table B-8

Spill Risk Estimate for the FPSO Located in Walker Ridge

Environmental Resource	Spill Occurrence Variable [1] (%)	Transport Variable [2] within 30 Days (%)	Spill Risk [3] [4] within 30 Days (%)
Counties/Parishes[5]			
Calhoun, TX	8.3	<0.5	<0.5
Matagorda, TX	8.3	1	<0.5
Brazoria, TX.	8.3	1	<0.5
Galveston, TX	8.3	2	<0.5
Jefferson, TX.	8.3	1	<0.5
Cameron, LA	8.3	2	<0.5
Vermilion, LA	8.3	1	<0.5
Iberia, LA	8.3	<0.5	<0.5
Terrebonne, LA	8.3	1	<0.5
LaFourche, LA	8.3	1	<0.5
Jefferson, LA	8.3	<0.5	<0.5
Plaquemines, LA	8.3	1	<0.5
Environmental Resource	Spill Occurrence Variable [1] %	Transport Variable [2] within 3/10/30 Days %	Spill Risk [3] [4] within 3/10/30 Days %
2. International Boundary Sea Segment (IBSS) [5]			
IBSS 1 (closest to Texas/Mexico)[6]	8.3	<0.5/<0.5/<0.5	<0.5/<0.5/<0.5
IBSS 2[6]	8.3	<0.5/<0.5/<0.5	<0.5/<0.5/<0.5
IBSS 3[6]	8.3	<0.5/<0.5/2	<0.5/<0.5/<0.5
IBSS 4[6]	8.3	<0.5/<0.5/4	<0.5/<0.5/<0.5
IBSS 5[6]	8.3	<0.5/1/9	<0.5/<0.5/1
IBSS 6[6]	8.3	<0.5/4/17	<0.5/<0.5/1
IBSS 7 (due south of the Walker Ridge Area) [6]	8.3	2/13/26	<0.5/1/2
IBSS 8 (due south of the Walker Ridge Area) [6]	8.3	6/16/23	<0.5/1/2
IBSS 9[6]	8.3	1/7/12	<0.5/1/1
IBSS 10[6]	8.3	<0.5/2/5	<0.5/<0.5/<0.5
IBSS 11[6]	8.3	<0.5/<0.5/1	<0.5/<0.5/<0.5
IBSS 12[6]	8.3	<0.5/<0.5/1	<0.5/<0.5/<0.5
IBSS 13[6]	8.3	<0.5/<0.5/1	<0.5/<0.5/<0.5
IBSS 14[6]	8.3	<0.5/<0.5/<0.5	<0.5/<0.5/<0.5
IBSS 15[6]	8.3	<0.5/<0.5/<0.5	<0.5/<0.5/<0.5
IBSS 16[6]	8.3	<0.5/<0.5/<0.5	<0.5/<0.5/<0.5
IBSS 17 (closest to Florida) [6]	8.3	<0.5/<0.5/<0.5	<0.5/<0.5/<0.5

(1) The percent chance of a spill event occurring from the proposed FPSO. This variable was determined assuming that 80,000 bbl of oil was processed per day on the FPSO and that the FPSO was in use for 8 years (Petrobras America Inc., 2007). Any additional production capacity that may be added in Phase 2 or 3, or additional years of service is not covered by this analysis.

Table B-8. Spill Risk Estimate for the FPSO Located in Walker Ridge (continued).

(2) The percent chance that winds and currents will move a point projected onto the surface of the Gulf beginning within Walker Ridge and ending at specified shoreline, international boundary sea segments, or environmental resources. These results are the results of a numerical model that calculates the trajectory of a drifting point projected onto the surface of the water using temporally and spatially varying winds and ocean current fields. These probabilities do not factor in the risk of spill occurrence, consideration of the spill size, any spill-response or cleanup actions, or any dispersion and weathering of the slick with time. For the coastal counties and parishes, a 30-day probability is all that is shown because the hypothetical Walker Ridge oil-spill launch area is located 140-160 nautical miles from the coast, which resulted in no probabilities of contact to county/parish land segments of >0.5% for 3-10 days. The international boundary sea segments are located in proximity to the hypothetical Walker Ridge oil-spill launch area; therefore, the probabilities for 3, 10, and 30 days are included. Refer to *Oil Spill Risk Analysis: Contingency Planning Statistics for Gulf of Mexico OCS Activities in the Walker Ridge Planning Area* for additional details (USDOI, MMS, 2007).

(3) The probability of a spill occurring and contacting identified environmental features represents the weighted risk that accounts for both the risk that a large spill will occur and the risk that it will contact locations where the resources occur, given the assumptions already described in (1) and (2).

(4) <0.5 = less than 0.5%.

(5) Counties with all values <0.5% are not shown.

(6) It should be noted that the international boundary segments do not terminate the trajectories as the county/parish boundaries do; therefore, one trajectory could contact more than one segment based upon changing wind and current histories. Additionally, these results do not indicate contact with a particular shoreline resource; instead, they indicate the possibility that a spill may traverse into international waters (USDOI, MMS, 2007).

Table B-9

Spill Risk Estimate for the Shuttle Tankering Activities Associated with the FPSO Located in Walker Ridge

Environmental Resource	Spill Occurrence Variable [1] %	Transport Variable [2] within 30 Days %	Spill Risk [3][4] within 30 Days %
Counties/Parishes[5]			
Calhoun, TX	24	<0.5	<0.5
Matagorda, TX	24	1	<0.5
Brazoria, TX	24	1	<0.5
Galveston, TX	24	2	<0.5
Jefferson, TX	24	1	<0.5
Cameron, LA	24	2	<0.5
Vermilion, LA	24	1	<0.5
Iberia, LA	24	<0.5	<0.5
Terrebonne, LA	24	1	<0.5
LaFourche, LA	24	1	<0.5
Jefferson, LA	24	<0.5	<0.5
Plaquemines, LA	24	1	<0.5
Environmental Resource	Spill Occurrence Variable [1] %	Transport Variable [2] within 3/10/30 Days %	Spill Risk [3][4] within 3/10/30 Days %
2. International Boundary Sea Segment (IBSS) [5]			
IBSS 1 (closest to Texas/Mexico)[6]	24	<0.5/<0.5/<0.5	<0.5/<0.5/<0.5
IBSS 2[6]	24	<0.5/<0.5/<0.5	<0.5/<0.5/<0.5
IBSS 3[6]	24	<0.5/<0.5/2	<0.5/<0.5/<0.5
IBSS 4[6]	24	<0.5/<0.5/4	<0.5/<0.5/1
IBSS 5[6]	24	<0.5/1/9	<0.5/<0.5/2
IBSS 6[6]	24	<0.5/4/17	<0.5/1/4
IBSS 7 (due south of the Walker Ridge Area) [6]	24	2/13/26	<0.5/3/6
IBSS 8 (due south of the Walker Ridge Area) [6]	24	6/16/23	1/4/6
IBSS 9[6]	24	1/7/12	<0.5/2/3
IBSS 10[6]	24	<0.5/2/5	<0.5/<0.5/1
IBSS 11[6]	24	<0.5/<0.5/1	<0.5/<0.5/<0.5
IBSS 12[6]	24	<0.5/<0.5/1	<0.5/<0.5/<0.5
IBSS 13[6]	24	<0.5/<0.5/1	<0.5/<0.5/<0.5
IBSS 14[6]	24	<0.5/<0.5/<0.5	<0.5/<0.5/<0.5
IBSS 15[6]	24	<0.5/<0.5/<0.5	<0.5/<0.5/<0.5
IBSS 16[6]	24	<0.5/<0.5/<0.5	<0.5/<0.5/<0.5
IBSS 17 (closest to Florida)[6]	24	<0.5/<0.5/<0.5	<0.5/<0.5/<0.5

(1) The percent chance of a spill event occurring from the proposed shuttle tankering associated at the proposed FPSO location. This variable was determined assuming that 80,000 bbl of oil was offloaded and transported per day at the FPSO site and that the FPSO was in use for 8 years (Petrobras America Inc., 2007). Any additional transported capacity that may be added in Phase 2 or 3, or additional years of service is not covered by this analysis.

Table B-9. Spill Risk Estimate for the Shuttle Tankering Activities Associated with the FPSO Located in Walker Ridge (continued).

(2) The percent chance that winds and currents will move a point projected onto the surface of the Gulf beginning within Walker Ridge and ending at specified shoreline, international boundary sea segments, or environmental resources. These results are the results of a numerical model that calculates the trajectory of a drifting point projected onto the surface of the water using temporally and spatially varying winds and ocean current fields. These probabilities do not factor in the risk of spill occurrence, consideration of the spill size, any spill-response or cleanup actions, or any dispersion and weathering of the slick with time. For the coastal counties and parishes, a 30-day probability is all that is shown because the hypothetical Walker Ridge oil-spill launch area is located 140-160 nautical miles from the coast, which resulted in no probabilities of contact to county/parish land segments of >0.5% for 3-10 days. The international boundary sea segments are located in proximity to the hypothetical Walker Ridge oil-spill launch area; therefore, the probabilities for 3, 10, and 30 days are included. Refer to *Oil Spill Risk Analysis: Contingency Planning Statistics for Gulf of Mexico OCS Activities in the Walker Ridge Planning Area* for additional details (USDOI, MMS, 2007).

(3) The probability of a spill occurring and contacting identified environmental features represents the weighted risk that accounts for both the risk that a large spill will occur and the risk that it will contact locations where the resources occur, given the assumptions already described in (1) and (2).

(4) <0.5 = less than 0.5%.

(5) Counties with all values <0.5% are not shown.

(6) It should be noted that the International boundary segments do not terminate the trajectories as the county/parish boundaries do; therefore, one trajectory could contact more than one sea segment based upon changing wind and current histories. Additionally, these results do not indicate contact with a particular shoreline resource; instead, they indicate the possibility that a spill may traverse into international waters (USDOI, MMS, 2007).

Table B-10

Spill Risk Estimate for the Cascade-Chinook Wells Located in Walker Ridge

Environmental Resource	Spill Occurrence Variable [1] %	Transport Variable [2] within 30 Days %	Spill Risk [3][4] within 30 Days %
Counties/Parishes[5]			
Calhoun, TX	1	<0.5	<0.5
Matagorda, TX	1	1	<0.5
Brazoria, TX	1	1	<0.5
Galveston, TX	1	2	<0.5
Jefferson, TX	1	1	<0.5
Cameron, LA	1	2	<0.5
Vermilion, LA	1	1	<0.5
Iberia, LA	1	<0.5	<0.5
Terrebonne, LA	1	1	<0.5
LaFourche, LA	1	1	<0.5
Jefferson, LA	1	<0.5	<0.5
Plaquemines, LA	1	1	<0.5
Environmental Resource	Spill Occurrence Variable [1] %	Transport Variable [2] within 3/10/30 Days %	Spill Risk [3][4] within 3/10/30 Days %
2. International Boundary Sea Segment (IBSS) [5]			
IBSS 1 (closest to Texas/Mexico)[6]	1	<0.5/<0.5/<0.5	<0.5/<0.5/<0.5
IBSS 2[6]	1	<0.5/<0.5/<0.5	<0.5/<0.5/<0.5
IBSS 3[6]	1	<0.5/<0.5/2	<0.5/<0.5/<0.5
IBSS 4[6]	1	<0.5/<0.5/4	<0.5/<0.5/<0.5
IBSS 5[6]	1	<0.5/1/9	<0.5/<0.5/<0.5
IBSS 6[6]	1	<0.5/4/17	<0.5/<0.5/<0.5
IBSS 7 (due south of the Walker Ridge Area) [6]	1	2/13/26	<0.5/<0.5/<0.5
IBSS 8 (due south of the Walker Ridge Area) [6]	1	6/16/23	<0.5/<0.5/<0.5
IBSS 9[6]	1	1/7/12	<0.5/<0.5/<0.5
IBSS 10[6]	1	<0.5/2/5	<0.5/<0.5/<0.5
IBSS 11[6]	1	<0.5/<0.5/1	<0.5/<0.5/<0.5
IBSS 12[6]	1	<0.5/<0.5/1	<0.5/<0.5/<0.5
IBSS 13[6]	1	<0.5/<0.5/1	<0.5/<0.5/<0.5
IBSS 14[6]	1	<0.5/<0.5/<0.5	<0.5/<0.5/<0.5
IBSS 15[6]	1	<0.5/<0.5/<0.5	<0.5/<0.5/<0.5
IBSS 16[6]	1	<0.5/<0.5/<0.5	<0.5/<0.5/<0.5
IBSS 17 (closest to Florida) [6]	1	<0.5/<0.5/<0.5	<0.5/<0.5/<0.5

(1) The percent chance of a spill event occurring from one of the proposed three wells associated with Phase 1 of the proposed FPSO activity. This variable was determined assuming that 27,000 bbl of oil (1/3 of the total production) was produced per day from each well for 8 years (Petrobras America Inc., 2007). This scenario assumes loss of control at only one of these wells due to the physical distance between the proposed subsurface wells. Any additional production capacity that may be added in Phase 2 or 3, or additional years of production is not covered by this analysis.

Table B-10. Spill Risk Estimate for the Cascade-Chinook Wells Located in Walker Ridge (continued).

(2) The percent chance that winds and currents will move a point projected onto the surface of the Gulf beginning within Walker Ridge and ending at specified shoreline, international boundary sea segments, or environmental resources. These results are the results of a numerical model that calculates the trajectory of a drifting point projected onto the surface of the water using temporally and spatially varying winds and ocean current fields.   These probabilities do not factor in the risk of spill occurrence, consideration of the spill size, any spill response or cleanup actions, or any dispersion and weathering of the slick with time. For the coastal counties and parishes, a 30-day probability is all that is shown because the hypothetical Walker Ridge oil-spill launch area is located 140-160 nautical miles from the coast, which resulted in no probabilities of contact to county/parisjh land segments of >0.5% for 3-10 days. The international boundary sea segments are located in proximity to the hypothetical Walker Ridge oil-spill launch area; therefore, the probabilities for 3, 10, and 30 days are included. Refer to *Oil Spill Risk Analysis: Contingency Planning Statistics for Gulf of Mexico OCS Activities in the Walker Ridge Planning Area* for additional details (USDOI, MMS, 2007).

(3) The probability of a spill occurring and contacting identified environmental features represents the weighted risk that accounts for both the risk that a large spill will occur and the risk that it will contact locations where the resources occur, given the assumptions already described in (1) and (2).

(4) < 0.5 = less than 0.5%.

(5) Counties with all values less than 0.5 percent are not shown.

(6) It should be noted that the International boundary segments do not terminate the trajectories as the county/parish boundaries do; therefore, one trajectory could contact more than one sea segment based upon changing wind and current histories. Additionally, these results do not indicate contact with a particular shoreline resource, instead, they indicate the possibility that a spill may traverse into international waters (USDOI, MMS, 2007).

Table B-11

Spill Risk Estimate for the Cascade-Chinook Oil Pipelines Located in Walker Ridge

Environmental Resoure	Spill Occurrence Variable [1] %	Transport Variable [2] within 30 Days %	Spill Risk [3][4] within 30 Days %
Counties/Parishes [5]			
Calhoun, TX	10	<0.5	<0.5
Matagorda, TX	10	1	<0.5
Brazoria, TX	10	1	<0.5
Galveston, TX	10	2	<0.5
Jefferson, TX	10	1	<0.5
Cameron, LA	10	2	<0.5
Vermilion, LA	10	1	<0.5
Iberia, LA	10	<0.5	<0.5
Terrebonne, LA	10	1	<0.5
LaFourche, LA	10	1	<0.5
Jefferson, LA	10	<0.5	<0.5
Plaquemines, LA	10	1	<0.5
Environmental Resource	Spill Occurrence Variable [1] %	Transport Variable [2] within 3/10/30 Days %	Spill Risk [3][4] within 3/10/30 Days %
2. International Boundary Sea Segment (IBSS) [5]			
IBSS 1 (closest to Texas/Mexico) [6]	10	<0.5/<0.5/<0.5	<0.5/<0.5/<0.5
IBSS 2 [6]	10	<0.5/<0.5/<0.5	<0.5/<0.5/<0.5
IBSS 3 [6]	10	<0.5/<0.5/2	<0.5/<0.5/<0.5
IBSS 4 [6]	10	<0.5/<0.5/4	<0.5/<0.5/<0.5
IBSS 5 [6]	10	<0.5/1/9	<0.5/<0.5/1
IBSS 6 [6]	10	<0.5/4/17	<0.5/<0.5/2
IBSS 7 (due south of the Walker Ridge Area) [6]	10	2/13/26	<0.5/1/3
IBSS 8 (due south of the Walker Ridge Area) [6]	10	6/16/23	1/2/2
IBSS 9 [6]	10	1/7/12	<0.5/1/1
IBSS 10 [6]	10	<0.5/2/5	<0.5/<0.5/1
IBSS 11 [6]	10	<0.5/<0.5/1	<0.5/<0.5/<0.5
IBSS 12 [6]	10	<0.5/<0.5/1	<0.5/<0.5/<0.5
IBSS 13 [6]	10	<0.5/<0.5/1	<0.5/<0.5/<0.5
IBSS 14 [6]	10	<0.5/<0.5/<0.5	<0.5/<0.5/<0.5
IBSS 15 [6]	10	<0.5/<0.5/<0.5	<0.5/<0.5/<0.5
IBSS 16 [6]	10	<0.5/<0.5/<0.5	<0.5/<0.5/<0.5
IBSS 17 (closest to Florida) [6]	10	<0.5/<0.5/<0.5	<0.5/<0.5/<0.5

(1) The percent chance of a spill event occurring from the proposed pipelines associated with Phase 1 of the proposed FPSO project. This variable was determined assuming that 27,000 bbl of oil was transported per day by the pipelines and that they were in use for 8 years (Petrobras America Inc., 2007). Any additional production transport that may be added in Phase 2 or 3, additional years of service, or other pipeline locations outside of Walker Ridge is not covered by this analysis.

Table B-11. Spill Risk Estimate for the Cascade-Chinook Oil Pipelines Located in Walker Ridge (continued).

(2) The percent chance that winds and currents will move a point projected onto the surface of the Gulf beginning within Walker Ridge and ending at specified shoreline, international boundary sea segments, or environmental resources. These results are the results of a numerical model that calculates the trajectory of a drifting point projected onto the surface of the water using temporally and spatially varying winds and ocean current fields. These probabilities do not factor in the risk of spill occurrence, consideration of the spill size, any spill-response or cleanup actions, or any dispersion and weathering of the slick with time. For the coastal counties and parishes, a 30-day probability is all that is shown because the hypothetical Walker Ridge oil-spill launch area is located 140-160 nautical miles from the coast, which resulted in no probabilities of contact to county/parisjh land segments of >0.5% for 3-10 days. The international boundary sea segments are located in proximity to the hypothetical Walker Ridge oil-spill launch area; therefore, the probabilities for 3, 10, and 30 days is included. Refer to *Oil Spill Risk Analysis: Contingency Planning Statistics for Gulf of Mexico OCS Activities in the Walker Ridge Planning Area* for additional details (USDOI, MMS, 2007).

(3) The probability of a spill occurring and contacting identified environmental features represents the weighted risk that accounts for both the risk that a large spill will occur and the risk that it will contact locations where the resources occur, given the assumptions already described in (1) and (2).

(4) <0.5 = less than 0.5%.

(5) Counties with all values <0.5% are not shown.

(6) It should be noted that the international boundary segments do not terminate the trajectories as the county/parish boundaries do; therefore, one trajectory could contact more than one segment based upon changing wind and current histories. Additionally, these results do not indicate contact with a particular shoreline resource; instead, they indicate the possibility that a spill may traverse into international waters (USDOI, MMS, 2007).

Spill Response

The MMS and USCG have extensive requirements both for the prevention of spills and preparedness to respond to a spill in the event of an accidental spill. This section presents information on the MMS and USCG requirements for spill response preparedness.

MMS Spill-Response Program

The MMS Oil-Spill Program oversees the review of oil-spill response plans, coordinates inspection of oil-spill response equipment, and conducts unannounced oil-spill drills. This program also supports continuing research to foster improvements in spill prevention and response. Studies funded by MMS address issues such as spill prevention and response, *in-situ* burning, and dispersant use.

In addition, MMS works with USCG and other members of the multiagency National Response System to further improve spill-response capability in the Gulf of Mexico. The combined resources of these groups and the resources of commercially contracted oil-spill response organizations result in extensive equipment and trained personnel for spill response in the Gulf of Mexico.

Spill Response for this Project

The USCG considers any FPSO to be a "vessel" based upon the definition of vessels as set forth in 46 U.S.C. 2101(45), referencing 1 U.S.C. 3. Crude oil produced from a subsea installation by an FPSO is "cargo" per the definition of "cargo" in the tank vessel regulations at 46 CFR 30.10-5. The crude that is produced and stored aboard any FPSO, regardless of the FPSO's mode of propulsion type or connection to the riser, is considered cargo. Therefore, cargo tanks aboard an FPSO are subject to the tank vessel requirements in 33 CFR 157. The USCG considers the offloading operations associated with the FPSO to be lightering operations; therefore, the lightering regulations in 33 CFR 156 are applicable. The USCG regulations presented in 33 CFR, Subchapter N, pertain to USCG responsibility in governing OCS activities and pollution prevention measures on the OCS. Various aspects of operations plans, vessel plans, safety systems, and contingency plans are subject to USCG review, inspection, and approval. Accordingly, Petrobras has submitted oil-spill response plans to USCG for the FPSO, the FPSO cargo, the shuttle vessel, and all offloading activity. These plans also identify the required contractual capability to respond to spills covered by these plans (i.e., worst-case discharge examples 2 and 9 of **Table B-3**). The USCG is responsible for the approval of these contingency plans.

Petrobras has a regional oil-spill response plan on file with MMS that includes the proposed FPSO production facilities and associated wells and pipelines and also has current contracts with an offshore oil-spill response organization, Clean Gulf Associates, which can respond to spills from these activities (i.e., worst-case discharge examples 1 and 3-8 of **Table B-3**). The MMS has determined that this contingency plan is adequate to respond to the FPSO-related activities under MMS jurisdiction.

Although not all of the following falls within MMS regulatory jurisdiction, potential spill sources for this project include an accidental blowout, a spill of liquid oil stored on the FPSO, a spill from an associated support vessel, a spill during offloading to a shuttle vessel, a spill from the shuttle vessel either en-route or at the FPSO or terminal, or a spill from one of the projects associated pipelines. **Table B-3** provides the worst-case discharge volume estimate that could potentially be spilled from each of the components associated with the proposed FPSO activity. The API gravity of the oil anticipated to be produced or transported is estimated to have a range of 17-29.

The TV indicates that there is a possibility that a spill occurring from the FPSO site and/or vicinity could traverse into international waters. The U.S. currently has an agreement in place with Mexico that addresses trans-boundary spill response, which is referred to as the "Joint United States-Mexico Contingency Plan" and its Mexican-United States (MEXUS) Gulf Annex. There are no such plans presently in place with Cuba. If a spill in the FPSO vicinity occurs and traverses into Mexican waters, the aforementioned MEXUS Gulf Annex would go into affect; however, the responsible party would be ultimately responsible no matter where the spill occurred. The MEXUS plan facilitates the movement of people and equipment across the border or into Mexican waters to respond to incidents affecting or threatening Mexican interests. The response would be a joint response involving both Mexican and U.S. Government representatives at the responsible party's expense. However, the response would most likely result in Mexican personnel and equipment being used in Mexican waters. Although U.S. personnel and equipment may be deployed to Mexico, unless a U.S. company has permits in place to work in Mexico, there are insurance, work permit, and other issues that would need to be addressed before doing so.

MEXUS identifies the use of dispersants in Mexican waters with that use being contingent upon the conditions of the Mexican National Contingency Plan. Results of bio-testing and use only in waters deeper than 50 m are two of the aforementioned conditions that must be met in order to use dispersants in Mexican waters. The Mexican On-Scene Commander will review any requests for the use of dispersants and may approve its use if the request meets the conditions set forth in Mexican policy. Despite the timeliness of the dispersant use request, approval from the Mexican government may not be obtained before the window for opportune dispersant application has passed.

The FPSO EIS indicated that there was a concern regarding the availability and quantity of dispersants needed to mitigate a large oil spill from an FPSO. The FPSO EIS indicated that USCG at that time shared the concern raised by the FPSO EIS regarding the availability of and quantity of dispersants. The USCG, in correspondence regarding the FPSO EIS, suggested that requirements for dispersant use be pursued with the Regional Response Team (USDOI, MMS, 2001).

To date, there are no USCG or MMS requirements in place requiring the use of dispersants. In addition, it now takes 30 days to begin dispersant manufacturing capability in Sugarland, Texas, compared with the 48 hours assumed in the FPSO EIS analysis. However, the FPSO analysis assumed that the Gulf of Mexico dispersant stockpile would be completely used within 48 hours; given the dispersant application equipment available at that time. This estimate has not significantly changed despite recent changes to the dispersant manufacturing capability and the relocation of Marine Spill Response Corporation dispersant application equipment outside of the Gulf of Mexico region. The changes in the dispersant manufacturing capability have been raised to the Regional Response Team, which includes the USCG for consideration.

The MMS will continue to verify the operators' capability to respond to oil spills via the MMS Oil-Spill Program. The operators are required to keep their oil-spill response plans up-to-date in accordance with MMS regulations. The operators must also conduct an annual drill to demonstrate the adequacy of their spill preparedness. The MMS also conducts unannounced drills to further verify the adequacy of an operator's spill-response preparedness. The USCG has a similar program in place by which they monitor and verify their operator's ability to respond to spills.

References

Anderson, C.M. and R.P. LaBelle. 2000. Update of Comparative Occurrence Rates for Offshore Oil Spills. Spill Science & Technology Bulletin 6(5/6):303-321.

Petrobras America Inc. 2007. Initial development operations coordination document for Walker Ridge Block 206 Unit and Walker Ridge Block 425 Unit, OCS Federal waters, Gulf of Mexico, offshore, Louisiana. (Plan Control No. N-9015).

U.S. Dept. of the Interior. Minerals Management Service. 2001. Proposed use of floating production, storage, and offloading systems on the Gulf of Mexico Outer Continental Shelf, Western and Central Planning Areasd – final environmental impact statement. U.S. Dept. of the Interior, Minerals Management Service, Gulf of Mexico OCS Region, New Orleans, LA. OCS EIS/EA MMS 2000-090. 782 pp.

U.S. Dept. of the Interior. Minerals Management Service. 2007. Oil-spill risk analysis: Contingency planning statistics for Gulf of Mexico OCS activities in the Walker Ridge Planning Area. U.S. Dept. of the Interior, Minerals Management Service, Herndon, VA. OCS Report MMS 2007-029.

The Department of the Interior Mission

As the Nation's principal conservation agency, the Department of the Interior has responsibility for most of our nationally owned public lands and natural resources. This includes fostering sound use of our land and water resources; protecting our fish, wildlife, and biological diversity; preserving the environmental and cultural values of our national parks and historical places; and providing for the enjoyment of life through outdoor recreation. The Department assesses our energy and mineral resources and works to ensure that their development is in the best interests of all our people by encouraging stewardship and citizen participation in their care. The Department also has a major responsibility for American Indian reservation communities and for people who live in island territories under U.S. administration.

The Minerals Management Service Mission

As a bureau of the Department of the Interior, the Minerals Management Service's (MMS) primary responsibilities are to manage the mineral resources located on the Nation's Outer Continental Shelf (OCS), collect revenue from the Federal OCS and onshore Federal and Indian lands, and distribute those revenues.

Moreover, in working to meet its responsibilities, the **Offshore Minerals Management Program** administers the OCS competitive leasing program and oversees the safe and environmentally sound exploration and production of our Nation's offshore natural gas, oil and other mineral resources. The MMS **Minerals Revenue Management** meets its responsibilities by ensuring the efficient, timely and accurate collection and disbursement of revenue from mineral leasing and production due to Indian tribes and allottees, States and the U.S. Treasury.

The MMS strives to fulfill its responsibilities through the general guiding principles of: (1) being responsive to the public's concerns and interests by maintaining a dialogue with all potentially affected parties and (2) carrying out its programs with an emphasis on working to enhance the quality of life for all Americans by lending MMS assistance and expertise to economic development and environmental protection.

www.ingramcontent.com/pod-product-compliance
Lightning Source LLC
Chambersburg PA
CBHW080259290526
45790CB00005B/1862